★★★★★★★★★★★★

The Recipe Hall of Fame Cookbook II

★

Winning Recipes from Hometown America

The fishin' is always good on quiet lakes under a big shady tree in Anywhere, USA.

The Recipe Hall of Fame Cookbook II

★

Winning Recipes from Hometown America

EDITED BY

Gwen McKee

AND

Barbara Moseley

Illustrated by Tupper England

QUAIL RIDGE PRESS

Preserving America's Food Heritage

Library of Congress Cataloging-in-Publication Data

The Recipe hall of fame cookbook II : winning recipes from hometown America /
    edited by Gwen McKee and Barbara Moseley ;
    illustrated by Tupper England.
        p. cm. — (Best of the best).
    ISBN 1-893062-38-4
     1. Cookery, American. 2. Cookery—Competitions—United States
I. McKee, Gwen. II. Moseley, Barbara. III. Quail Ridge Press cookbook series.
TX715 .R289 2003
641.5973—dc21   2002036905

Manufactured in the United States of America
Book design by Cynthia Clark
Cover photo by Greg Campbell

First printing, March 2003 • Second, November 2004 • Third, January 2005

On the cover: Yuletide Punch Bowl (p.13), Hot Pepper Jelly (p.36), Feather Beds (p.38),
Bunker Hill Brown Bread (p.41), Strawberry Bread with Spread (p.43), Sweet Red Pepper Soup (p.68),
Craisin-Spinach Salad (p.81), Special Indoor Barbecued Spare Ribs with Sauce (p.187),
Snow-Capped Broccoli Spears (p.106), Three Layered Cheesecake (p.209),
Sue's Apple Pie in a Jar (p.246), Cold Lime Soufflé (p.274).

QUAIL RIDGE PRESS
P. O. Box 123 • Brandon, MS 39043 • e-mail: info@quailridge.com
www.recipehalloffame.com • www.quailridge.com

Contents

Preface 7

Beverages & Appetizers 9

Bread & Breakfast 37

Soups, Stews, & Chilies 61

Salads 77

Vegetables 99

Pasta, Rice, Etc. 119

Poultry 133

Seafood 151

Meats 169

Cakes 193

Cookies & Candies 217

Pies & Other Desserts 239

List of Contributing Cookbooks 277

Index 293

Barbara fills the van tank once again on one of the tours she and Gwen have taken researching cookbooks all across the country, endeavoring to Preserve America's Food Heritage. This stop was somewhere around lovely Eureka Springs, Arkansas.

★★★★★★★★★★ ★★★★★★★★★★

When the selections for the original *Recipe Hall of Fame Cookbook* were made, we found so many recipes from our BEST OF THE BEST STATE COOKBOOKS deserving of Hall-of-Fame status, that we immediately knew we had to establish an on-going list of recipes from our growing database that also deserved to be in The Recipe Hall of Fame. And now its time has come. Here is *The Recipe Hall of Fame Cookbook II!* But though its name says "II," this outstanding collection is indeed second to none. As with the original inductees, and in the *Recipe Hall of Fame Dessert Cookbook* and the *Recipe Hall of Fame Quick & Easy Cookbook,* each recipe has already been selected to be in the BEST OF THE BEST STATE COOKBOOK SERIES. They are American classics, each one upholding our slogan of Preserving America's Food Heritage.

In our travels around the country, we have gone down many roads. We invite you to go with us by way of our chapter opening photos. In preceding books, we have showcased many famous places in America; this time we take you to the back roads where we often go in search of recipes from each state. We look for the kind of recipe you would want to have for dinner . . . or to take to the church picnic . . . or to have for an office party . . . or to bring as a "happy" to a friend who needs a little cheering up. We are partial to these kinds of recipes, having grown up in households where Mama stayed home and did all the cooking. She had lots of practice and perfected so many dishes that never failed to bring smiles and "yums" and compliments. We got downright excited when the aromas drifted beyond the kitchen—"Mama's making her stuffed peppers and peas tonight!" These "perfected" recipes aren't usually fancy—they're just good! And they're not all old recipes . . . some of the best ones have surprising new twists that we delight in discovering. Our goal is to find and preserve classic recipes so that they can be enjoyed for generations to come.

We wish to thank many talented people: our illustrator, Tupper England, our photographer, Greg Campbell, and our dedicated staff. In *The Recipe Hall of Fame Cookbook II,* we are not only including more of our personal favorites, but the selections of our loyal customers who use the BEST OF THE BEST STATE COOKBOOKS all the time. Responses came in from cooks all over America, and along with our survey came a bonus of many, many compliments on the original *Recipe Hall of Fame Cookbook,* including, "When will you publish another volume?"

So with much researching, testing, commenting, judging, and voting, we have come up with another collection of exceptional recipes—434 in all. We are proud to present the latest inductees into The Recipe Hall of Fame. Enjoy.

Our Best to you,
Gwen McKee and Barbara Moseley

P. S. Please note that the title of each contributing cookbook is listed below the recipe along with the state name in parenthesis, indicating the BEST OF THE BEST STATE COOKBOOK where the recipe appears. Beginning on page 277, you can find a list of the cookbooks who have contributed the recipes that are inductees into The Recipe Hall of Fame. Throughout the book we've added some of our own comments as "Editor's Extras."

Charming country stores—where everything you could possibly need is on five or six rows of shelves—are commonplace when driving through Vermont, especially on historic Route 7A.

Coffee Mocha Punch

Heavenly delicious!

2 quarts brewed coffee, chilled
1 quart chocolate milk
¹/₂ gallon vanilla ice cream

1 cup heavy cream, whipped
1 ounce semisweet chocolate,
  grated

Stir coffee and chocolate milk together in a punch bowl. Spoon in vanilla ice cream. Stir slightly to combine. Place dollops of whipped cream on top and sprinkle with grated chocolate for garnish. Serves 16–20.

Kay Ewing's Cooking School Cookbook (Louisiana II)

Creamy Hot Chocolate

Delicious! This is deluxe!

1 (14-ounce) can sweetened
  condensed milk
¹/₂ cup unsweetened cocoa
1¹/₂ teaspoons vanilla extract

¹/₈ teaspoon salt
6¹/₂ cups hot water
Marshmallows (optional)

In large saucepan, combine sweetened condensed milk, cocoa, vanilla, and salt; mix well. Over medium heat, slowly stir in water; heat through, stirring occasionally. Top with marshmallows, if desired. Makes about 2 quarts.

Sleigh Bells and Sugarplums (Washington)

Dixie Tea

It's been around a long time with good reason.

8 cups boiling water
5 tablespoons tea leaves
Juice of 1 lemon
Juice of 6 oranges

2 cups sugar
8 cups water
1 teaspoon whole cloves

Add the boiling water to the tea; let stand 5 minutes and strain the tea off the leaves. Add the fruit juices. Make a syrup by boiling the sugar, water, and cloves; strain and add to tea. This makes about 18 cups.

Two Hundred Years of Charleston Cooking (South Carolina)

Mock Sangria

Tastes better than the real thing.

1 (40-ounce) bottle unsweetened
  white grape juice, chilled
1 (32-ounce) bottle apple-cranberry
  juice, chilled
½ cup lime juice, chilled

1 (33.8-ounce) bottle club soda,
  chilled
Seedless green grapes
Sliced limes
Sliced oranges

Combine juices. Just before serving, add club soda; stir and garnish. Yields 14 cups.

Per serving: Cal 47; Fat 0g; Chol 0mg; Sod 10mg.

Simply Colorado (Colorado)

Want to see the world's largest coffee pot? It's in Stanton, Iowa, which is the home of Virginia Christine, who played Mrs. Olsen in Folger's Coffee television commercials. Modified from the original water tower, the "Swedish-style" pot, painted with decorative hearts and flowers, is 35 feet tall and holds 40,000 gallons—of water, that is.

★★★★★★★★★★★ ★★★★★★★★★★★

Texas Sunrise

4 cups cran-raspberry juice
2 cups pineapple juice
2 cups orange juice

2 cups club soda
1 lime
1 cup whole strawberries

Combine cran-raspberry, pineapple, and orange juices in punch bowl or large pitcher. Add club soda. Cut lime into thin round slices, discarding ends. Float some or all of slices in punch. Stir in strawberries. Add ice, if desired, and serve. Makes approximately 10 cups.

Per ½-cup serving: Cal 62; Prot .31g; Carb 15.5g; Fat .1g; Chol 0mg; Sod 6.58 mg.

The Second Typically Texas Cookbook (Texas II)

Peachy Twirl Cooler

So refreshing...as pretty as it is peachy!

3 medium peaches
1 tablespoon lemon juice
1 teaspoon almond extract
2 tablespoons sugar

1 cup milk
1 cup peach ice cream
Mint sprigs for garnish

Peel, pit, and slice peaches. Reserve 2 slices; dip in lemon juice. Place remainder of the sliced peaches in the blender and purée. Add remaining lemon juice, almond extract, sugar and milk; cover and blend thoroughly. Mix in peach ice cream. Pour into large glasses; garnish each with reserved peach slice and a sprig of mint. Serve immediately. Makes 2 (12-ounce) servings.

The Peach Sampler (South Carolina)

Yuletide Punch Bowl

2 pints raspberry sherbet, divided
1 cup lemon juice
1 cup orange juice
¾ cup sugar
1 large bottle cranberry juice
 cocktail
2 bottles ginger ale

Soften 1 pint sherbet in punch bowl. Combine softened sherbet, lemon juice, orange juice, and sugar; stir to dissolve sugar. Add cranberry juice and ginger ale, all of which have been chilled. With ice cream scoop, float remaining 1 pint sherbet over top of punch. Makes about 30-36 (6-ounce) servings. (Pictured on cover.)

Jasper County Extension Homemakers Cookbook (Indiana)

Beachcomber's Gold

This drink has been one of my most pleasant surprises and has become the favorite of many who have tried it. With very few exceptions, most customers who try this drink seldom switch to another. The drink is relatively simple, but the combination of these ingredients produces a most exotic drink. Once you try it, I think you'll agree.

1½ ounces Grand Marnier
2 ounces orange juice
1 ounce coconut cream
¼ ounce orgeat syrup

Place all ingredients in blender over ice selection. Select the proper blender speed and blend until consistently smooth. Garnish with orange wedge and cherry. One 12-ounce serving.

Pool Bar Jim's (South Carolina)

★ **Editor's Extra:** Orgeat syrup is made from almonds, sugar, and rose water or orange-flower water. It is used in many cocktails for its distinctive almond flavor. Orgeat syrup can be hard to find, but may be available in stores that sell coffee syrups and flavorings. Almond syrup is an acceptable substitute.

Frozen Peach Margaritas

Margarita fans, you're going to love these! They are always a hit at summer parties. Make them ahead of time; keep them in the freezer—ready to serve to your guests as they arrive.

1 (16-ounce) can frozen limeade
6 ounces tequila
6 ounces Triple Sec
6 tablespoons lime juice

2 cups fresh peaches, peeled and
  sliced
4 cups ice cubes

Combine all ingredients except ice in blender. Blend well. Pour half of mixture into a container. Then add 2 cups ice to the mixture in blender and blend well. Pour blended margarita into container for the freezer. Pour remaining half of mixture into the blender and add 2 cups ice to blend. Place in freezer until ready to serve. Serves 6–8.

Note: Fresh peaches are a must. Put a supply of peaches in your freezer to enjoy throughout the year!

The Peach Tree Family Cookbook (Texas II)

Parmesan Chicken Fingers

A tailgate great!

8 boneless chicken breast halves
2 cups dry bread crumbs
¾ cup grated Parmesan cheese
1 teaspoon salt

½ teaspoon pepper
¼ cup chopped fresh parsley
2 garlic cloves, chopped
1 cup butter, melted

Remove skin and cut each chicken breast into 3–4 fingers. In large bowl, combine bread crumbs, cheese, salt, pepper, and parsley. Sauté garlic in butter. Remove from heat; add chicken fingers and let set for 3 minutes.

Dip chicken in bread crumbs and place in a 9x12x2-inch baking dish. Top fingers with more bread crumbs and pour remaining butter over all. Bake at 400° for 18–20 minutes. Cool slightly and cover loosely with foil. Refrigerate until well-chilled, and transport in cooler. Yields 24 chicken fingers.

Uptown Down South (South Carolina)

★ **Editor's Extra:** Don't hesitate to serve these hot for lunch or dinner.

Turkey Tidbits with Cranberry Dip

Tangy and terrific.

½ cup sour cream
1 teaspoon lemon juice
1 teaspoon horseradish
¼ teaspoon salt
1 pound uncooked turkey breast,
   cut into pieces

⅔ cup dry bread crumbs
⅔ cup ground walnuts
2 tablespoons margarine, melted
Cranberry Dip

Combine sour cream, lemon juice, horseradish, and salt in non-metal bowl; blend well. Add uncooked turkey breast pieces. Toss to coat. Cover; marinate in refrigerator 2–24 hours.

In shallow pan, combine bread crumbs and ground walnuts. Remove turkey from marinade. Roll in crumbs. Place on greased 10x15-inch pan. Drizzle melted margarine over turkey. Bake at 350° for 35 minutes or until golden brown. Serve warm or cold with Cranberry Dip.

CRANBERRY DIP:
1 (8-ounce) can jellied cranberry
   sauce

¼ cup sour cream
2 tablespoons horseradish

Mix all ingredients.

Savor the Flavor (New York)

★★★★★★★★★★★ ★★★★★★★★★★★

Appetizer Chicken Wings

5 pounds chicken wings
2 (4-ounce) jars strained apricot
  baby food

6 ounces soy sauce
2 teaspoons ground ginger
1 clove garlic, minced

Disjoint wings; discard tips. Rinse well; pat dry. Place in single layer in baking pan. Pour mixture of remaining ingredients over chicken. Marinate, covered with plastic wrap, in refrigerator for 24 hours. Bake, uncovered, at 350° for 1 hour or until tender. Serve hot. Yields 10 servings.

Approx Per Serving: Cal 520; T Fat 33g; 59% Calories from Fat; Prot 46g; Carb 6g; Fiber <1g; Chol 145mg; Sod 1114mg.

Pioneer Pantry (Illinois)

Teriyaki Chicken Wings

A richly glazed appetizer that can also be served as a main dish.

16 chicken drumettes (the meaty leg
  portion of wings)
$\frac{1}{4}$ cup reduced-sodium soy sauce
$\frac{3}{4}$ cup firmly packed light brown
  sugar

1 tablespoon honey
4 thin slices fresh ginger
2 green onions, cut into 1-inch pieces

Clean wings; trim off excess fat and skin. Place in medium bowl. Combine remaining ingredients; stir to dissolve sugar. Pour over chicken. Cover; chill at least 3 hours, turning occasionally. When ready to bake, place chicken in foil-lined shallow baking pan. Bake at 350° for 15 minutes. Baste with marinade; bake 30–35 minutes or until tender, basting frequently. Makes 8 hors d'oeuvre servings, 2 per person.

Six Ingredients or Less: Cooking Light & Healthy (Washington)

Waikiki Meatballs

Wonderful is a weak word to describe these.

1½ pounds ground beef
⅔ cup cracker crumbs
⅓ cup minced onion
1 egg
1½ teaspoons salt
¼ teaspoon ginger
¼ cup milk
1 tablespoon shortening

2 tablespoons cornstarch
½ cup brown sugar
1 (13½-ounce) can pineapple
   tidbits; drain and reserve syrup
⅓ cup vinegar
1 tablespoon soy sauce
⅓ cup chopped green pepper

Mix thoroughly the beef, crumbs, onion, egg, salt, ginger, and milk. Shape mixture into ½-inch balls. Melt shortening in large skillet. Brown and cook meatballs until done. Remove meatballs and keep warm. Pour fat from skillet.

Mix cornstarch and sugar. Stir in reserved pineapple syrup, vinegar, and soy sauce until smooth. Pour into skillet; cook over medium heat, stirring constantly, until mixture thickens and boils. Add meatballs, pineapple tidbits, and green pepper. Heat thoroughly. Can be stored and/or frozen in plastic zipper bags. Serves 6 (main dish); 10–12 (hors d'oeuvres).

Amarillo Junior League Cookbook (Texas)

★★★★★★★★★★★ ★★★★★★★★★★★

Savory Ham Balls

This has long been a favorite hot hors d'oeuvre. I have seen men scoop up the dredges with whatever crackers they could find.

1/3 cup fine dry bread crumbs
1/4 cup milk
1/4 cup catsup
1/4 cup minced onion
1 egg, slightly beaten

1/4 teaspoon salt
Dash pepper
1 pound ground ham
1 pound ground pork

In large bowl, combine bread crumbs, milk, 1/4 cup catsup, onion, egg, salt, and pepper. Add meats and mix thoroughly. Shape into about 5 dozen small meatballs. Place in 9x13x2-inch baking pan. Bake in 350° oven for 25–30 minutes. Cool. Refrigerate or wrap and freeze.

SAUCE:
1 cup apricot preserves
1/4 cup water
1 tablespoon Worcestershire sauce

1 tablespoon prepared mustard
2 tablespoons catsup
2 tablespoons vinegar

To serve, combine Sauce ingredients in large skillet. Add meatballs. Cook, stirring occasionally, till meatballs heat through. Turn into blazer pan or baking dish; place over hot water to keep warm.

Encore (Georgia)

★ **Editor's Extra:** I use my food processor (steel blade) to "grind" ham and pork. This also keeps warm nicely in a crockpot.

★★★★★★★★★★★★ ★★★★★★★★★★★★

Rolled Tortillas

2 (8-ounce) packages cream cheese,
  softened
1 package ranch dressing mix
2 green onions
$\frac{1}{2}$ cup diced red peppers
$\frac{1}{2}$ cup diced celery
1 cup black olives, chopped
4 (12-inch) flour tortillas

Mix together cream cheese and dressing mix. Add remaining ingredients and spread on tortillas. Roll tightly and wrap in plastic wrap. Chill at least 2 hours. Cut in 1-inch slices and serve.

Seasoned with Love (Wisconsin)

★ **Editor's Extra:** Have salsa nearby for dipping. Soooo good.

Tamale Bites

A real taste treat.

2 cups crumbled corn bread
1 (10-ounce) can mild enchilada
  sauce, divided
$\frac{1}{2}$ teaspoon salt
$1\frac{1}{2}$ pounds ground beef
1 (8-ounce) can tomato sauce
$\frac{1}{2}$ cup shredded Monterey Jack
  cheese

Combine bread crumbs, $\frac{1}{2}$ cup enchilada sauce, and salt. Add beef and mix well. Shape into 1-inch balls. Place in shallow baking pan. Bake, uncovered, in 350° oven for 18-20 minutes or until done. Meanwhile, in small saucepan, heat together tomato sauce and the remaining enchilada sauce. Place cooked meatballs in chafing dish; pour sauce over and top with shredded cheese. Keep warm over low heat. Serve with wooden picks. Make these ahead, chill, and bake when you need them. Yields 90 bites.

Huntsville Entertains (Alabama)

Armadillo Eggs

1 dozen fresh whole large jalapeños
1/2 pound marbled (Jack and
   Cheddar) cheese

2 pounds sausage (pork breakfast
   roll)
1 box original flavor Shake-n-Bake
   Coating Mix

Wash jalapeños; leave stems intact. Slit side of each pepper with paring knife. Gently squeeze peppers by ends to open; remove all seeds. Set aside. Cut cheese into 1/4-inch square strips. Stuff cheese strips into peppers. Set aside. Make 1 dozen sausage patties, 1/4 inch thick, making diameter large enough to cover entire patty. Place each pepper slit-side-down in middle of patty; wrap patty around pepper. Roll all peppers in coating mix and place on cookie sheet. Bake for 25–30 minutes at 350°, or until done.

What's Cookin' at Casa (New Mexico)

★ **Editor's Extra:** For a tamer taste, try using banana peppers; half of each lets your guests choose.

Crab Stuffed Mushrooms

1/3 cup minced green pepper
1/3 cup minced red pepper
1/4 cup minced onion
2 cloves garlic, minced
1/2 cup unsalted butter, divided
1 egg, beaten

1/4 cup freshly grated Parmesan
   cheese
1/3 cup lump crabmeat
1/8 teaspoon cayenne pepper
1/2 cup bread crumbs
24 firm white mushrooms

Sauté peppers, onion, and garlic in 1/4 cup butter until soft. Remove from heat and add egg, cheese, crabmeat, cayenne, and bread crumbs. Remove stems from mushroom caps. Melt remaining butter and dip each cap in melted butter. Stuff with crabmeat stuffing. At this point, it can be refrigerated up to 3 days. Bake at 400° until lightly browned on top. Serve immediately. Makes 2 dozen.

Steamboat Entertains (Colorado)

Coconut Shrimp

This is a great "do-ahead" hors d'oeuvre.

1 pound medium shrimp	**2 tablespoons cream**
$\frac{1}{4}$ cup flour	**$\frac{3}{4}$ cup flaked coconut**
$\frac{1}{2}$ teaspoon salt	**$\frac{1}{3}$ cup dry bread crumbs**
$\frac{1}{2}$ teaspoon dry mustard	**Vegetable oil**
1 egg	**Chinese Mustard Sauce**

Shell and devein shrimp, but leave tails intact. Combine flour, salt, and dry mustard in a small bowl. Beat egg and cream in another small bowl. Combine coconut and bread crumbs in a shallow dish. Dip shrimp in flour mixture, then in egg-cream mixture and finally in coconut-crumb mixture (coat well). At this point shrimp can be arranged in single layer and refrigerated.

When ready to cook, pour oil in medium saucepan (or wok) to 2-inch depth. Heat oil to 350°. Fry shrimp (6 or less at a time) for about 2 minutes. Turn once, cooking until golden brown. Remove with slotted spoon and drain on paper towels or paper bag. Keep warm in slow oven until all shrimp are cooked. Serve with Chinese Mustard Sauce and duck sauce.

Note: Can freeze and reheat in 350°–370° oven for about 10 minutes. Serve on doilies to absorb any remaining grease.

CHINESE MUSTARD SAUCE:

$\frac{1}{3}$ cup dry mustard	**1 tablespoon honey**
2 teaspoons vinegar	**$\frac{1}{4}$ cup cold water (maybe less)**

Mix all ingredients until well blended. Refrigerate.

Jaycee Cookin' (Mid-Atlantic/Maryland)

The Mount Horeb Mustard Museum, in Mount Horeb, Wisconsin, is the home of the world's largest collection of prepared mustards—nearly 4,000 jars, bottles, and tubes from all 50 states and more than 60 countries. Founder Barry Levenson started collecting mustards in 1986, and opened the museum to the general public on April 6, 1992. National Mustard Day, celebrated at the Mustard Museum on the first Saturday in August, annually attracts approximately 3,000 mustard lovers.

★★★★★★★★★★★★   ★★★★★★★★★★★★

Shrimp Appetizer Platter

Always a hit!

1 (8-ounce) package cream cheese,
  softened
1/2 cup sour cream
1/4 cup mayonnaise
2 (4 1/4-ounce) cans shrimp, drained

1 cup seafood cocktail sauce
2 cups shredded mozzarella cheese
1 green pepper, chopped
3 green onions, chopped
1 large tomato, diced

Combine cream cheese, sour cream, and mayonnaise. Spread over 12-inch pizza pan or platter, plate, etc. Scatter shrimp over cheese layer; cover with seafood sauce. Then layer on the mozzarella, green pepper, green onions, and tomatoes. Cover and chill. Serve with crackers.

Cookin' for the Crew (Iowa)

Peter Rabbit's Pizza

Turn your food processor loose on this one.

2 (8-ounce) cans refrigerated
  crescent dinner rolls
2 (8-ounce) packages cream cheese,
  softened
1 (1-ounce) package ranch-style
  dressing mix
3/4 cup salad dressing
3/4 cup finely chopped broccoli

3/4 cup finely chopped cauliflower
3/4 cup finely chopped celery
3/4 cup finely chopped onion
3/4 cup finely chopped radishes
3/4 cup finely chopped carrots
3/4 cup finely chopped green pepper
3/4 cup grated Cheddar cheese

Grease an 11x15-inch cookie sheet with sides or a jellyroll pan. Unroll crescent rolls into 8 rectangles. Line bottom of cookie sheet with rectangles of dough, pinching perforations together to make a seal. Bake according to directions; cool.

Combine cream cheese, dressing mix, and salad dressing. Spread over the crust. Mix chopped vegetables, and layer over cream cheese mixture. Top with cheese. Cover with plastic wrap and refrigerate overnight. Cut into 1x3-inch pieces.

Note: Make the day before and refrigerate. For best results, chop green pepper by hand.

Homecoming (Texas II)

Smoked Salmon Paté

1 (1-pound) can salmon
1 (8-ounce) package cream cheese, softened
2 tablespoons grated or finely chopped onion
1/4 teaspoon salt
1 tablespoon lemon juice

1/4 teaspoon pepper or dash of Tabasco
1 tablespoon liquid smoke
1 teaspoon prepared horseradish (optional)
Chopped nuts
Parsley or paprika

Drain salmon and remove skin and bones. Flake and combine with next 7 ingredients. Chill several hours. Decorate with chopped nuts and parsley or paprika. Serve with crackers. Serves 16–20.

Three Rivers Cookbook I (Pennsylvania)

Please with Cheese

Sure to please indeed.

1 (16-ounce) box cheese crackers, crushed, divided
1 (8-ounce) package cream cheese, softened
1 cup sour cream
1/2 cup stuffed green olives, chopped

1/2 cup chopped celery
1/2 cup chopped green pepper
1/2 cup chopped onion
2 tablespoons lemon juice
1 teaspoon salt
Dash of Tabasco

Grease a 9-inch springform pan. Cover the bottom of pan with half the crushed crackers. Mix cream cheese and sour cream; blend in olives, celery, green pepper, onion and seasonings. Spread cheese mixture over cracker crumbs. Top with remaining cracker crumbs. Cover and refrigerate overnight. To serve, remove sides of pan. Garnish with a border of sliced stuffed olives, cut into wedges, and serve with fresh fruit.

Fillies Flavours (Kentucky)

 The 10-day Kona Coffee Cultural Festival in Kona, Hawaii, started in 1970, is recognized as the oldest product festival in Hawaii and is the only coffee festival in the United States.

★★★★★★★★★★★ ★★★★★★★★★★★

Cheese Cookies

Whoa! These are good.

2 sticks (¹/₂ pound) butter or
  margarine
16 ounces shredded Cheddar
  cheese (New York Sharp)

2 cups flour
1 teaspoon salt
1 teaspoon cayenne pepper
1¹/₂ cups chopped pecans

Cream butter and cheese together. Add flour, salt, and pepper, then blend in pecans. It will be a very stiff dough. With wax paper, make small, long rolls of the dough and refrigerate overnight. Slice thin and bake on ungreased cookie sheet in 275° oven for 45–50 minutes. Cool on a rack. Dough will keep several days in refrigerator or a couple of months in the freezer. Serves 50 for cocktails or with coffee or tea.

Golliwogg Cake (Louisiana II)

Spinach Cheese Pastries

This is a great make-ahead-freeze-bake-as-needed dish.

PASTRY:

¹/₂ pound soft cream cheese
1 cup soft salted butter

2 cups plain flour

Combine cream cheese and butter, using pastry blender. Cut in flour. Use hands to work dough until it holds together. Place on wax paper. Form into a ball and chill overnight. Roll dough to ¹/₃-inch thickness with floured rolling pin on a generously floured surface. Cut into 2-inch rounds with cutter.

FILLING:

1 (10-ounce) package frozen
  spinach, thawed and drained
1 medium onion, finely chopped
¹/₄ cup olive oil
1¹/₄ teaspoons salt

¹/₄ teaspoon white pepper
1 cup feta cheese
¹/₂ cup pot cheese or cottage cheese
1 egg, beaten

Sauté onion in olive oil. Add spinach and seasonings while cooking. Mix cheeses and egg. Combine spinach with egg mixture. Be sure to mix thoroughly. Cool to lukewarm. Place teaspoonful of Filling in center of each round of Pastry. Fold over to make crescent shape. Edges may be pressed with fork. Place on ungreased cookie sheet. Bake at 425° for 15-20 minutes. May be served warm or at room temperature.

Waddad's Kitchen (Mississippi)

Christmas Cheese Ball

For many years I have made this cheese ball for gifts to my friends at Christmas. The red and green ingredients seem to go with the season.

3 (8-ounce) packages cream cheese
1 (4-ounce) package blue cheese
½ teaspoon garlic salt
2 tablespoons chopped pimiento

2 tablespoons chopped green pepper
2 tablespoons chopped celery
Chopped pecans

Allow the cheese to come to room temperature. Mix all the ingredients except pecans. Shape into a ball (or two small balls). Roll cheese ball in chopped pecans. Decorate the top of the cheese ball with strips of pimiento and green pepper to represent poinsettias.

By Special Request (Louisiana II)

Cherry Tomatoes Filled with Pesto

24 firm cherry tomatoes
2 cups fresh basil leaves
½ cup fresh parsley leaves
2 cloves garlic, minced
¼ cup pine nuts or walnuts

¼ cup grated Parmesan cheese
⅓ cup olive oil
Salt and pepper
1 (3-ounce) package cream cheese,
   softened

Cut off tops of tomatoes. Carefully loosen the insides and scoop out with a small spoon or melon ball scoop. Turn tomatoes upside down and drain. To make the pesto, combine basil and parsley in food processor or blender. Add garlic, nuts, Parmesan cheese, and olive oil. Blend until almost smooth, but still a bit crunchy. Taste and season. Add pesto to cream cheese and mix well. Use about 1 teaspoon of this mixture to stuff each tomato. Refrigerate tomatoes for several hours and let stand at room temperature about 30 minutes before serving.

More Than Delicious (Pennsylvania)

★★★★★★★★★★★   ★★★★★★★★★★★

Spinach Dip

Your guests will love you for serving this.

1 (16-ounce) carton (2%) low-fat
  cottage cheese
2 tablespoons skim milk
3 tablespoons lemon juice
1 (8-ounce) can water chestnuts,
  drained, chopped fine

1 package Knorr Vegetable Soup
  Mix
1/2 cup finely chopped onions
1 (10-ounce) package frozen
  spinach, thawed and
  well-drained

Blend cottage cheese, milk, and lemon juice in blender until smooth. Add remaining ingredients and stir well. Serve with raw vegetables. Yields 3 cups (24 servings).

Per Serving (2 tablespoons): Calories 35; Cholesterol Tr; Fat Tr; Sodium 235mg; ADA Exchange Value: 1/4 cup = 1 meat.

Take it to Heart (Arkansas)

Tonia's Spinach Dip Supreme

2 large green onions with tops,
  minced
1 pint sour cream
1 (8-ounce) package cream cheese,
  softened
1 cup shredded Cheddar cheese
1 cup chopped pecans
1/2 teaspoon lemon juice

1 teaspoon Worcestershire sauce
1 package dry ranch-style dressing
  mix
1 (10-ounce) package frozen
  spinach, thawed, drained well and
  squeezed dry
1 can water chestnuts, chopped fine

Mix all ingredients and chill thoroughly several hours, preferably overnight. Serve in hollowed loaf of rye or pumpernickel bread, with cubes of bread in basket to the side. It is also pretty in a red cabbage shell.

A Cooking Affaire II (Great Plains/Kansas)

Hot Crawfish Dip

Delicious in patty shells, too.

1 onion, chopped
3 stalks celery, chopped
1 bell pepper, chopped
1 clove garlic, minced
1 stick butter
1 pound ground crawfish tails
1 (8-ounce) package cream cheese

¼ cup mayonnaise
1 teaspoon dry mustard
1 teaspoon sugar
3 tablespoons Sauterne wine
Salt and pepper to taste

Sauté onion, celery, bell pepper, and garlic in butter. Add crawfish and cream cheese; cover and simmer until cream cheese is melted. Add mayonnaise, mustard, sugar, and wine. Simmer; add salt and pepper to taste. Optional: You may also add onion tops, parsley, and crawfish fat.

The Louisiana Crawfish Cookbook (Louisiana)

★ **Editor's Extra:** Buy frozen packages of peeled crawfish tails and thaw enough to separate. Easy and yummy!

Spicy Hot Crab Dip

An elegant entrée when served over rice or in pastry shells.

1 (8-ounce) package cream cheese,
  softened
1 tablespoon milk
8 ounces fresh lump crabmeat
2 tablespoons sherry
1 teaspoon Worcestershire sauce
¼ teaspoon garlic powder

1 teaspoon Tabasco sauce
Juice of ½ lemon
2 tablespoons grated onion
2 teaspoons prepared horseradish
¼ teaspoon salt
Dash cayenne pepper

Preheat oven to 375°. Combine cream cheese and milk. Blend thoroughly. Add remaining ingredients. Blend well. Spread mixture in a baking dish. Bake 15–20 minutes. Serve with assorted crackers. Serves 12–15.

Necessities and Temptations (Texas II)

★ **Editor's Extra:** Also nice to sprinkle a few sliced almonds on top before baking.

★★★★★★★★★★★ ★★★★★★★★★★★

Five-Layer Mexican Dip

You'll find they won't leave this dip alone.

1 (15-ounce) can fat-free refried
  beans
¹/₂ cup mild salsa
¹/₂ ripe avocado, mashed
¹/₂ cup plain nonfat yogurt

2 cups shredded lettuce
¹/₂ cup chopped tomatoes
1 ounce reduced-fat sharp Cheddar
  cheese, shredded

In a small bowl, mix together beans and salsa. In a separate bowl, blend together avocado and yogurt. In a shallow serving dish, layer ingredients beginning with bean mixture; top with avocado sauce, then cover with lettuce, tomato, and cheese. Yields 5 cups.

Per serving: Cal 45; Fat 1g; Chol 0mg; Sod 36mg.

Simply Colorado (Colorado)

Debbie's Chile Con Queso

¹/₄ cup butter or margarine
¹/₂ cup finely chopped onion
1 (1-pound) can tomatoes, undrained
1¹/₂ or 2 (4-ounce) cans green
  chiles, drained and chopped (more,
  if you like it hotter)

Salt to taste
1 pound Monterey Jack cheese,
  cubed
¹/₂ cup heavy cream

Heat butter in medium skillet; sauté onion until tender. Add tomatoes, chiles, and salt. Mash tomatoes with a fork. Simmer, stirring occasionally, for 15 minutes. Add cheese cubes, stirring until cheese is melted. Stir in cream. Cook, stirring constantly for 2 minutes. Remove from heat and let stand for 15 minutes. Serve warm in casserole over candle warmer as dip with veggies and corn chips. Makes 10–12 servings.

Pleasures from the Good Earth (Arizona)

 The Barber Vintage Motorsports Museum, in Birmingham, Alabama, showcases over 700 motorcycles (not all are on display at the same time), with some models dating back to as early as 1904. This is the largest motorcycle museum in the world.

★★★★★★★★★★★ ★★★★★★★★★★★

Coyote Caviar

A very Southwestern appetizer. Sure to be a hit.

1 (15-ounce) can black beans,
  drained, rinsed
1 (4-ounce) can chopped black
  olives, drained
¼ cup chopped onion
1 (4-ounce) can chopped green
  chiles
1 clove of garlic, chopped
¼ cup chopped cilantro
2 tablespoons vegetable oil
2 tablespoons freshly squeezed
  lime juice

2 teaspoons chili powder
¼ teaspoon salt
¼ teaspoon crushed red pepper
  flakes
¼ teaspoon cumin
1 teaspoon black pepper
8 ounces cream cheese, softened
2 hard-cooked eggs, peeled,
  chopped
Salsa to taste
1 green onion, sliced

Combine the black beans, black olives, onion, green chiles, garlic, cilantro, oil, lime juice, chili powder, salt, red pepper flakes, cumin and black pepper in a bowl; mix well. Chill, covered, for 2 hours. Spread the cream cheese on a round serving plate. Cover with black bean mixture. Arrange the eggs and salsa around the edge of the black bean mixture. Sprinkle with the green onion. Serve with tortilla chips. Serves 12.

Reflections Under the Sun (Arizona)

Black-Eyed Pea and Pepper Salsa

Easy, zesty appetizer with a Southwestern flavor.

2 (15-ounce) cans black-eyed peas,
  rinsed and drained
2 sweet red peppers, diced
1 (11½-ounce) jar hot salsa
3 tablespoons minced onion

4 tablespoons olive oil or vegetable
  oil
4 tablespoons red wine vinegar
2 tablespoons snipped fresh parsley
1 tablespoon minced jalapeño chiles

Combine all ingredients and refrigerate. Allow flavors to blend in refrigerator for 2 hours or overnight. Serve with corn chips or tortillas. Yields 5 cups.

Five Star Sensations (Ohio)

★★★★★★★★★★★★ ★★★★★★★★★★★★

Pepperoni Pizza Dip

The first to disappear.

1 (8-ounce) package cream cheese,
  softened
$^1/_2$ cup dairy sour cream
1 teaspoon crushed dried oregano
$^1/_8$ teaspoon garlic powder
$^1/_8$ teaspoon crushed red pepper
  (optional)

$^1/_2$ cup pizza sauce
$^1/_2$ cup chopped pepperoni
$^1/_4$ cup sliced green onion
$^1/_4$ cup chopped green pepper
$^1/_2$ cup (2 ounces) shredded
  mozzarella cheese

In a small mixer bowl, beat together cream cheese, sour cream, oregano, garlic powder, and red pepper. Spread evenly in a 9- or 10-inch quiche dish or pie plate. Spread pizza sauce over top. Sprinkle with pepperoni, green onions, and green pepper. Bake in a 350° oven for 10 minutes. Top with cheese; bake 5 minutes more, or until cheese is melted and mixture is heated through. Serve with sweet pepper strips, broccoli flowerets, or crackers. Makes $1^1/_2$ cups (12 servings).

Favorite Recipes from Poland Women's Club (Ohio)

Beef in a Bread Bowl

$^1/_2$ cup chopped onion
2 tablespoons butter
1 tablespoon cornstarch
1 cup Carnation evaporated milk,
  undiluted
$^1/_2$ cup water
1 (3-ounce) package cream cheese

1 (5-ounce) package dried beef,
  rinsed and diced
$^1/_4$ cup chopped green pepper
8–10 drops Tabasco sauce
1 teaspoon prepared mustard
1 large or 2 small uncut loaves
  round crusty bread

Sauté onion in butter over medium heat. Stir in cornstarch and mix thoroughly. Gradually add milk and water. Cook mixture over medium heat, stirring constantly until the mixture just comes to a boil and thickens. Stir in cream cheese, dried beef, green pepper, Tabasco sauce, and mustard. Continue to cook and stir until the cheese is melted. Cut the top off the crusty bread and pull the center of the bread out to form a bread bowl. Tear the bread top and center pieces up to use as dippers. Just before serving, spoon the hot beef mixture into the hollowed bread and serve. Makes $2^2/_3$ cups.

Recipes & Remembrances/Buffalo Lake (Great Plains/South Dakota)

Chipped Beef Spread

This party-dip recipe has been around for years, and seems to get better with age. It is always a hit at gatherings large and small.

1 (8-ounce) package cream cheese, softened
2½ ounces dried beef, shredded
¼ cup finely chopped green pepper
¼ cup finely chopped red bell pepper

1 medium onion, finely chopped
½ teaspoon black pepper
½ cup sour cream
¾ cup chopped pecans

Mix cream cheese well with dried beef, green and red peppers, onion, and black pepper. Fold in sour cream. Spoon into casserole dish. Top with pecans. Bake at 350° for 20 minutes. Serve with crackers. Serves 8–10.

Savannah Collection (Georgia)

Benedictine

A favorite sandwich spread, or can be thinned with milk or sour cream to make a delightful vegetable chip dip. Benedict's, the home of Benedictine, was made famous by caterer and cookbook writer, Jennie Carter Benedict. The opulent decor of the Fourth Street establishment is remembered by many. The Blue Ribbon Cookbook of Jennie Benedict was popular at the turn of the century. The author was a civic leader as well as an astute businesswoman.

1 large cucumber
1 (8-ounce) package cream cheese, softened
1 small onion, grated

¼ teaspoon salt
1 tablespoon mayonnaise
2–3 drops green food coloring

Pare, grate, and drain cucumber. Combine cucumber with remaining ingredients.

The Cooking Book (Kentucky)

Vidalia Onion Spread

1 cup coarsely chopped Vidalia
  onions
1 cup Hellmann's Mayonnaise

1 cup grated Cheddar cheese
Paprika

Combine onions, mayonnaise, and cheese. Pour into 1-quart baking dish. Sprinkle with paprika. Bake at 350° for 25 minutes. Blot with paper towels to remove excess oil. Serve hot with Triscuits. Yields 6–8 servings.

Second Round, Tea-Time at the Masters® (Georgia)

Sun-Dried Tomato Spread

3 ounces sun-dried tomatoes
2 large garlic cloves
1 teaspoon dried basil
$^{1}/_{2}$ teaspoon salt
$^{1}/_{2}$ cup olive oil

2 parsley sprigs
$^{1}/_{4}$ teaspoon red pepper
1 green onion, chopped
6 ounces cream cheese
2 ounces butter, softened

Cover dried tomatoes with boiling water and let stand for 20 minutes to rehydrate. Drain. Combine all but cream cheese and butter in processor, then let marinate for 2 hours.

Combine cream cheese and butter. Whip until smooth. In small bowl lined with plastic wrap, layer mixtures: cheese, tomato, cheese, tomato, and cheese. This keeps for several days in refrigerator. Unmold and serve with Cayenne Toast.

CAYENNE TOAST:
$^{1}/_{2}$ teaspoon sugar
$^{1}/_{2}$ teaspoon pepper
$^{1}/_{2}$ cup olive oil
$^{1}/_{2}$ teaspoon cayenne pepper

$^{1}/_{2}$ teaspoon salt
$^{1}/_{2}$ teaspoon paprika
$^{1}/_{2}$ teaspoon garlic powder
1 loaf French bread

Whisk ingredients (except bread) together. Cut bread into $^{1}/_{4}$-inch slices. Spread oil mixture on each slice with a pastry brush. Bake on ungreased sheet in a 200° oven for 1 hour.

Steppingstone Cookery (Mid-Atlantic/Maryland)

★ **Editor's Extra:** The Cayenne Toast is good with anything! Or by itself! I like to use light olive oil. Frozen French bread cuts more neatly than fresh, and be sure to use a serrated knife.

Amber Glow

1 (8-ounce) package cream cheese, softened
1 (10-ounce) jar (¾ cup) apricot preserves
1½ teaspoons dry mustard
1 teaspoon prepared horseradish
¼ cup chopped salted peanuts
Crackers

Press cream cheese into an 8-ounce plastic margarine tub or a small bowl. Loosen edges with a spatula and invert onto the center of a shallow serving dish. Smooth surface with a spatula.

In a small bowl, mix preserves, mustard, and horseradish until well blended. Pour over cheese. Sprinkle with nuts. Serve with crackers.

Chefs and Artists (Pennsylvania)

Kahlúa Pecan Brie

3 tablespoons packed brown sugar
¼ cup Kahlúa or strong, freshly brewed coffee, cooled
¾ cup pecan halves, toasted
1 (16-ounce) round brie cheese

In medium skillet, combine brown sugar and Kahlúa. Heat, stirring constantly, until blended. Add pecans; simmer until hot, but not runny. Remove from heat.

Place brie on microwave-safe serving plate and spoon warm pecan mixture on top. Microwave on HIGH for 1–2 minutes, or until cheese softens. Watch carefully, cheese will melt quickly. Serve with crackers and fresh fruit. Makes 8–10 servings.

Colorado Collage (Colorado)

★★★★★★★★★★★   ★★★★★★★★★★★

Crab Quiche Squares

Great for a crowd.

Double pie crust pastry	1 pint half-and-half
10–12 ounces shredded Swiss cheese	1 (10-ounce) package frozen chopped spinach
2 tablespoons grated Romano cheese	1 large onion, chopped
3–4 tablespoons flour	1 tablespoon minced garlic
5 eggs	½ cup butter
	1 (12-ounce) can crabmeat

Press double pie crust pastry into a 15x10x1-inch jellyroll pan and come up the sides. Puncture crust with a fork. Pre-bake at 350° for 10 minutes. Cool crust.

Toss shredded Swiss and Romano cheeses with flour. Beat eggs; add half-and-half. Add spinach that has been well squeezed. Sauté onion and garlic in butter. Add sautéed mixture to egg mixture. Add crabmeat. Then add to Swiss and Romano cheese mixture. Bake at 400° for 40–45 minutes, until brown. Yields 60 (1½-inch) squares.

Note: This can also be placed into 2 pre-baked pie shells. Freezes well.

Treat Yourself to the Best Cookbook (West Virginia)

Curious about which kind of crabmeat to choose from when preparing recipes? Lump crabmeat is the largest pieces of meat from the crab's body; it is the most expensive form of crabmeat. Backfin is white body meat in lump and large flakes and is best for dishes where appearance is important. Special, which is flakes of white body meat other than lump, is good for casseroles and crabcakes. Claw is small, brownish meat from the claws; as the least expensive type of crabmeat, it is good for appetizers, soups, and dips.

Helen's Nuts and Bolts

Fun snack to take on trips.

4 sticks margarine or 2 cups corn oil
2 level teaspoons garlic salt
2 level teaspoons celery salt
5 teaspoons Worcestershire sauce
1 (8-ounce) box Rice Chex
4 ounces Corn Chex

4 ounces Wheat Chex
1 (7-ounce) box Cheerios
1 pound pecan halves
10 ounces pretzel sticks
1 small can mixed party nuts
   (optional)

Melt butter with all seasonings. Mix remaining ingredients well, using wooden spoon to stir. Try to coat evenly. Bake, uncovered, in 250° oven for 1½–2 hours. Stir every 15 minutes while baking. Let cool overnight in pan that it was baked in.

Our Favorite Recipes (Tennessee)

Baked Caramel Goodstuff

Set this near your cookie jar and you will find it cuts down on your cookie baking. Great for nibbling!

8 cups puffed wheat cereal
½ cup walnut pieces
½ cup dry roasted peanuts
½ cup pecan pieces
½ cup butter or margarine

1 cup packed brown sugar
¼ cup corn syrup
¼ teaspoon salt
¼ teaspoon baking soda
1 teaspoon vanilla

In large bowl, combine first 4 ingredients. Melt butter in saucepan; stir in sugar, syrup, and salt. Bring to boil, stirring constantly. Boil 5 minutes. Remove from heat and stir in baking soda and vanilla. Gradually pour over cereal mixture. Stir to coat thoroughly. On greased cookie sheet, spread evenly. Bake at 300° for 15 minutes. Stir well and bake 15 minutes more. Cool completely on pan. Break into desired size pieces and store in airtight container.

Savoring the Southwest (New Mexico)

★ **Editor's Extra:** The first time you make this will be the first of many. I like some Chex in it, too!

Cranberry Jalapeño Jelly

Red instead of the usual green.

6 jalapeño peppers
2½ cups cranberry juice cocktail
7 cups sugar

6 ounces liquid fruit pectin
1 cup vinegar
Red food coloring (optional)

Wearing lightweight rubber gloves, quarter and remove seeds from peppers. Place peppers and cranberry juice in blender and process until peppers are very finely chopped. Combine with sugar in a 4-quart simmer pot. Cover with plastic wrap (so that you can see mixture as it cooks). Microwave on HIGH 18–20 minutes, or until mixture comes to a full rolling boil. Add pectin and microwave on HIGH 2–3 minutes, or until mixture returns to a boil. Add vinegar and, if desired, food coloring. Pour mixture into sterilized jelly glasses and seal. Yields 8 (8-ounce) jars.

Serving Suggestion: Spread ½ cup jelly over an 8-ounce block of cream cheese. Serve with assorted crackers.

Micro Quick! (Texas)

Hot Pepper Jelly

This is great!

4 large bell peppers (1⅓ pounds)
½ cup fresh hot red peppers (12)
   or 4 tablespoons crushed dried red
   peppers

7 cups sugar
1½ cups white vinegar
Green food coloring (6–8 drops)
2 (6-ounce) bottles liquid pectin

In large pot, place peppers that have been ground fine (use juice and pulp), sugar, and vinegar. Bring to full boil; reduce heat to low and simmer 10 minutes. Add green food coloring and pectin. Stir well. Bring mixture to a boil over high heat; reduce heat and boil 1 minute. Remove from heat and pour mixture into hot dry, sterilized half-pint jars. Seal while hot. Makes 8 pints. To use as hors d'oeuvre, spread crackers with cream cheese and top with dab of pepper jelly. (Pictured on cover.)

Rivertown Recipes (Tennessee)

★★★★ ★★★★

*When there is a whale sighting on the Seward Highway in Alaska,
the cars pull off the road to catch a glimpse of these magnificent
mammals. Gwen and Barney linger in this beautiful setting long after
the whales have gone.*

Cheese Biscuits

This is a raised biscuit—delicious served with a salad meal.

2 cups flour
4 teaspoons baking powder
1 teaspoon salt

4 tablespoons Crisco
1 cup grated cheese
²/₃ cup milk (or more)

Sift dry ingredients; add shortening and cheese. Mix into a wet dough with milk. Place on floured board and work only enough to handle well. Cut biscuits and bake (about 10–12 minutes) in 425°– 450° oven.

The Junior Welfare League 50th Anniversary Cookbook (Kentucky)

Feather Beds

These may also be made into crescent rolls and clover rolls. They are very light and most delicious.

¹/₃ cup sugar
1 teaspoon salt
³/₄ cup hot potato water
¹/₄ cup margarine

4–4¹/₂ cups flour
1 package yeast
¹/₂ cup warm mashed potatoes
1 egg

Stir together sugar, salt, potato water, and margarine. Let cool. Add the rest of the ingredients and knead well. Let rise until double in bulk. Then roll out and cut into circles. Put close together on a baking sheet. Let rise again until double. Bake at 350° for 18–30 minutes until golden. (Pictured on cover.)

Grandmother's Cookbook (Pennsylvania)

★ **Editor's Extra:** When boiling potatoes for another dish, save enough to have ³/₄ cup water and ¹/₂ cup mashed potatoes. If making for this recipe alone, boil one medium-sized, peeled, cut potato in 1¹/₂ cups of water.

Mexican Spoon Bread

A Southwestern classic.

1 (16-ounce) can cream-style corn
¾ cup milk
⅓ cup vegetable oil
2 eggs
1 cup yellow cornmeal

½ teaspoon baking soda
1 teaspoon salt
1 (4-ounce) can chopped green chiles
2 cups shredded longhorn cheese
  or Cheddar cheese, divided

Combine the corn, milk, oil, eggs, cornmeal, baking soda, and salt in a mixer bowl. Beat until well mixed. Pour ½ of the mixture into a buttered 1½-quart casserole. Sprinkle green chiles and 1 cup of the cheese over the corn mixture. Spoon the remaining corn mixture over the cheese. Top with remaining cheese. Bake at 400° for 45 minutes or until puffed and golden. Serves 4.

Reflections Under the Sun (Arizona)

Spinach Corn Bread

1 stick margarine
1 large onion, chopped fine
8 ounces cottage cheese
1 package Jiffy or Mexican corn
  bread mix (Mexican is best)

1 package frozen chopped spinach,
  drained and squeezed
½ teaspoon salt
4 eggs, well beaten

Melt margarine; add onion, cheese, corn bread mix, spinach, and salt. Add eggs last and mix well. Bake at 400° for 30 minutes in greased dish or corn bread pan. Does not brown on top, so run under broiler a few minutes to brown.

Top Rankin Recipes (Mississippi)

Stretched across the Royal Gorge and the raging Arkansas River is the Royal Gorge Bridge in CaZon City, Colorado, the world's highest suspension bridge. The bridge, constructed in 1929, measures 1,053 feet high, 1,260 feet long and 18 feet wide.

Classic Bruschetta

Use a good, dense, crusted loaf of bread, sliced thin, but thick enough to hold as finger food. Great with a salad meal.

1 loaf crusty bread	**Parmesan cheese**
Olive oil	

Cut bread into ½-inch slices. Brush both sides with olive oil. Place on an ungreased baking sheet and bake at 425° for 5 minutes, or until crisp and lightly browned, turning once. (Can be covered and stored for up to 24 hours at room temperature.)

Spread each toast with a thin layer of Olive Paste. Top with Tomato Topping; sprinkle with Parmesan cheese. Return to baking sheet and bake at 425° for 2-3 minutes, or until cheese melts and toppings are heated through.

OLIVE PASTE:

1 cup pitted, ripe olives	**1 teaspoon olive oil**
1 teaspoon balsamic vinegar	**2 cloves garlic, minced**
1 teaspoon capers, drained	

Blend (in blender) the above ingredients until nearly smooth paste forms. (If desired, can be made ahead and refrigerated up to 2 days.)

TOMATO TOPPING:

2 medium red tomatoes, chopped	**½ cup chopped green pepper**
2 medium yellow tomatoes, chopped	**½ cup chopped yellow pepper**
⅓ cup sliced green onions	**1 tablespoon olive oil**
½ cup chopped red pepper	**1 tablespoon chopped fresh basil**
	⅛ teaspoon black pepper

Combine tomatoes, onions, peppers and olive oil. Add basil and black pepper. Can be covered and chilled for up to 2 days.

Where There's a Will... (Mid-Atlantic/Maryland)

Monte Cristo Club

A celebration in a sandwich.

6 slices whole-wheat bread
4 tablespoons strawberry preserves
4 slices boiled ham
4 slices cooked turkey
4 slices Swiss cheese

1 egg
¼ cup milk
Salt to taste
Butter for grilling

Spread each of 4 slices of bread with 1 tablespoon preserves. Top each of 2 of these slices with a slice of ham, turkey, and cheese and a plain slice of bread. Place another slice of ham, turkey, and cheese on the plain slice.

Place the remaining preserve-coated bread, preserve-side-down, on top. Beat together the egg, milk, and salt. Dip the sandwiches in the egg mixture, then grill in a buttered skillet until golden brown and hot enough. Serve at once. Makes 2 servings.

Love Yourself Cookbook (North Carolina)

Bunker Hill Brown Bread

An easy bread with a delicious flavor. Spread with cream cheese or serve plain.

1½ cups flour
1½ teaspoons salt
2 teaspoons baking soda
1 cup wheat germ
1 cup graham cracker crumbs

2 eggs
½ cup vegetable oil
1 cup molasses
2 cups buttermilk

Preheat oven to 350°. Sift flour, salt, and baking soda into a mixing bowl. Add wheat germ and graham cracker crumbs. Stir to combine. In a second bowl combine eggs, vegetable oil, molasses, and buttermilk. Blend.

Add liquid ingredients to dry ingredients. Stir until well blended. Pour batter into 2 well-greased and floured, tall, one-pound coffee cans (or prepared Bundt pan). Bake for 50–55 minutes or until bread tests done. Makes 2 loaves or 1 Bundt pan. (Pictured on cover.)

Stirring Performances (North Carolina)

★★★★★★★★★★★ ★★★★★★★★★★★

Spicy Pineapple Zucchini Bread

3 eggs, beaten
1 cup oil
2 cups sugar
2 teaspoons vanilla
2 cups shredded, unpeeled zucchini
 squash
1 (8¼-ounce) can crushed
 pineapple, well drained

3 cups plain flour
2 teaspoons baking soda
1 teaspoon salt
½ teaspoon baking powder
1½ teaspoons cinnamon
¾ teaspoon nutmeg
1 cup finely chopped nuts
½ cup raisins

Beat eggs with oil, sugar, and vanilla until thick and foamy. Stir in zucchini and pineapple. Sift flour with baking soda, salt, baking powder, and spices. Stir nuts and raisins into flour mixture, then add to zucchini. Stir together just until blended. Divide evenly between 2 greased and floured 9x5-inch loaf pans. Bake at 350° until done, about 1 hour. Yields 2 loaves.

Potlucks and Petticoats (Georgia)

Applesauce Bread Baked in a Jar

Great take-along and have-on-hand dessert.

⅔ cup shortening
3⅓ cups sugar, divided
4 eggs
2 cups applesauce
3⅓ cups flour
2 teaspoons baking soda

1 teaspoon cinnamon
⅔ cup chopped nuts
½ teaspoon baking powder
1½ teaspoons salt
1 teaspoon cloves

Cream the shortening and 2⅔ cups sugar together. Beat in eggs, remaining ⅔ cup sugar, and applesauce. Sift together and blend into first mixture the remaining ingredients. Mix well. Pour into well-greased pint jars (wide mouth with no neck), filling half full. Bake at 325° for about 45 minutes. Remove one jar at a time from oven; wipe the sealing edge clean. Put on lid and ring and screw tight. Jar will seal as bread cools. Store as you would regular canned goods. Delicious! Enjoy!

Centennial Cookbook (Michigan)

Strawberry Bread with Spread

2 (10-ounce) packages frozen sliced
  strawberries, thawed
3 cups all-purpose flour
1 teaspoon baking soda
1 teaspoon cinnamon
2 cups sugar

1 teaspoon salt
1¼ cups vegetable oil
4 eggs, beaten
1 teaspoon red food coloring
Spread (recipe below)

Measure out ½ cup strawberry juice and reserve for Spread. Mix all dry ingredients together. Make a hole in center of mixture. Pour strawberries, oil, and eggs into the hole. Mix by hand until all ingredients are combined. Add food coloring. Mix well. Pour into 2 greased and floured 9x5x3-inch loaf pans. Bake at 350° for 1 hour. Cool thoroughly.

SPREAD:
1 (8-ounce) package cream cheese,
  softened

½ cup reserved strawberry juice

Mix until spreading consistency is obtained. Spread on cooled slices of strawberry bread. (Pictured on cover.)

Amazing Graces (Texas II)

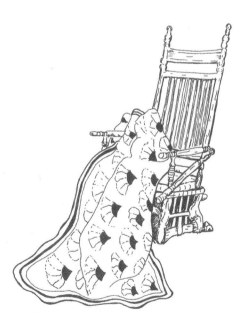

Glazed Cranberry Orange Nut Bread

1 cup sugar
2 cups plus 2 tablespoons flour
1 teaspoon salt
2 teaspoons baking powder
1/2 teaspoon baking soda
1 cup orange juice

Grated peel from 1 orange
1/4 cup shortening, melted
1 cup chopped cranberries
1/2 cup chopped nuts
1 egg, beaten

Sift dry ingredients together. In separate bowl, combine remaining ingredients. Lightly mix all the ingredients together. Bake in a lightly greased loaf pan for 40–50 minutes at 375°. Toothpick should come out clean when it is done. Before loaf cools, pour Glaze over the top.

GLAZE:
1/4 cup sugar
2 tablespoons orange juice

2 tablespoons coarsely chopped
  cranberries

Cook slowly until a thick syrup forms. Pour over loaf while hot.

The Best Cranberry Recipes (Wisconsin)

Cooperstown B&B Banana Jam Bread

1/2 cup margarine
1 cup sugar
2 eggs
1 cup mashed bananas
1 teaspoon lemon juice
2 cups flour

1 tablespoon baking powder
1/2 teaspoon salt
1/2 cup strawberry jam
1 cup chopped pecans or walnuts
1 cup raisins

Cream margarine. Gradually add sugar and beat until fluffy. Add eggs. Combine bananas and lemon juice. Stir into creamed mixture. Combine flour, baking powder, and salt. Add to creamed mixture, stirring until moistened. Stir in jam, nuts, and raisins. Pour into greased 9x5-inch loaf pan. Bake at 350° for 50 minutes. Cool 10 minutes. Remove from pans. Cool on wire rack.

Trinity Catholic School Cookbook (New York)

"The Best" Pumpkin Bread

A very moist, tasty bread—the best I have ever eaten.

2½ cups flour
2 teaspoons baking soda
1 teaspoon salt
1 teaspoon cinnamon
½ teaspoon nutmeg
¼ teaspoon ginger
1 (3½-ounce) package butterscotch instant pudding
1 (3½-ounce) package lemon instant pudding
5 eggs
1½ cups sugar
1½ cups cooking oil
1 (1-pound) can pumpkin (2 cups)
3 teaspoons vanilla
1 cup chopped pecans (optional)

Sift first 8 ingredients together in large bowl. Beat eggs; add sugar, oil, pumpkin, and vanilla. Stir into dry ingredients and mix well. Stir in nuts, if desired. Pour into 2 greased 8½x4½-inch loaf pans. Bake at 350° for 1 hour or until tests done (tester should come out clean), but do not bake too brown. Cool in pan 10 minutes; carefully turn out onto cake rack to cool.

Tip: Make pumpkin-wiches by spreading softened cream cheese between pumpkin bread slices.

Holiday Treats (Virginia)

Over 60% of the nation's entire furniture production is crafted within a 200-mile radius of High Point, North Carolina, the furniture capital of the world. There are more than 125 manufacturing plants in the area, many of which are the largest factories in the world.

★★★★★★★★★★★★ ★★★★★★★★★★★★

Morning Glorious Bread or Muffins

Served at Ramblewood in Camdenton.

2 cups flour
1¼ cups granulated sugar
½ teaspoon salt
2 teaspoons baking soda
2 teaspoons baking powder
2 teaspoons cinnamon
3 tablespoons Tang

¾ cup coconut
1½ cups grated carrots
  (4 medium)
3 eggs
1 cup oil
1 teaspoon vanilla
1½ cups chopped apples

Combine dry ingredients; add remaining ingredients. Bake at 350° in 2 greased loaf pans for 1 hour (20 minutes for 2-inch muffins; 15 minutes for mini-muffins).

Breakfasts Ozark Style (Missouri)

Bran Muffins with Maple Syrup

Great muffins!

¾ cup maple syrup
2 eggs
2½ cups bran flakes, crushed
1 cup sour milk (buttermilk)

1 cup flour
1 teaspoon baking soda
½ cup chopped nuts

Combine maple syrup and eggs, then crushed bran flakes. Let the mixture stand for 5 minutes. Using a wooden spoon, beat in the sour milk. Stir in flour and baking soda and fold in chopped nuts. Pour batter into greased muffin pans. Bake for about 20 minutes at 400°. Makes 12 servings.

Recipe from Sugarbush Bed and Breakfast, Barneveld, New York
Bed & Breakfast Leatherstocking Welcome Home Recipe Collection
(New York)

★ **Editor's Extra:** I like to use raisin bran flakes. I put about 3 cups in a plastic bag and crush with my hands, then measure in case you need more. Batter can be refrigerated if you want to make half today and half a few days later. This a repeat favorite.

Leslie's Blueberry Cinnamon Muffins

Have some sweet butter and a mug of coffee ready—you're in for a glorious morning!

Preheat the oven to 375°. Grease the muffin pan with butter or cooking spray. In one bowl, blend the liquids:

1 egg, lightly beaten
2 tablespoons soft butter or
  vegetable oil

¾ cup milk

In another bowl, blend the solids:

½ cup sugar
1 cup flour
1 teaspoon baking powder
½ teaspoon ground cinnamon
¼ teaspoon ground cloves

½ teaspoon salt
1½ cups fresh or frozen wild
  blueberries (if frozen, drain
  well)

In a small cup, mix the topping:

2 tablespoons sugar

1 teaspoon ground cinnamon

Add the liquids to the solids and quickly blend the ingredients with a rubber spatula. Do not overmix. Fill the muffin cups, sprinkle with the topping, and bake for 20–25 minutes. Makes 8 muffins.

Recipes from a New England Inn (New England/Maine)

Raspberry Muffins

"The room, the fire, the town...everything was great! But could we have a dozen muffins to go, please?"

2½ cups flour
¼ cup sugar
¼ cup packed brown sugar
1 tablespoon plus 1 teaspoon baking powder
½ teaspoon cinnamon

2 eggs, slightly beaten
1 cup milk
½ cup margarine or butter, melted
1 tablespoon flour
6 ounces raspberries, fresh or frozen

In a large bowl, mix together flour, sugar, brown sugar, baking powder, and cinnamon. In another bowl, combine eggs, milk, and margarine or butter. Add to dry ingredients and stir until just blended, being careful not to overmix. Coat raspberries with a small amount of flour and fold into batter. Spoon into muffin tins.

TOPPING:

½ cup chopped walnuts
1 cup packed brown sugar
½ cup flour

1 tablespoon grated orange peel
1 tablespoon cinnamon

Combine Topping ingredients and top each muffin with 1 teaspoon of the mixture. Bake at 350° for 20–25 minutes, until tester comes clean.

Mendocino Mornings (California)

★ **Editor's Extra:** These were declared the best in "Muffindom!"

Bite-Size Applesauce Muffins

Little jewels.

$^{1}/_{2}$ cup butter or margarine
$^{1}/_{2}$ cup sugar
2 eggs
$^{3}/_{4}$ cup applesauce
$1^{3}/_{4}$ cups all-purpose flour
1 tablespoon baking powder

$^{1}/_{2}$ teaspoon salt
$^{1}/_{4}$ cup butter or margarine,
  melted
$^{1}/_{4}$ cup sugar
$^{1}/_{8}$ teaspoon ground cinnamon

Cream $^{1}/_{2}$ cup butter; gradually add $^{1}/_{2}$ cup sugar, beating until light and fluffy. Add eggs, one at a time, beating well after each addition. Stir in applesauce. Combine flour, baking powder, and salt; add to creamed mixture and stir just until moistened. Spoon batter into lightly greased miniature muffin pans. Fill two-thirds full. Bake at 425° for 10–15 minutes or until done.

Remove from pan immediately and dip muffin tops into melted butter. Combine $^{1}/_{4}$ cup sugar and cinnamon. Sprinkle sugar mixture over each muffin. Yields about $3^{1}/_{2}$ dozen.

The Bonneville House Presents (Arkansas)

Peach Pudding Coffee Cake

This is a great Sunday morning brunch treat, served warm.

2 cups sliced peaches
Lemon juice
Cinnamon
$^{3}/_{4}$ cup sugar
1 teaspoon baking powder

1 cup flour
$^{1}/_{2}$ teaspoon salt
4 tablespoons butter
$^{1}/_{2}$ cup milk

In an 8-inch-square pan, slice 2 cups fresh peaches. Sprinkle with lemon juice and cinnamon. Combine sugar, baking powder, flour, and salt in mixing bowl. Blend in butter and add milk. Spread this batter on top of peaches. Sprinkle the batter with Topping.

TOPPING:
$^{3}/_{4}$ cup sugar
1 tablespoon cornstarch

1 cup boiling water

Sprinkle sugar and cornstarch over batter. Add boiling water over top. Do not stir. Bake at 350° for 45 minutes.

Blue Willow's "Sweet Treasures" (Iowa)

Pineapple Coffee Cake

2 cups flour
1¾ cups sugar
2 teaspoons baking soda
2 eggs

1 (20-ounce) can crushed pineapple
  with juice
½ cup chopped nuts
2 teaspoons vanilla

Mix flour, sugar, baking soda, and eggs by hand and add remaining ingredients. Pour into greased 9x13-inch pan and bake at 350° for 35–40 minutes.

TOPPING:

1 (8-ounce) package cream cheese,
  softened
1 stick butter, softened

1¾ cups powdered sugar
1 teaspoon vanilla

Combine all ingredients until well blended and spread over cooled cake.

Somethin's Cookin' at LG&E (Kentucky)

Apple Biscuit Coffee Cake

2 tablespoons butter or margarine
2 cooking apples, peeled and sliced
¼ cup raisins
1 can refrigerated ready-to-bake
  biscuits
¼ cup brown sugar

½ teaspoon cinnamon
¼ cup light corn syrup
1 egg
¼ cup walnuts
1 tablespoon butter or margarine

Melt 2 tablespoons butter in bottom of 9-inch-round cake pan. Arrange sliced apples over butter. Sprinkle raisins over apples. Cut each of the biscuits into fourths and place over apples.

Mix together brown sugar, cinnamon, corn syrup, and egg until well blended and sugar is dissolved. Pour over biscuits. Sprinkle walnuts over top. Dot with 1 tablespoon butter.

Bake at 350° for 25–30 minutes. Invert on serving plate, spooning juices over top. Yields 6–8 servings.

From the Apple Orchard (Missouri)

Blueberry Streusel Coffee Cake

CAKE:

2¾ cups flour
1½ teaspoons baking powder
1½ teaspoons baking soda
½ teaspoon salt
¾ cup butter or margarine, softened

1 cup sugar
3 eggs
1 pint sour cream (may use plain
  yogurt)
2 teaspoons vanilla extract

Grease and flour a 10-inch tube pan. Combine flour, baking powder, baking soda, and salt. Set aside. In a large bowl, cream butter or margarine and sugar until light and fluffy. Add eggs one at a time, beating well after each addition. Add flour mixture alternately with sour cream and vanilla to batter.

STREUSEL:

¾ cup brown sugar
¾ cup chopped walnuts
1 teaspoon cinnamon

2–2½ cups blueberries (if frozen,
  drain before using)

Combine Streusel ingredients (except blueberries). Set aside ½ cup Streusel for topping. Toss remaining Streusel with berries. Spread ⅓ of the batter in prepared pan; sprinkle with ½ of the berry mixture. Spread ⅓ of the batter over that and sprinkle with remaining berry mixture. Top with remaining batter and reserved Streusel. Bake at 375° for 60–65 minutes or until toothpick inserted in center comes out clean. Cool in pan on wire rack for 10 minutes. Remove from pan and serve. Serves 16.

Savor the Flavor of Oregon (Oregon)

Butterscotch Breakfast Ring

This is a good recipe to have for holidays. Sweet enough to be dessert!

1 cup butterscotch morsels,
  divided
2 tablespoons butter
2 tablespoons flour
$1/8$ teaspoon salt

$1/2$ cup chopped pecans
1 (10-ounce) package refrigerated
  crescent rolls
7 teaspoons corn syrup

Preheat oven to 375°. Melt half of the butterscotch morsels and the butter in the top of a double boiler over hot, not boiling, water. Remove from heat. Stir in flour, salt, and nuts, mixing gently with a fork. Set aside.

Separate the rolls into triangles. Arrange on a greased cookie sheet so the triangles form a circle. The edges should overlap slightly and the long ends point outward.

Spread 2 teaspoonfuls of butterscotch mixture on each triangle. Roll up, jellyroll fashion, toward the center. Slash the inside half of each roll. Bake for 15 minutes, or until golden brown.

Meanwhile, combine the remaining $1/2$ cup butterscotch morsels with the corn syrup. Melt over hot water, stirring to blend. Let cool slightly, then drizzle over the Breakfast Ring. Serve hot or cold. Makes 1 ring.

Love Yourself Cookbook (North Carolina)

★★★★★★★★★★★★   ★★★★★★★★★★★★

Breakfast Bundt Cake

¹/₄ cup chopped nuts
1 package yellow cake mix
1 package vanilla instant pudding
³/₄ cup oil
³/₄ cup water

4 eggs
1 teaspoon vanilla
1 teaspoon butter extract
2 teaspoons cinnamon
¹/₄ cup sugar

GLAZE:
1 cup confectioners' sugar
¹/₂ teaspoon vanilla

¹/₂ teaspoon butter extract
1 tablespoon plus ¹/₂ teaspoon milk

Grease and flour Bundt pan; sprinkle nuts in bottom. Combine cake mix, pudding, oil, and water, and mix well. Add eggs, one at a time, and mix well. Add vanilla and butter extract. Beat at high speed for 8 minutes. Pour ¹/₃ of batter into pan; sprinkle with half mixture of cinnamon and sugar. Add another ¹/₃ batter and sprinkle again. Add remaining batter. Bake 40–45 minutes at 350°. Cool and remove from pan. Mix Glaze ingredients till smooth. Drizzle with Glaze while still warm.

Watsonville Community Hospital 40th Anniversary Edition (California)

Curried Fruit

Delicious with breakfast, lunch, or supper . . . or as a dessert!

¹/₃ cup butter
³/₄ cup brown sugar
4 teaspoon curry powder
1 tall can pear halves

1 tall can peeled apricot halves
1 tall can pineapple chunks
1 tall can peach halves

Mix butter, sugar, and curry powder. Drain the canned fruits and place in baking dish. Other fruits such as kumquats or cherries may be added. Spread sugar mixture over fruits and bake for 1 hour at 325°. Can be baked once and reheated and it's even better! Serves 6–8.

Gator Country Cooks (Florida)

 The honor system is alive and well in Washington at the Orchard Run Fruit Stand on the Blewett Pass Highway (U.S. Route 97), where customers can pay by stuffing dollar bills into a slot at the front of the wooden stand.

Stuffed French Toast

1 (8-ounce) package cream cheese,
  softened
1/4 cup crushed pineapple
1/2 cup chopped pecans
1 (16-ounce) loaf French bread
4 eggs

1 cup whipping cream
1/2 teaspoon vanilla
1 teaspoon ground nutmeg
1 (12-ounce) jar (1 1/2 cups) apricot
  preserves
1/2 cup orange juice

Beat cream cheese and pineapple together until fluffy. Stir in nuts; set aside. Cut bread into 10–12 (1 1/2-inch) slices; cut a pocket in the top of each. Fill each with 1 1/2 tablespoons of the cheese mixture. Beat together eggs, whipping cream, vanilla, and nutmeg. Using tongs, dip the filled bread slices in egg mixture, being careful not to squeeze out the filling. Cook on lightly greased griddle until both sides are golden brown. Meanwhile, heat together preserves and juice. To serve, drizzle apricot mixture over hot French toast. Yields 10–12 slices.

Recipe from Annie's Bed and Breakfast, Big Sandy
Texas Historic Inns Cookbook (Texas)

Overnight Caramel French Toast

1/2 cup (1 stick) butter
1 cup firmly packed brown sugar
2 tablespoons light corn syrup
6 slices thick Texas toast

6 eggs
1 1/2 cups milk
1 teaspoon vanilla
Dash of salt

Melt butter in 9x13-inch glass baking dish in microwave for 1–2 minutes. Add brown sugar and corn syrup; mix well and microwave 1 minute more. Stir again. Lay thick bread slices on top of sugar mix. In a separate bowl, combine eggs, milk, vanilla, and salt; whip well. Pour egg mixture over bread. Cover and refrigerate overnight.

Bake, uncovered, at 350° for 45–60 minutes (should be puffed and brown). When serving portions, invert so caramel is on top. Makes 8 servings.

Recipe from Meadow Creek Bed & Breakfast Inn, Pine
Colorado Columbine Delicacies (Colorado)

Heavenly Pancakes

1 cup sour cream
1 cup cottage cheese
¾ cup flour

4 eggs, separated
¼ teaspoon salt
1 tablespoon sugar

Mix cream and cheese; stir in flour and well-beaten egg yolks. Beat until smooth; add salt and sugar. Fold in stiffly beaten egg whites. Cook on hot, greased griddle. Delicious served with creamed chicken.

Bucks Cooks (Pennsylvania)

Blueberry Hill Wild Blueberry Pancakes

This was and continues to be the most requested breakfast entrée, as attested to by the many "blue" smiles of guests leaving the dining room.

1¼ cups unbleached white flour
1 tablespoon sugar
1 tablespoon baking powder
½ teaspoon salt
4 eggs, separated
2 cups milk

¼ cup sweet butter, melted
1 cup wild blueberries, rinsed and
   picked over
Butter
Maple syrup

In a large mixing bowl, mix together all the dry ingredients. Set aside. Lightly beat the egg yolks, then add the milk and melted butter and mix well. Set aside.

Beat the egg whites until they form stiff—but not dry—peaks. Set aside. Make a hollow in the center of the dry ingredients. Pour in the milk mixture and blend batter well. Don't worry about a few lumps—they will work themselves out. Carefully fold in the egg whites until well incorporated. Gently stir in the blueberries.

Ladle the batter onto a lightly greased hot skillet or griddle to form 3-inch circles. Cook till bubbles form, flip, and cook until golden brown, about 1 minute. Serve with butter and heated Vermont syrup. Serves 4.

Tony Clark's New Blueberry Hill Cookbook (New England/Maine)

Sour Cream Rollups

As anyone who visits the Steamboat Inn knows, this dish is our "House Breakfast Special"—we couldn't remove it from the menu even if we wanted to without having a battle on our hands!

1 cup white flour	2 eggs
1 cup whole-wheat flour	2½ tablespoons oil
½ teaspoon salt	2 cups sour cream, divided
1½ teaspoons sugar	1 cup preserves, homemade or
1½ teaspoons baking powder	purchased, divided
1½ teaspoons baking soda	Powdered sugar
2 cups buttermilk	

Combine dry ingredients. Combine buttermilk, eggs, and oil together and add to dry ingredients, beating just until all is incorporated.

To cook on a griddle: Ladle out a 10-inch strip of batter, using ½ cup of batter. Cook until batter starts to bubble and firm up. Flip over to cook on other side.

To cook in a skillet: Pour batter in a round pancake shape and cook as above. When pancake is finished cooking, remove from pan.

Spoon ⅓ cup sour cream along the pancake and top with 3 tablespoons preserves. Roll up in jellyroll fashion and top with a dollop of sour cream and jam. Dust with powdered sugar. Makes 6–8 rollups.

Thyme & the River, Too (Oregon)

Apple Pan Dowdy

An old recipe that continues to please. Also good as a dessert.

White bread (about 10–12 slices)	½ teaspoon cinnamon
Melted butter (1–2 sticks)	½ cup water
4 large green apples	Whipped cream
½ cup dark brown sugar	

Remove crust from bread and slice each piece into 3 fingers. Dip each finger into melted butter and line bottom and sides of a baking dish with half of the fingers. Peel and core apples. Slice. Place in center of bread fingers. Sprinkle apples with mixture of the sugar and cinnamon. Add water and cover the top with a layer of well-buttered fingers of bread. Sprinkle top with additional sugar. Cover and bake 1 hour in a 350° oven. Serve hot with whipped cream. Serves 6.

Recipes from Smith-Appleby House (New England/Rhode Island)

Sausage-Grits Casserole

A Southern classic.

1 cup quick grits
3 cups beef bouillon
$^1/_2$ teaspoon salt
1 pound hot sausage
2 sticks butter

4 beaten eggs
1 cup milk
$^1/_2$ cup grated sharp cheese, divided
  (use half and sprinkle with
  remainder)

Cook grits in bouillon and salt until thick, about 3–4 minutes. In skillet, cook sausage until well done; drain on paper towels. Add sausage to cooked grits, mixing thoroughly. Add remainder of ingredients to grits and sausage, again mixing thoroughly. Pour into greased casserole. Sprinkle with remaining grated cheese before cooking. (This looks very soupy before cooking; it thickens as it bakes.) Bake for 30–45 minutes at 350°. Serves 8.

Gardeners' Gourmet II (Mississippi)

Garlic Cheese Grits

$^1/_2$ teaspoon salt
2 cups water
1 cup quick grits
8 ounces garlic cheese
$^1/_2$ cup butter or margarine

2 egg yolks, beaten
Salt and pepper to taste
Dash of Tabasco sauce
Worcestershire sauce to taste
2 egg whites, stiffly beaten

Preheat oven to 350°. Bring salted water to a boil and stir in grits, slowly. Cook for 2 minutes. Remove from heat and add cheese (cut into 6–8 pieces) and butter or margarine. Place back on medium heat and continue to cook until cheese is completely melted. Remove from heat and add egg yolks, and salt and pepper to taste. Mix thoroughly, then add Tabasco sauce and Worcestershire sauce, mixing well. Fold in stiff egg whites and then pour into greased casserole. Bake at 350° for 30 minutes or until browned. Serves 6.

Kiss My Grits (Tennessee)

Sausage and Egg Brunch Bake

Make-ahead marvelous!

2 cups herb croutons
1 pound bulk sausage, cooked and
  well drained
4 eggs, lightly beaten
2$^1/_2$ cups milk

1 teaspoon dry mustard
1$^1/_2$ cups (6 ounces) shredded
  Cheddar cheese
1 (10$^3/_4$-ounce) can cream of
  mushroom soup

Line bottom of greased 9x13-inch glass baking dish with croutons. Cover with sausage. Combine eggs, milk, mustard, cheese, and soup. Pour over sausage. Run a knife cross-wise through mixture as you would to marble cake batter. Cover and refrigerate overnight.

When ready to bake, preheat oven to 325°. Bake, uncovered, for 1 hour and 15 minutes or until firm in center and brown on top. Let stand 5 minutes before cutting into squares. Serves 8.

Becky's Brunch & Breakfast Book (Texas)

Potato Egg Bake

$^1/_2$ cup margarine
1 (16-ounce) package frozen hash
  browns
1 cup shredded Cheddar cheese
2 cups shredded Swiss cheese

2 cups diced ham
4–5 eggs
1 cup milk
1 cup chopped onion, or to taste

Melt margarine in 9x13-inch pan. Add hash browns. Bake at 425° for 30 minutes. Mix balance of ingredients together and pour over browned hash browns. Bake at 350° for 30 minutes. This can be made the day before serving. Let stand 5 minutes before cutting into pieces.

Red, White & Blue Favorites (Arizona)

The World's Largest Santa statue, weighing 900 pounds and standing 48 feet tall, is located quite naturally in North Pole, Alaska. The fiberglass Santa was built for the 1962 World's Fair in Seattle, Washington. Santa stood near the Space Needle for a few years and was later moved to the Seattle Shopping Center before finding his current home.

Baked Eggs in Pepper Rings

Pretty with red peppers, too.

1 large green pepper
1 tablespoon butter
4 eggs
1/4 teaspoon salt
1/8 teaspoon pepper
1/8 teaspoon oregano

1/8 teaspoon basil
4 tablespoons cream
4 tablespoons fresh bread crumbs
2 teaspoons Parmesan cheese
2 tablespoons butter, melted

Cut pepper into 4 rings, 1/2 inch thick. Cook in lightly salted water for 3–5 minutes. Drain. Melt 1 tablespoon butter in a shallow 1-quart casserole in oven. Place pepper rings in casserole. Break 1 egg into each ring. Sprinkle with seasonings. Pour 1 tablespoon cream over each. Combine crumbs, Parmesan, and butter; sprinkle over. Bake at 350° for 15–20 minutes, or until eggs are set. This doubles, triples, and more for a large brunch. Can easily be prepared ahead.

Flavors of Cape Henlopen (Mid-Atlantic/Delaware)

Cheese Strata

A Christmas morning favorite.

8 slices white bread, buttered, crusts removed
3 cups shredded Cheddar cheese, divided

4 eggs, slightly beaten
2 1/2 cups milk
1 teaspoon salt
1/4 teaspoon dry mustard

Cut bread slices into quarters. Alternate layers of bread and cheese in greased 7x11-inch baking dish, ending with cheese. Mix eggs, milk, salt, and mustard. Pour over cheese and bread layers. Cover. Chill 6 hours or overnight.

Bake uncovered in a preheated 325° oven for 45 minutes or until firm. Let stand a few minutes and cut into squares. May be frozen after baking. Defrost before reheating. Serves 6–8.

Gulfshore Delights (Florida)

Quiche Cargo Boat

This luscious "boat" will please every crew member.

1 loaf French bread, unsliced	2 teaspoons cornstarch, divided
2 tablespoons butter	2 eggs, lightly beaten
$1/2$ cup chopped scallions	$1/4$ teaspoon dry mustard
$1^1/2$ teaspoons flour	$1/4$ teaspoon salt
1 cup shredded Swiss or Cheddar	$1/4$ teaspoon pepper
cheese	1 tablespoon grated Parmesan
$1/2$ cup light cream, divided	cheese

Preheat oven to 425°.

Cut off top of bread and hollow out, leaving about 1 inch of bread on bottom. Cover with foil. Place on baking sheet and bake 5 minutes. While bread is in oven, melt butter in saucepan and sauté scallions until tender. Mix in flour and set aside. Layer shredded cheese and any cooked meats or vegetables you might want to add in the bottom of the bread shell. Reduce heat to 375°.

In a medium bowl, stir small amount of the cream into cornstarch, blending until smooth. Add remaining cream, eggs, seasoning, and remaining starch, blending until smooth. Mix well and add to the scallion mixture. Pour cream mixture over cheese in bread shell. Sprinkle with Parmesan. Bake 40 minutes or until inserted knife comes out clean. Let stand 10 minutes before slicing. Serve or wrap to go. Serves 8–10.

Variations: Crumbled bacon, ham, basil, mushrooms, cooked shrimp, broccoli, or spinach may be added to the egg mixture.

Moveable Feasts Cookbook (New England/Connecticut)

Soups, Stews & Chilies

★★★★ ★★★★

A farm girl herself, Barbara couldn't resist seeing what it felt like to sit in an old wooden bathtub like the one here at the John Deere Home in Grand Detour, Illinois.

Ox-Tail Vegetable Soup

Knuckle soup bone or ox-tail chuck
  roast of beef
1 (29-ounce) can tomatoes, put
  through blender
$1/4$ cup chopped fresh carrots,
  small pieces
$1/4$ cup chopped celery, small pieces
$1/4$ cup chopped onion, small pieces
$1/4$ cup corn (fresh, if possible)
$1/4$ cup fresh green beans
$1/4$ cup finely cut cabbage
1 teaspoon sugar
$1/3$ cup barley
1 tablespoon chopped fresh parsley
Salt to taste
1 cup V-8 or tomato juice
1 potato, chopped in small pieces
$1/2$ cup rice

Cover meat with water and blended tomatoes; bring to a boil, skim, then add all vegetables and ingredients except potato and rice. May vary amount of vegetables as desired. Cook at least 2 hours. Then add potato and rice and cook an additional $1/2$ hour. May serve meat separately or shred throughout soup. Add more juice or water, if more liquid is needed.

McNamee Family & Friends Cookbook (Washington)

Goulash Soup

This easy, do-ahead recipe is the best treasure I brought home from Germany. It has become an American classic.

1–$1^1/2$ pounds beef chuck, cut into
  bite-size pieces
$1/2$ stick margarine, melted
4 medium onions, chopped
2 cloves garlic, minced
3 tablespoons flour
4 tablespoons paprika
1 ($10^1/2$-ounce) can tomato purée
2 quarts beef bouillon
1 (10-ounce) can beef consommé
2–3 potatoes, cubed
Salt and pepper to taste

Brown beef well in large heavy pot in margarine. Add and sauté onions and garlic. Add flour, paprika, tomato purée, bouillon, consommé, and potatoes. Add salt and pepper. Simmer for 3 hours. Serve with hot French bread and a salad.

Culinary Classics (Georgia)

★★★★★★★★★★ ★★★★★★★★★★

Hearty Split Pea, Bean and Barley Soup

This soup is wonderful reheated and will keep for 4–5 days refrigerated.

15 cups water
1 meaty ham bone, or 2 large pork
  hocks (about 2 pounds total)
2 cups (1 pound) dry green split
  peas, picked over and rinsed
$\frac{1}{2}$ cup pearl barley
$\frac{1}{2}$ cup dry black-eyed peas, picked
  over and rinsed
$\frac{1}{2}$ cup dry navy beans, picked over
  and rinsed
3 bay leaves

2 beef bouillon cubes (or up to 5 as
  needed)
2 large onions, coarsely chopped
2 large carrots, thinly sliced
2 large celery stalks, including
  leaves, thinly sliced
2 garlic cloves, minced
$\frac{1}{2}$ teaspoon (generous) dried thyme
$\frac{1}{2}$ teaspoon ground celery seed
$\frac{1}{2}$ teaspoon black pepper
Salt to taste

In a large, heavy soup pot, combine water, ham bone, split peas, barley, black-eyed peas, and beans. Bring to a boil over high heat. Add bay leaves, 2 bouillon cubes, onions, carrots, celery, garlic, thyme, celery seed, and pepper. Cover and lower heat. Simmer, stirring occasionally, until beans are tender and split peas have thickened the soup, about 2–$2\frac{1}{2}$ hours.

As soup thickens, lower heat and stir more frequently to prevent split peas from sticking to bottom of pot. Taste the soup. If more bouillon cubes are needed (for richer flavor), add them, along with salt, if desired.

When beans are tender, remove ham bone or pork hocks. If pork hocks have been used, discard them. If a ham bone has been used, reserve and cool slightly. Meanwhile, remove soup from heat and skim fat off top and discard. Then, if ham bone has been used, cut meat into bite-size pieces and return it to soup. Bring soup to a boil again. Stir well before serving. Serves 12–14.

Get Cookin' with Sound Construction (Oregon)

Richard Hollingshead opened America's first drive-in movie theater in Camden, New Jersey, on June 6, 1933—it is no longer in operation. Wilson Shankweiler opened the second drive-in theater in America, in Orefield, Pennsylvania, on April 15, 1934. It is the longest-running outdoor cinema in America, having opened consecutively for every season since 1934.

Lentil Soup

1¼ cups lentils
5 cups water
4 slices bacon
1 medium onion, diced
1–2 medium carrots, finely chopped
1 medium green pepper, finely
  chopped

1 medium tomato, peeled, coarsely
  chopped
3 tablespoons margarine
3 tablespoons all-purpose flour
1 (10½-ounce) can beef consommé
2 teaspoons salt
2 tablespoons vinegar

Wash lentils and cook in water for 1 hour. Cut bacon into little pieces and fry in large skillet. Place vegetables in bacon fat and cook until limp, about 5 minutes. Add vegetable mixture to lentils and continue cooking over low heat. Do not clean skillet. In same skillet in which bacon was cooked, melt margarine. Add flour, stirring to make a smooth paste. Add consommé, salt, and vinegar, stirring constantly. Add this sauce to the lentils and stir well. Cook over low heat for 30 minutes or longer, until cooked to taste. Serve with crusty rolls and a green salad for a satisfying meal.

Mountain Laurel Encore (Kentucky)

Mexican Corn & Bean Sopa

One of the most popular soups ever to come from the Colophon, this Mexican Corn & Bean Sopa has been featured in many publications since we created it. It's vegetarian and low in fat.

1 medium onion, finely diced
3 cloves garlic, minced
Olive oil
1 (15-ounce) can diced tomatoes, or
  equal amount of fresh tomatoes
  and juice
2 (15-ounce) cans red kidney beans,
  drained
1 (24-ounce) can vegetable juice

3 teaspoons chili powder
1 teaspoon sugar
½ teaspoon black pepper
1 teaspoon cumin
Hot water
1 (1-pound) bag frozen corn
Sour cream for garnish
Tortilla chips for garnish

Sauté onion and garlic in a little olive oil in a large pot. Add tomatoes, beans, and vegetable juice to pot and heat to a slow boil. Mix chili powder, sugar, black pepper, and cumin in a small bowl, then add hot water to make a paste-like consistency; add to pot. Add corn to pot; heat to slow boil, reduce heat, and simmer for about 20 minutes. Garnish with sour cream and tortilla chips.

The Colophon Cafe Best Soups (Washington)

Southwest Taco Soup

1½ pounds lean ground beef
1 (23-ounce) can ranch-style beans
1 (15-ounce) can pinto beans
1 (15-ounce) can kidney beans
1 (15-ounce) can corn, drained
1 (14-ounce) can Mexican-style
  tomatoes
1 large onion, chopped
3 ribs celery, chopped
2 (1-ounce) envelopes taco seasoning
1 (1-ounce) envelope ranch-style
  salad dressing

Brown the ground beef in a skillet, stirring until crumbly; drain.

Combine the browned beef, undrained ranch-style beans, undrained pinto beans, undrained kidney beans, corn, undrained tomatoes, onion, and celery in a slow cooker and mix well. Stir in the taco seasoning mix and salad dressing mix. Cook, covered, on LOW for 8 hours. Serves 10.

Tucson Treasures (Arizona)

★ **Editor's Extra:** This can be done on the stovetop—simmer an hour or so.

Sopa de Tortilla

2 (10¾-ounce) cans Campbell's
  Chicken Broth, diluted according
  to instructions
½ cup chopped celery
1 teaspoon chili powder
1 small tomato, peeled, seeded, and
  chopped
1 teaspoon chopped onion
3 small cloves garlic, minced
1 teaspoon chopped parsley
1 tablespoon olive oil
1 (6¾-ounce) package Doritos,
  regular flavor
1 cup grated sharp Cheddar cheese

Boil broth, celery, and chili powder until celery is tender. Fry tomato, onion, garlic, and parsley in oil until onion is soft. Add tomato mixture to broth. Break the Doritos into medium pieces and add to soup, boiling briefly until the Doritos are soft. Add cheese just before serving.

Flavors (Texas)

★★★★★★★★★★★   ★★★★★★★★★★★

Italian Sausage Soup

1 pound Italian sausage
1 cup coarsely chopped onion
2 garlic cloves, sliced
5 cups beef broth
$1/2$ cup water
$1/2$ cup red (burgundy) wine
2 cups stewed tomatoes
1 cup sliced carrots (or grated)

$1/2$ teaspoon basil leaves
3 tablespoons parsley
$1/2$ teaspoon oregano leaves
1 medium green pepper, chopped
Regular or cheese tortellinis
  (optional)
Parmesan cheese

Cook sausage. Sauté onion and garlic in drippings; drain. When fully cooked, add remaining ingredients. Simmer 35–45 minutes. You can add cut-up regular or cheese tortellinis to soup. Sprinkle Parmesan cheese on each serving.

Maple Hill Cookbook (Minnesota)

Sweet and Sour Cabbage Soup

6 cups shredded and diced cabbage
1 onion, coarsely chopped
5 cups beef broth
5 cups chicken broth
2–3 cups chopped cooked meat*
1 teaspoon minced garlic
$1/4$ teaspoon dried thyme
$1/4$ teaspoon ground allspice

$1/2$ teaspoon ground cayenne, or to
  taste
Salt and pepper to taste
2 cups chopped tomatoes
$1/4$ cup tomato paste
$1/4$ cup brown sugar
$1/4$ cup cider vinegar
$1/8$ cup lemon juice

Simmer cabbage and onion in the broth in a big soup pot until tender, about $1/2$ hour. Add the meat, garlic, spices, tomatoes, and tomato paste, and simmer until reduced slightly and the flavors are blended. Add the brown sugar, vinegar, and lemon juice and reheat.

This soup improves with 24 hours chilling and reheating. While the recipe makes a lot of hearty soup, it freezes well. Serves 10.

*Note: Smoked sausage, ham, beef, pork roast, pot roast—any kind of cooked meat will work in this recipe.

More to Love...from The Mansion of Golconda (Illinois)

Garlic Soup

Don't be put off by the title. This is an aromatic, beautiful and delicious soup. When the garlic is boiled, it loses the familiar pungency, and instead, flavors the soup subtly and almost indefinably.

20 pods of garlic, peeled and sliced
4 tablespoons butter
2 fresh tomatoes, peeled, seeded, and diced
$^1\!/_2$ cup scraped and sliced carrots
$^1\!/_4$ cup sliced celery

$^1\!/_4$ cup diced onion
4 cups chicken broth
1 egg, separated
$^1\!/_2$ tablespoon cider vinegar
Salt and pepper to taste

In a large saucepan, sauté the garlic in butter until very soft. Stir in the tomatoes and cook briefly. Add carrots, celery, and onion and cook until onion is soft. Stir in broth and simmer, uncovered, until vegetables are cooked through. Remove from heat. In a separate bowl, combine egg yolk and vinegar and beat slightly. Carefully stir in 2 or 3 ladlesful of the soup mixture. Stir slowly back into soup a little at a time. Without beating beforehand, whisk egg white into soup mixture. Season to taste with salt and pepper. Reheat, if necessary, but do not allow to boil. Serves 4.

Galley Buffet Soup Cookbook (Texas)

Sweet Red Pepper Soup

2 tablespoons unsalted butter
2 large onions, chopped
2 medium carrots, peeled and sliced
6 cups chicken broth
2$\frac{1}{2}$ pounds sweet red peppers, chopped

1 cup skim milk
Salt and pepper to taste
$\frac{1}{4}$ teaspoon thyme
Sour cream or yogurt for garnish

Melt butter in large saucepan and sauté onions over low heat until soft. Add carrots and chicken stock and bring to a boil. Reduce heat and simmer for 20 minutes. Add chopped red peppers and cook for 20 minutes, until peppers are soft. Remove from heat and add milk, salt, pepper, and thyme. When soup is cool, purée in batches in blender or food processor. To serve, reheat, but do not boil. Add a dollop of sour cream or yogurt, if desired. Yields 6 adult servings. (Pictured on cover.)

Best of Friends (Mid-Atlantic/Maryland)

Down Home Cheddar Cheese Soup

Flavor is outstanding.

$\frac{1}{2}$ cup margarine
$\frac{1}{2}$ cup each finely chopped:
  celery, green pepper, onion, carrot, cauliflower
1 tablespoon granulated chicken bouillon (or 2 cubes)

2 cups water
$\frac{1}{2}$ cup margarine
$\frac{2}{3}$ cup flour
4 cups milk
$\frac{1}{2}$ pound (2 cups) sharp Cheddar cheese, shredded

Heat $\frac{1}{2}$ cup margarine over medium heat. Add vegetables; cook until tender, stirring often. Add chicken bouillon and water; heat to boiling. Cover; cook over low heat 10 minutes.

Meanwhile, heat $\frac{1}{2}$ cup margarine in saucepan. Stir in flour; cook until bubbly. Remove from heat. Gradually stir in milk. Cook over medium heat, stirring often, until thickened, but do not boil. Stir in cheese till fully blended. Stir cheese mixture into vegetables and chicken broth mixture. Serves 8–10.

The Country Mouse (Mississippi)

Broccoli-Cheese Soup

A scrape-the-bottom-of-the-bowl soup.

**4 cups fresh or frozen chopped
  broccoli**
2 (14-ounce) cans chicken broth
2 cups chopped onions
**1 clove garlic, minced, or
  ⅛ teaspoon garlic powder**

½ cup margarine
½ cup flour
2 cups milk
2 cups grated Cheddar cheese
1 teaspoon basil

Simmer until tender the broccoli, broth, onions, and garlic. Melt in saucepan the margarine, flour, milk, and cheese. Mix the cheese sauce into the broccoli mixture and add basil. Heat; simmer awhile, and enjoy.

Four Square Meals a Day (Colorado)

Cream of Broccoli Soup

4 slices bacon
⅓ cup chopped onion
**6 cups shredded raw potatoes
  (6 medium)**
2 teaspoons salt
3 cups boiling water
**1 (10-ounce) package frozen
  chopped broccoli (or 1½ cups
  fresh)**

1 cup water
3 tablespoons butter
4 tablespoons flour
**1 tablespoon instant chicken
  bouillon**
1½ cups milk
1 (13-ounce) can evaporated milk
½ teaspoon pepper
2 teaspoons Accent (optional)

Fry bacon in deep skillet; remove slices, drain, and reserve. Add to the bacon fat, onions potatoes, salt, and boiling water. Cover and simmer about 15 minutes; last 5 minutes, add the broccoli that has been puréed with the cup of water in blender. Melt butter in separate saucepan; blend in flour and bouillon. Add milks and cook until thickened. Add to broccoli mixture and heat. Add pepper and Accent, if desired. Crumble bacon fine; can be added to the soup or sprinkled on top of servings. Serves 6–8.

Through Our Kitchen Windows (Florida)

Tomato Bisque

In earlier days, it was common practice to "home can" tomatoes, not only by themselves, but also in the form of concentrated soup base. To make tomato soup, all you had to do was heat the soup base in one pan and an equal amount of milk in another, then combine them. Most older community cookbooks in Ohio contain at least one recipe for Cream of Tomato Soup, sometimes called Tomato Bisque.

2 cups chicken broth or stock
1 (14½-ounce) can whole tomatoes,
  undrained and broken up
½ cup chopped celery
½ cup chopped onion
3 medium tomatoes, peeled, seeded,
  and chopped

3 tablespoons butter or
  margarine
3 tablespoons flour
2 cups half-and-half or light coffee
  cream
1 tablespoon sugar

In large saucepan, combine broth, canned tomatoes, celery, and onion; bring to a boil. Reduce heat, cover, and simmer 20 minutes. In blender or food processor, purée mixture in small batches until all mixture is puréed. In same pan, cook fresh tomatoes in butter about 5 minutes; stir in flour. Add half-and-half; over low heat, cook and stir until thickened. Stir in broth mixture and sugar; heat through (do not boil). Makes about 1½ quarts.

Bountiful Ohio (Ohio)

The World's Largest Buffalo, located at the Frontier Village in Jamestown, North Dakota ("The Buffalo City"), is a concrete statue 26 feet high, 46 feet long, and weighs 60 tons. The Jamestown Chamber of Commerce's tourist promotion committee, as a monument to commemorate the vast herds of bison that once roamed the prairies of North America, conceived the idea for the buffalo in 1957. The statue, sculpted by Elmer Paul Peterson, was dedicated in 1959.

Seafood Bisque

This is the best seafood bisque ever!

2 sticks butter (no substitute)
1/3 cup finely chopped celery
1/3 cup finely chopped onion
1/2 bay leaf
Pinch of Italian seasoning
1/2 pinch tarragon
4 drops Tabasco sauce

3 tablespoons clam juice
1/3 cup flour
2 tablespoons sherry
1 quart half-and-half
1 pound seafood chunks (shrimp, crab, scallops, white fish)
1 1/2 teaspoons salt

Melt butter in skillet; add celery, onion, and bay leaf. Sauté until tender. Add Italian seasoning, tarragon, Tabasco sauce, clam juice, and flour. Stir to make a roux (remove bay leaf). Remove from heat; add sherry and set aside.

In top of double boiler, heat the half-and-half. Stir in roux and heat (stirring) until thickened, 7–10 minutes. Add mixed seafood. Heat until seafood is cooked through, 10 minutes. Add extra clam juice if it gets too thick. Salt to taste.

Manna by the Sea (Oregon)

★★★★★★★★★★   ★★★★★★★★★★

Seafood Gumbo II

½ cup salad oil
½ cup flour
1 large onion, chopped
2–3 garlic cloves, minced
1 (1-pound) can tomatoes, undrained
1½ pounds frozen okra, or
  equivalent fresh
Oil for frying okra (2 tablespoons)
2 quarts hot water
3½ tablespoons salt
¾ teaspoon red pepper

1 large bay leaf
¼ teaspoon thyme
8–10 allspice berries
Few grains chile pepper
2 pounds headless raw shrimp,
  peeled
1 pound claw crabmeat, picked
1 pint oysters
½ cup chopped green onions
½ cup chopped parsley

Make a very dark roux with oil and flour in a large heavy pot. Add onions and garlic. Cook slowly until onions are transparent. Add tomatoes and cook on low heat until oil rises to the top (about 30 minutes), stirring frequently.

In separate skillet, fry okra in oil on moderately high heat, stirring constantly until okra is no longer stringy. Add the okra to the other mixture; stir and simmer about 10 minutes. Add water, salt, and pepper. Simmer partially covered for 45 minutes. Add other seasonings and simmer an additional 20 minutes; then add shrimp—simmer 15 minutes; then add crabmeat, simmering 15 minutes more. Add the oysters the last 5 minutes of cooking. Taste carefully for seasoning, adding more, if necessary. Remove from fire and stir in green onions and parsley. Serve over rice. Variations may be made by adding different seafoods, sausages, or poultry. Serves 8–10.

River Road Recipes II (Louisiana)

★★★★★★★★★★★ ★★★★★★★★★★★

Grandma Smith's Clam Chowder

We have been told by a customer—who claims to be an absolute authority on clam chowder—to be sure not to change even a grain of pepper in the recipe.

2½–3 slices bacon, diced
1 cup diced celery
3 tablespoons diced onion
3 cups water
3 medium potatoes, peeled and diced
1¾ teaspoons Worcestershire sauce
1 teaspoon salt
Pinch pepper

2 (6½-ounce) cans minced clams, undrained
¼ cup butter
6 tablespoons flour
½ cup evaporated milk and ½ cup water, or 1 cup milk
Fresh parsley sprigs

Cook bacon in skillet until crisp. Remove bacon, drain on paper towels, and set aside. Reserve drippings. Sauté celery and onion in reserved drippings over low heat for 5–10 minutes, or until vegetables are translucent. Drain and set aside.

Combine potatoes, Worcestershire sauce, salt and pepper with water in medium pot. Add clams and reserved bacon and vegetables. Cover and simmer for 20–30 minutes, or until potatoes are tender.

Melt butter in heavy skillet. Blend in flour and stir over low heat for 5–6 minutes. Do not brown. Add milk slowly, stirring until mixture is smooth and thick. Add gradually to clam-vegetable mixture. Heat, but do not boil. Garnish each serving with a parsley sprig. Makes 6 servings.

The Elsah Landing Restaurant Cookbook (Illinois)

Midwest Corn Chowder

A meal in itself.

2 cups diced potatoes
½ cup chopped carrots
½ cup chopped celery
¼ cup chopped onion
2 cups boiling water
¼ cup margarine

¼ cup flour
2 cups milk
10 ounces mild Cheddar cheese, divided
1 (16-ounce) can cream-style corn

Simmer potatoes, carrots, celery, and onion in water 15–20 minutes, till tender. Make a cream sauce with margarine, flour, and milk. Stir shredded cheese into cream sauce until melted. Add cheese sauce and corn to vegetables and their broth. Heat through, but do not let boil. Serves 6–8.

Sharing our Best (Colorado)

Chilies

White Grass Chili

This is by far the most popular dish served at White Grass. We should have a sign reading "Over A Billion Bowls Served."

2½ cups dried or 2 (16-ounce) cans pinto beans
2 teaspoons salt
2 medium onions, chopped
4 cloves garlic, chopped
3 stalks celery, chopped
4 carrots, peeled and grated
1 large green pepper, chopped
2 tablespoons olive oil
⅓ cup raw bulgur
1 tablespoon ground cumin

1 teaspoon dried basil
1 teaspoon dried oregano
3 tablespoons chili powder
¼ teaspoon or dash cayenne pepper
1 cup water
1 (16-ounce) can whole tomatoes, chopped
1 (16-ounce) can tomato purée
Salt and pepper to taste
Grated Jack or Cheddar cheese

If using dried beans, soak them overnight in 2 quarts water (plus a dash of baking soda). Rinse and cook in fresh water with salt. Cook until tender, about 1 hour. Reserve 1 cup broth.

In a large saucepan, sauté onions, garlic, celery, carrots, and green pepper in olive oil. Add bulgur, herbs, spices, and water. Mix well and add cooked beans, 1 cup of bean broth (or canned beans), tomatoes, and purée. Let simmer 45 minutes, or until bulgur is softened. Season to taste. It may be necessary to add more water to determine thickness. Serve topped with grated Jack or Cheddar cheese. Serves 6.

White Grass Cafe Cross Country Cooking (West Virginia)

The world's largest kaleidoscope, Kaatskill Kaleidoscope, in Mt. Tremper, New York, was originally built inside a silo, but the silo was later replaced with a larger 65-foot-tall structure to accommodate more visitors. Viewers actually step inside the giant kaleidoscope with its 37.5-foot-tall, 50-foot-wide Pyramid of Mirrors towering over their heads.

Chili Blanco

1 large onion, chopped
1 tablespoon oil
2 (16-ounce) cans white beans
2 (14-ounce) cans chicken broth
1 teaspoon chicken soup base
2–3 cloves garlic, minced
2 (4-ounce) cans diced green chiles

1–2 teaspoons ground cumin
1 teaspoon dried oregano leaves
½ teaspoon pepper
4 cups cooked and diced chicken
1 cup sour cream
3 cups shredded Monterey Jack
   cheese

Sauté onion in oil. In crockpot, combine all ingredients except sour cream and cheese. Simmer several hours (at least 3) so flavors are blended. Just before serving, stir in sour cream and cheese, heating until cheese melts.

Years and Years of Goodwill Cooking
(Great Plains/North Dakota)

Bowl of Red

The exact origin of chili is still debated today, but New Mexicans claim it was a chuckwagon cook who ran out of black pepper. Looking for a substitute, he tried the little red peppers commonly used by the local Indians and Mexicans, and thus "Bowl of Red" was born.

2 tablespoons vegetable oil
1 large white onion, coarsely chopped
3 garlic cloves, finely chopped
3 pounds lean beef, coarse
4 tablespoons ground hot New
   Mexico red chile

4 tablespoons ground mild New
   Mexico red chile
2 teaspoons ground cumin
1½ teaspoons salt
3 cups water

In a 4-quart Dutch oven or heavy pot, heat oil; add onion and garlic. Cook until soft. Add beef, ground chiles, and cumin; cook until meat is evenly browned, breaking any lumps with fork. Add salt and water; bring to a boil and reduce heat. Simmer uncovered 2–3 hours, stirring occasionally, until meat is very tender and flavors are fully blended. Add more water as necessary. Makes 6 servings.

Sassy Southwest Cooking (New Mexico)

No Peep Stew

2 pounds lean beef	3 cans Snap-E-Tom tomato cocktail
2 cups Irish potatoes	3 tablespoons tapioca
2 cups celery	Salt and pepper
2 cups chopped onions	Lawry's Seasoned Salt
2 cups chopped carrots	

Cube and mix together meat and vegetables. Season to taste with salt, pepper, and Lawry's, and any other desired seasoning. Place in a Dutch oven. Dissolve tapioca in the tomato juice and pour over mixture. Bake for 5 hours at 250°. Do not peep! Serves 6–8.

Maury County Cookbook (Tennessee)

★ **Editor's Extra:** This works well in an electric roaster in less time—about 2$^{1}/_{2}$ hours. Superb!

Crock Pot Barbecued Beef Stew

A meaty stew, so delicious, so easy.

2 pounds stew beef	$^{1}/_{3}$ cup barbecue sauce
2 tablespoons oil	2 cups beef stock
1 cup sliced onions	$^{1}/_{2}$ teaspoon salt
1 large clove garlic, minced	1 (4-ounce) can mushrooms,
$^{1}/_{2}$ cup chopped bell pepper	drained
$^{1}/_{8}$ teaspoon pepper	3 tablespoons cornstarch
1 cup diced tomatoes	1$^{1}/_{4}$ cup cold water

Brown beef in oil. Put sliced onions, garlic, and pepper in bottom of crock pot. Add beef and remaining ingredients except the cornstarch and water. Cook on LOW 8–10 hours. Dissolve cornstarch in water; add to crock pot, and simmer until thick. Serve over rice.

Carolina Cuisine Encore! (South Carolina)

★ **Editor's Extra:** An outstanding, light barbecue taste that everybody seems to enjoy. This can be done in the oven at 250° for about 4 hours.

Salads

Multnomah Falls on Larch Mountain in Oregon is the second highest year-round waterfall in the nation. Benson Bridge, where you can feel the falls' cool mists, crosses between the upper and lower cataracts.

Strawberry & Romaine Salad

A wonderful salad. The combination of strawberries and onion is simply delicious—everyone's favorite.

DRESSING:

2 cups mayonnaise	**$^1/_3$ cup raspberry vinegar**
$^2/_3$ cup sugar	**2 tablespoons poppy seeds**
$^1/_3$ cup light cream	**2–3 tablespoons raspberry jam**

Combine Dressing ingredients.

Romaine, washed and torn	**Fresh strawberries, sliced**
Red onion, sliced	**Slivered almonds for garnish**

Toss romaine, onion, and strawberries. Just before serving, drizzle Dressing over salad. Dressing can be kept at least a week in refrigerator. Good on fruit, too.

If It Tastes Good, Who Cares? I (Great Plains/North Dakota)

Roasted Hazelnut Salad

The warm smell of roasting hazelnuts will remind you of the cozy atmosphere in your grandmother's kitchen. Serve with salmon or steelhead.

SALAD:

$^1/_2$ cup Oregon hazelnuts, roasted	**2 tomatoes, seeded and cubed**
1 head romaine lettuce, torn into	**$^1/_2$ cup alfalfa sprouts**
bite-size pieces	**$^1/_3$ cup sliced green onions**
1 avocado, peeled and cubed	**$^1/_2$ cup shredded mozzarella cheese**

To roast hazelnuts, place on a cookie sheet in a 275° oven for 20–30 minutes, until skins crack. To remove skins, rub warm nuts between your hands or in a towel. (Or microwave 3–4 minutes on FULL power.) Chop nuts, saving a few whole nuts for garnish.

In a large salad bowl, toss romaine, avocado, tomatoes, nuts, sprouts, onions, and cheese.

DRESSING:

2 tablespoons white wine vinegar	**$^1/_3$ cup olive oil**
1–2 tablespoons Dijon mustard	**Freshly ground pepper to taste**

In a small bowl, whisk together vinegar and mustard. Gradually drizzle in olive oil. Whisk; add pepper. Chill and pour over Salad just before serving. Garnish with whole roasted hazelnuts. Yields 10 servings.

Rogue River Rendezvous (Oregon)

Cobb Salad with Buttermilk Herb Dressing

Light, pretty salad with an excellent dressing.

1/2 head iceberg lettuce	4 scallions, chopped
1/2 head red leaf lettuce	2 hard-cooked eggs, chopped
1/2 bunch watercress, chopped	2 whole chicken breasts, cooked
2 medium tomatoes, diced	and cubed
1/2 cup crumbled blue cheese	1 large avocado, diced
6 slices bacon, cooked and crumbled	Chopped parsley for garnish

Cut lettuce into small pieces. Toss lightly in a bowl with watercress and arrange on a serving platter. Arrange tomatoes, blue cheese, bacon, scallions, eggs, chicken, and avocado in rows across lettuce. Garnish with parsley and chill.

BUTTERMILK HERB DRESSING:

1/2 cup buttermilk	1/2 teaspoon freshly ground pepper
1/2 cup mayonnaise	1 tablespoon minced chives
1 large shallot, minced	1/2 teaspoon ground thyme
1 large clove garlic, minced	1 teaspoon minced parsley
1/2 teaspoon coarse salt	

Whisk buttermilk, mayonnaise, shallot, and garlic in a medium bowl. Add the salt, pepper, chives, thyme, and parsley, blending well. To serve, pass the salad with dressing on the side. Yields 6 servings.

Note: Dressing best made at least 24 hours before serving.

Five Star Sensations (Ohio)

★★★★★★★★★★★ ★★★★★★★★★★★★

Greek Salad

Greek cook Pauline Georges is a good friend always willing to share a recipe. When I asked about the secret of her delicious Greek salads, she said it in two words: lemon juice. She promptly sent me a recipe for a basic Greek salad and salad dressing. I serve it often, and each time, I appreciate the delicate blend of herbs and lemon all over again.

1 small head lettuce (romaine preferred), washed and chopped	**1 cucumber, chopped**
2 green onions, chopped in 1-inch pieces	**1 fresh tomato, chopped**
	1 green pepper, cut in strips
	Feta cheese, crumbled
2 stalks celery, chopped	**Calamata olives (large Greek olives)**

Mix salad ingredients, except feta and olives. Pour dressing over salad. Toss to coat. Top each salad serving with feta cheese and an olive.

GREEK SALAD DRESSING:

¹/₂ cup olive oil	**¹/₄ teaspoon freshly ground black pepper**
¹/₄ cup vegetable oil	
¹/₃ cup fresh lemon juice (about 3 lemons)	**1 clove garlic, minced or pressed**
	³/₄ teaspoon dried oregano
1 teaspoon salt	**¹/₄ teaspoon sugar**

Place in jar. Shake well. Store in refrigerator. Allow to come to room temperature before using. Makes 1 cup.

Note: Double or triple for large groups.

Savannah Collection (Georgia)

 Mississippi's Canton Flea Market, the South's oldest and largest arts and crafts show, is held twice a year, on the second Thursday in May and October. Visitors come from as far as Europe to enjoy a great variety of crafts from more than 1,100 vendors.

Craisin-Spinach Salad

3 bunches spinach, washed and
  torn into bite-size pieces
2 Gala apples, washed and chopped

$^3/_4$ cup craisins
$^1/_2$ cup almonds

Combine ingredients in a large bowl. Add Dressing and toss well.

DRESSING:

$^1/_2$ cup sugar
2 teaspoons salt
2 tablespoons chopped onion
$1^1/_2$ cups oil

2 teaspoons dry mustard
$^2/_3$ cup apple cider vinegar
2 tablespoons poppy seeds

Combine well. Extra Dressing keeps well for a couple of weeks in refrigerator. (Pictured on cover.)

Taste of Balboa (Washington)

Twenty-Four Hour Spinach Salad

1 pound fresh spinach, washed,
  dried, and torn
Salt and pepper to taste
4 hard-cooked eggs, peeled and
  sliced
1 pound bacon, cooked and crumbled
1 small head iceberg lettuce, shredded

2 Bermuda onions, thinly sliced
1 large bag frozen English peas
$^1/_2$ cup mayonnaise
$^1/_2$ cup Miracle Whip
12 ounces baby Swiss cheese,
  shredded

Place spinach into a large glass salad bowl so that the layers may be seen. Sprinkle with salt and pepper. Add a layer of eggs, crumbled bacon, lettuce and another sprinkle of salt and pepper. Add a layer of onions and uncooked frozen peas. Repeat this process until the bowl is filled. Cover and refrigerate overnight.

    Early in the morning of the day the salad is to be used, mix mayonnaise and Miracle Whip and spoon over the top of the salad. This topping should penetrate through the salad. Sprinkle with shredded Swiss cheese over top and refrigerate until serving time. Serves 12.

The Gulf Gourmet (Mississippi)

Turkey Salad with Strawberries

This dressing is so good, you'll want to use it on all your salads!

1 pound asparagus
2 cups fresh strawberries, sliced
6 cups assorted salad greens

3 cups cooked turkey, cut into
  $^1/_2$-inch cubes
$^1/_4$ cup pecan halves for garnish

Cut asparagus into 1-inch pieces. Discard woody ends. Cover with water and cook until crisp-tender, about 5 minutes. Drain and rinse with cold water. Combine asparagus, berries, greens, and turkey.

DRESSING:
$^3/_4$ cup sugar
1 teaspoon dry mustard
1 teaspoon salt
$^1/_3$ cup cider vinegar
2 tablespoons minced onion

1 cup oil
1 tablespoon orange juice
1 teaspoon grated orange zest
$1^1/_2$ tablespoons poppy seeds

In a food processor, combine sugar, mustard, salt, vinegar, and onion. Gradually add oil, orange juice, orange zest, and poppy seeds. Toss the dressing with salad ingredients. Top with pecans. Serves 6–8.

Beyond Chicken Soup (New York)

★ **Editor's Extra:** I like to arrange this salad on individual plates—so pretty and colorful.

Turkey Waldorf Salad

A great way to serve Washington's abundant apples and tasty turkey for a luncheon.

3 Red Delicious apples, cored
  cut into $^1/_2$-inch chunks
3 Granny Smith apples, cored,
  cut into $^1/_2$-inch chunks
2 tablespoons lemon juice
4 stalks celery, diced
$^3/_4$ cup chopped pitted dates

3 cups cubed roast turkey
$^1/_2$ cup whipping cream
$^1/_2$ cup mayonnaise
$^3/_4$ cup coarsely chopped walnuts
Salt and freshly ground pepper to
  taste

Toss apple chunks with lemon juice in mixing bowl. Mix in celery, dates, and turkey. In separate bowl, whip the whipping cream; gently fold in mayonnaise. Blend into salad ingredients until well combined. Fold in walnuts and season to taste. Cover; refrigerate until serving.

Christmas in Washington Cook Book (Washington)

Chinese Chicken Salad

SALAD:

1 head napa cabbage, shredded
1 each red and green bell pepper,
  cut in strips
$1/2$ cup thinly sliced radishes
$1/2$ cup chopped green onions
$1/2$ cup chopped cilantro

Snow peas (optional)
2 or 3 chicken breasts, cut in strips
2 tablespoons sesame oil
2 tablespoon soy sauce
$1/2$ cup peanuts or cashews

In a large bowl, combine napa cabbage, bell peppers, radishes, onions, cilantro and snow peas, if desired. Brown chicken strips in sesame oil and soy sauce until done. Set aside.

SESAME DRESSING:

2 tablespoons sesame seeds
1 tablespoon sugar
1 teaspoon salt

2 teaspoons sesame oil
$1/3$ cup rice vinegar
$1/4$ cup salad oil

Brown sesame seeds in a small dry (no oil) nonstick pan; combine with remaining ingredients in covered jar. Shake well until sugar is dissolved. Just before serving, add chicken and peanuts to salad; mix. Add Sesame Dressing and mix well. Good without chicken, too!

Tasty Temptations (California)

Chicken Wedding Salad

1 (7½-ounce) package macaroni
  rings, cooked
2 cups cooked chicken or turkey
1 cup green grapes, cut in half
1 (11-ounce) can Mandarin oranges,
  cut in half
⅓ cup slivered almonds

1 cup diced celery
1 teaspoon salt
1 cup salad dressing (mayonnaise-
  type)
1 (8-ounce) carton frozen whipped
  topping

Cool the macaroni and chicken. Mix all, folding in whipped topping last. Chill and serve.

North Dakota American Mothers Cookbook
(Great Plains/North Dakota)

★ **Editor's Extra:** Small macaroni or any small pasta works well for this salad.

Chicken Salad in Melon Rings

This dish can be prepared up to four hours before serving. In fact, the flavors improve. Keep everything chilled, and assemble just before serving.

2 cups cooked chicken breast, cut
  into bite-size pieces
1½ cups seedless grapes, halved
½ cup chopped celery
½ cup toasted slivered almonds
⅔ cup mayonnaise
1 teaspoon soy sauce
½ teaspoon curry powder (optional)

Salt and freshly ground black
  pepper to taste
Chilled lettuce leaves
2 medium cantaloupes
Toasted slivered almonds for
  garnish
Green and red seedless grapes
  and/or strawberries for garnish

In a large bowl, combine chicken, grapes, celery, and ½ cup almonds. In a small bowl, combine mayonnaise, soy sauce, curry powder, salt and pepper; mix thoroughly. Toss with the chicken mixture and chill.

Just before serving, place lettuce leaves on individual plates. Cut the cantaloupe into 1- to 1½-inch-thick circular slices. Remove rind, seeds, and stringy pulp. Place on top of lettuce leaves. Fill each with chicken salad. Garnish with toasted almonds on top of salad and red and green grapes and/or whole strawberries on side of plate. Serves 6.

Variation: Honeydew melon or peach slices can be substituted for the cantaloupe. Red leaf lettuce adds a nice color to the plate.

Plain & Fancy Favorites (Ohio)

Crab Salad

This is for crab lovers. It has a mild flavor so as not to cover up the crab. Also great for a luncheon or light dinner.

1 pound lump crabmeat
4 cups shredded lettuce
½ cup minced celery
¼ cup minced scallions
2 hard-boiled eggs, chopped
¼ cup mayonnaise
¼ cup sour cream
½ teaspoon dry mustard

1 teaspoon Worcestershire sauce
1 small jar pimento, diced
1 teaspoon chopped fresh parsley
1 teaspoon chopped fresh chives
½ teaspoon salt
2 teaspoons Old Bay Seasoning
2 tomatoes, cut into wedges

Pick through crabmeat and set aside. Soak shredded lettuce in ice water; set aside. Add celery, scallions, and eggs to crabmeat; set aside. In small bowl, mix mayonnaise, sour cream, dry mustard, Worcestershire sauce, pimento, parsley, chives, salt, and Old Bay Seasoning until well combined. Drain lettuce well. Mix mayonnaise mixture and crab mixture together. Chill lettuce and crab salad (separately) for 1 hour. To serve, place lettuce on 4 plates and top with ¼ of crab salad. Arrange tomato wedges around. Serves 4.

A Taste of Tradition (Mid-Atlantic/Delaware)

Northwest Seafood Salad

SESAME DRESSING:

$1/3$ cup white vinegar
$1/4$ cup vegetable oil
3 tablespoons soy sauce
2 tablespoons dry mustard

2 tablespoons sesame oil
2 tablespoons sherry
1 tablespoon sugar
$1/3$ cup water

Combine all ingredients in a jar. Shake well to mix; set aside.

SALAD:

2 dozen large shrimp, shelled and
  deveined
$1^1/2$ pounds scallops
$1/2$ pound snow peas

2 cucumbers, peeled and sliced
4 celery stalks, sliced
1 lemon, quartered, for garnish

Cook shrimp in boiling water for 2 minutes or until they are pink. Drain well and transfer to a small bowl. Cool slightly. When they are cool, spoon 3 tablespoons Sesame Dressing over shrimp and refrigerate until serving.

Cook scallops in boiling water until white and opaque. Drain well and chill. Place snow peas in a colander and pour boiling water over them. Drain well. Transfer snow peas to a salad bowl and add cucumbers and celery. Toss slightly and chill.

To assemble, add scallops and shrimp to the salad bowl. Pour Sesame Dressing over all and toss to coat. Garnish each serving of this colorful main dish salad with a lemon quarter. Let it be the focus of a summer party. Makes 4 servings.

Simply Whidbey (Washington)

Greek Shrimp Salad

2 (6-ounce) packages frozen
  cocktail shrimp
2 medium tomatoes, cut in pieces
1 cucumber, unpeeled, sliced thin
1/2 red onion, sliced thin
1/4 cup prepared Italian or herb
  dressing

1/2 cup crumbled feta cheese
1/2 teaspoon dill weed
1/2 tablespoon chopped parsley
Black pepper to taste
1 (2 1/4-ounce) can sliced black
  olives

Add thawed and drained shrimp to all other ingredients. Mix gently. Serve chilled in a bowl of lettuce, spinach, or red cabbage leaves. Serves 4.

Applause Applause (Iowa)

Creamy Gazpacho Salad

A great discovery!

1 can tomato soup
1 envelope plain gelatin
1/4 cup cold water
1 (8-ounce) package cream cheese,
  softened
1/2 cup chopped celery

1/2 cup chopped bell pepper
1 tablespoon finely chopped onion
1 teaspoon lemon juice
1/2 cup chopped pecans
1 cup mayonnaise
1/3 cup sliced green olives

Heat soup, gelatin, and water; blend. Add cream cheese and stir constantly while leaving on medium heat. Blend well. Cool and add remaining ingredients. Pour mixture into a mold or a 9x9-inch Pyrex dish and let set overnight. Cut into squares to serve. Serves 8. To make a main dish, add 1 cup cooked shrimp.

A Little Taste of Texas (Texas II)

Veggie Lovers' Salad

Delicious! Special flavor is given to this salad by the nutmeg.

1/2 package rainbow rotini
1 cup chopped carrots
1 cup chopped cucumber
1 cup frozen peas

1 stem fresh broccoli, chopped
1/2 cup chopped onions
1/2 cup cut celery
3/4 cup sliced ripe olives

DRESSING:
1 cup salad dressing (not mayonnaise)
1/2 cup sugar
1/4 cup cider vinegar

1/4–1/2 teaspoon nutmeg
Salt and pepper

Cook noodles according to package directions. Rinse with cold water and drain. Add noodles to chopped vegetables. Pour Dressing over and refrigerate. Makes a large salad.

Old Westbrook Evangelical Lutheran Church Cookbook (Minnesota)

A Tomato Well Stuffed

2 cups canned artichoke hearts, chopped
1/2 cup chopped celery
1/2 cup chopped green onions and tops
1 cup Hellmann's mayonnaise

1 1/2 cups cooked shrimp, shelled and deveined
8 tomatoes
Lettuce leaves
12 slices bacon, cooked

Combine artichoke hearts with celery, green onions, and mayonnaise. Just before serving, add shrimp to stuffing. Peel and scoop out tomatoes; stuff with mixture. Place on lettuce. Sprinkle with crumbled bacon on top. Filling is better if made ahead. Yields 8 servings.

Quail Country (Georgia)

 Castroville, California, is known as the Artichoke Capital of the World. Marilyn Monroe was crowned Artichoke Queen there in 1947.

Broccoli Salad Supreme

4 cups chopped raw broccoli
1 cup chopped celery
¼ cup chopped green onions
1 cup seedless green grapes
1 cup seedless red grapes
⅓ cup sugar

1 cup good quality mayonnaise
1 tablespoon red wine vinegar
½ pound bacon, fried crisp and
  crumbled
⅔ cup almonds (slivered or sliced)
  toasted

Toss together the vegetables and grapes in a large salad bowl. Mix the sugar, mayonnaise, and vinegar in a separate small bowl to make dressing. Pour dressing over vegetables and grapes and stir gently to allow dressing to coat evenly. Refrigerate overnight before serving, if time allows, for flavors to mix. Just before serving, add crumbled bacon and toasted almonds. Serves 10–12.

Amazing Graces (Texas II)

Broccoli-Peanut Salad

SALAD:
1 bunch broccoli
1 cup chopped celery
8 strips bacon, crisped and crumbled

¾ cup raisins
¼ cup peanuts

Break broccoli into small flowerets. Mix broccoli, celery, and bacon. Add raisins and peanuts.

DRESSING:
1 cup mayonnaise
2 tablespoons vinegar

¼ cup sugar

Mix Dressing ingredients thoroughly. Combine with Salad. Refrigerate. This salad keeps nicely for several days. Adjust the amount of Dressing, if desired.

Treasured Recipes (Oregon)

Sweet and Sour Slaw

1 large cabbage, shredded
3 stalks celery, chopped
1 bell pepper, chopped
1 (4-ounce) jar chopped pimiento
1 large red onion, shredded
1/2 cup red wine vinegar

1/2 cup white wine vinegar
3/4 cup sugar
1 1/2 teaspoons salt
3/4 cup salad oil
Coarsely ground black pepper

Layer cabbage, celery, bell pepper, pimiento, and onion in bowl. Boil vinegars, sugar, and salt for 2 minutes. Remove from heat; add salad oil and coarsely ground black pepper. Return to heat and bring to a boil. Pour over vegetables while hot. Cover tightly. Refrigerate overnight. If refrigerated, this will keep for many days. Serves 10–12.

When Dinnerbells Ring (Alabama)

Golden Raisin Coleslaw

VINAIGRETTE:
4 tablespoons golden raisins
3 tablespoons red wine vinegar
2 tablespoons olive oil
1/2 cup water

2 tablespoons finely chopped onion
1 teaspoon Dijon mustard
Salt and pepper to taste

In a small saucepan, combine the above ingredients and boil the mixture, stirring, for 30 seconds. In a blender, purée the Vinaigrette until it is smooth.

COLESLAW:
2 cups grated cabbage
1 carrot, coarsely grated

1/2 cup golden raisins

Combine the cabbage, carrot, and raisins. Pour Vinaigrette over Coleslaw and toss. Serves 6.

Light Kitchen Choreography (Ohio)

Corn Salad

1 can whole-kernel corn
1 can shoe-peg white corn
1 small jar chopped pimento
1 large onion, chopped finely
1/2 cup finely chopped celery
1/2 cup finely chopped green pepper
1/2 cup sugar
1/2 cup vinegar
1 teaspoon garlic salt

Drain corn and pimento. Combine the corn, pimento, onion, celery, and green peppers, and set aside. Combine sugar, vinegar, and garlic salt; stir until sugar dissolves. Pour over vegetables and toss lightly. Cover and chill 8 hours.

WYVE's Bicentennial Cookbook (Virginia)

Baja Salad

Great for a festive luncheon on the patio.

CUMIN-LIME DRESSING:
1/2 cup lime or lemon juice
1 tablespoon Dijon mustard
2 tablespoons ground cumin
1 teaspoon minced garlic
1 teaspoon pepper
1/2 teaspoon salt
3/4 cup olive oil
3/4 cup vegetable oil

Mix together dressing ingredients and let stand for 1 hour or more.

1 (16-ounce) package dried black beans, picked over, soaked overnight in cold water to cover, and drained
1 red bell pepper, diced
1 green bell pepper, diced
1/3 cup chopped green onions
1 (10-ounce) package frozen corn, thawed
1/3 cup chopped cilantro
8 chicken breast halves, skinned and grilled
1–2 avocados, sliced, for garnish
1 cup salsa for garnish
1/2 cup sour cream for garnish
Chopped cilantro for garnish

In large saucepan, combine black beans and enough cold water to cover by 2 inches. Bring water to boil and simmer 45 minutes to 1 hour, or until tender, but not too soft. Drain black beans and mix with vegetables in large mixing bowl. Toss with Cumin-Lime Dressing. Place vegetables with dressing on large round platter. Cut chicken into strips and arrange on top with sliced avocado. Drizzle salsa on top. Put extra salsa, sour cream, and cilantro in bowls.

Note: This can also be made with grilled shrimp instead of chicken.

California Sizzles (California)

Groff's Potato Salad

Guests at Groff's Farms have asked for this recipe for years. Charlie has finally consented to printing his specialty. Bravo! It's definitely his claim to fame!

10 pounds potatoes, preferably new	**2 tablespoons lemon juice**
4 cups heavy mayonnaise	**1/2 cup chopped fresh parsley**
2 cups sour cream	**2 tablespoons chopped chives**
1/2 cup apple cider vinegar	**1 cup minced onion**
1 cup sugar	**1 cup minced celery**
1/2 tablespoon white pepper	**2 tablespoons Worcestershire sauce**
2 tablespoons dry mustard	**1/4 cup salt**
1/4 cup celery seed	

Peel and cook the potatoes until medium soft, then drain, slice and cool. Mix the mayonnaise and sour cream together, then add the remaining ingredients. Let the salad stand for at least 3 hours, overnight, if possible. This recipe can be cut in half for a smaller number of servings.

Betty Groff's Up-Home Down-Home Cookbook (Pennsylvania)

Sour Cream Potato Salad

There is none better.

5 cups diced, boiled potatoes	**3 hard-cooked eggs, whites diced,**
1 tablespoon grated onion	**yolks mashed**
1/2 cup diced cucumber	**1 1/2 cups sour cream**
3/4 teaspoon celery seed	**1/2 cup Hellmann's mayonnaise**
1 1/2 teaspoons salt	**1/4 cup vinegar**
1/2 teaspoon freshly ground pepper	**1 teaspoon prepared mustard**
1 tablespoon chopped parsley	

Potato salad is best made from red waxy potatoes, cooked in their jackets and peeled and marinated while still warm. Combine potatoes, onion, cucumber, celery seed, salt, pepper, and parsley and mix together lightly. Add diced egg whites to potato mixture. Combine mashed yolks with sour cream, mayonnaise, vinegar, and mustard; add to potatoes and gently blend together. Refrigerate several hours. Taste; some like a little more salt and pepper. Serves 10.

Cook and Deal (Florida)

Deviled Potato Salad

8 hard-boiled eggs
3 tablespoons vinegar
3 tablespoons prepared mustard
1 cup mayonnaise
$^{1}/_{2}$ cup sour cream

$^{1}/_{2}$ teaspoon celery salt
1 teaspoon salt
2 teaspoons chopped onion
6 medium potatoes, cooked and
  cubed

Cut eggs in half; remove yolks and mash. Blend yolks, vinegar, mustard, mayonnaise, sour cream, celery salt, and salt. Mix well. Chop egg whites and onions. Combine with mixture and add to potatoes. Chill and garnish with tomato wedges, cucumber slices, and/or hard-boiled egg slices. Yields 6–8 servings.

Sharing Our Best/Elizabeth House (Ohio)

Macaroni Salad

This will make you forget potato salad.

8 ounces macaroni
$^{3}/_{4}$ cup Kraft Italian low-calorie
  dressing
$^{3}/_{4}$ cup chopped carrots
1 cup chopped celery
$^{1}/_{4}$ cup chopped onion

$^{1}/_{4}$–$^{1}/_{2}$ cup chopped green pepper
$^{1}/_{2}$ cup cubed or grated cheese
1 (8-ounce) carton sour cream
Celery seed
Seasoned salt
Pepper

Cook macaroni according to package directions. Drain and marinate at least overnight in Italian dressing. Add vegetables and cheese. Mix with sour cream and seasonings to taste. Refrigerate. Keeps well up to a week or 10 days. Flavor improves with age.

Sam Houston Schoolhouse Cookbook (Tennessee)

The U.S. Postal Service lists the post office in Ochopee, Florida, as their smallest. The building, once a tool shed, is a steel shed about 7x8 feet. The building was converted into the post office after a fire in 1953 destroyed the original Ochopee Post Office located in the Gaunt Company Store.

Taffy Apple Salad

Use both red and green apples for a more colorful salad. Garnish the top with additional peanuts.

1 (16-ounce) can crushed pineapple
4 cups miniature marshmallows
1 tablespoon flour
½ cup sugar
1 egg, beaten

1½ tablespoons white vinegar
8 ounces whipped topping
2–3 cups coarsely chopped
  unpeeled apples
1 cup chopped Spanish peanuts

Drain the pineapple, reserving the juice. Combine the pineapple with the marshmallows in a bowl; set aside.

Combine the reserved juice with the flour, sugar, egg, and vinegar in a saucepan; mix well. Cook until slightly thickened, stirring constantly. Cool to room temperature. Fold in the whipped topping, marshmallow mixture, apples, and peanuts. Chill for several hours. Serves 6–8.

Generations (Illinois)

Creamy Frozen Salad

2 cups dairy sour cream (or 1½
  cups or to suit taste)
2 tablespoons lemon juice or
  Realemon
¾ cup sugar

1 banana, sliced
⅛ teaspoon salt
1 (9-ounce) can crushed pineapple,
  drained
¼ cups sliced maraschino cherries

Blend sour cream, lemon juice and sugar and stir in remaining ingredients. Pour into 1-quart mold or baking cups for cupcakes. It's nicer to put in baking cups so you can serve in the cups. Put in freezer. If you have muffin pans, set the paper cups in muffin pans till they freeze. Take out; put in plastic bags or wrap. Will keep in freezer 2 weeks or over. Take out a few minutes before serving.

Mountain Recipe Collection (Kentucky)

Easy Strawberry Salad

1 large package strawberry Jell-O
1 envelope plain gelatin
2 cups boiling water
1 large package frozen strawberries
1 large can crushed pineapple,
  drained
1 cup chopped nuts
½ (6-ounce) package small
  marshmallows
1 cup sour cream
1 (8-ounce) package cream cheese
½ cup sugar

Combine dry Jell-O and plain gelatin. Add boiling water and stir well.
Add strawberries, drained pineapple, nuts, and marshmallows. Pour into
long casserole and congeal. Mix sour cream, cream cheese, and sugar
with mixer. Spread on top of salad; chill.

Seasoned with Light (South Carolina)

Strawberry Pretzel Salad

3/4 cup butter or margarine
3 tablespoons sugar
$1\frac{2}{3}$ cup finely crushed pretzels

Cream butter and sugar; add pretzels. Press dough into a 9x13-inch pan.
Bake for 10 minutes at 350°. Let cool.

1 (9-ounce) carton Cool Whip
1 (8-ounce) package cream cheese
1 cup sugar

Mix together and spread on top of dough mixture that has cooled.

1 large package strawberry Jell-O
2 cups boiling water
1 pint frozen strawberries, thawed

Dissolve Jell-O in boiling water. Mix with strawberries when partially
set, then spread on top of other 2 layers. Refrigerate till firm.

Tasting Tea Treasures (Mississippi)

Blueberry Salad

An exceptional dessert, too!

1 large can crushed pineapple;
  drain and reserve juice
1 large package black cherry or
  blackberry Jell-O

1 cup cold water
1 can blueberry pie filling

Add enough water to pineapple juice to make 2 cups. Bring to a boil and add to gelatin. Stir until dissolved. Add 1 cup cold water. Add pineapple and blueberry pie filling and let congeal. Cover with Topping:

TOPPING:
1 (8-ounce) package cream cheese
½ cup sour cream

½ cup sugar
1 cup chopped nuts

Mix together and spread over congealed gelatin mixture.

Feeding the Faithful (South Carolina)

Orange Soufflé Gelatin Salad

2 (3-ounce) packages orange Jell-O
2 cups boiling water
1 cup reserved pineapple and
  orange juices
1 pint orange sherbet

1 (9-ounce) can crushed pineapple
  (juice reserved)
1 (11-ounce) can Mandarin oranges
  (juice reserved)
½ cup chopped nuts (optional)

Mix together Jell-O and boiling water to dissolve, then add drained juices. Allow to partially set. Fold in sherbet, crushed pineapple, oranges, and nuts. Pour into 9x13-inch glass dish. Refrigerate until firm. Serve on lettuce leaf with dollop of sour cream.

Traditionally Wesleyan (Georgia)

 Bridge Street, which connects Central Avenue and Malvern Street in Hot Springs, Arkansas, is only about twice as long as it is wide. It was listed in *The Guinness Book of World Records* as the World's Shortest City Street.

Holiday Cranberry Salad

Beautiful. May be served as a salad or a dessert. Either way, this dish does not stay around long!

2 (3-ounce) packages cream cheese
2 tablespoons mayonnaise
2 tablespoons sugar
1 cup canned whole cranberry
  sauce

1 cup crushed pineapple
1/2 cup chopped nuts
1 cup whipping cream, whipped
1/2 cup confectioners' sugar
1 teaspoon vanilla

Soften cream cheese. Blend with mayonnaise and sugar. Add cranberry sauce, pineapple, and nuts. Fold in cream which has been whipped with confectioners' sugar. Add vanilla. Pour into 9x13-inch container and freeze 6 hours. Cut into squares. Serves 6–8 people. Triple recipe for 3-quart container. Keeps in freezer. Seal well.

A Doctor's Prescription for Gourmet Cooking (Texas)

Hot Pepper Jelly Salad

1 (3-ounce) box lemon Jell-O
1 cup boiling water
1 (10-ounce) jar green hot pepper
  jelly
1 small can crushed pineapple
1 small jar pimentos, chopped

1 (3-ounce) package cream cheese,
  softened
1–2 tablespoons half-and-half
Tabasco
Mayonnaise to taste
1/4 cup chopped pecans

Dissolve Jell-O in boiling water. Dissolve hot pepper jelly in hot Jell-O. Add crushed pineapple with juice, and pimentos. Mash cream cheese and add half-and-half, a dash of Tabasco, mayonnaise to taste, and pecans. Grease muffin cups with oil. Add small amount Jell-O mix. Put in spoonful of cream cheese mixture. Fill with remaining Jell-O mix. Refrigerate. Serves 6.

Natchez Notebook of Cooking (Mississippi)

Pickled Beet Salad

1 (16-ounce) jar whole pickled
  beets; drain and reserve liquid
1 (3-ounce) package lemon gelatin
1 cup boiling water
1 teaspoon vinegar
1 cup chopped celery

1 teaspoon prepared
  horseradish
1½ teaspoons minced onion, divided
3 hard-cooked eggs, sieved
3 tablespoons mayonnaise

Chop beets to measure 1 cup; set aside. Reserve remaining beets. Dissolve gelatin in boiling water. Stir in ½ cup of reserved beet liquid and vinegar. Chill until consistency of unbeaten egg white. Stir in chopped beets, celery, horseradish, and ½ teaspoon onion; pour into 10x6x2-inch baking dish (loaf pan). Chill until firm. Combine eggs, mayonnaise, and remaining 1 teaspoon onion; spread over salad. Decorate with extra beet slices. Makes 8 servings.

Jubilee Cookbook (Texas II)

Beet Pickles

1 (28-ounce) can sliced beets,
  drained
½ cup sugar
½ cup vinegar

½ cup water
¾ teaspoon cinnamon
¼ teaspoon allspice
¼ teaspoon cloves

Combine and simmer for 15 minutes. Good hot, or jar and refrigerate.

Heavenly Delights (Missouri)

Vegetables

★★★★ ★★★★

This beautiful mountain waterfall touched us physically as well as visually as we slowly wound our way upward to Highlands, North Carolina. This area is truly blessed with natural beauty that continually wraps itself around you at every turn.

Golden Parmesan Potatoes

6 large potatoes (3 pounds)
$^1/_4$ cup sifted flour
$^1/_4$ cup grated Parmesan cheese
$^3/_4$ teaspoon salt

$^1/_8$ teaspoon pepper
$^1/_3$ cup butter
Parsley

Peel potatoes; cut into quarters. Combine flour, cheese, salt, and pepper in a bag. Moisten potatoes with water and shake a few at a time in bag, coating potatoes well. Melt butter in a 9x13-inch pan. Place potatoes in a layer in pan. Bake at 375° for 1 hour, turning once. When golden brown, sprinkle with parsley.

Home Cookin' is a Family Affair (Illinois)

Make-Ahead Mashed Potatoes

5 pounds potatoes, peeled and
  cooked
$^1/_2$ cup butter or margarine
$^1/_2$ cup sour cream
1 (8-ounce) package cream cheese

$^1/_2$–1 cup milk
2 eggs, beaten
1 package Good Seasons Italian
  Dressing* (optional)

Mash potatoes; add remaining ingredients. Whip together and put in a buttered casserole dish. Set in refrigerator overnight (a couple of days doesn't matter). Bake at 350° for 45 minutes to 1 hour, uncovered.

* The Good Seasons Dressing mix is optional, but it surely is good. Also good with just salt and pepper.

Heavenly Dishes (Ohio)

★★★★★★★★★★★★ ★★★★★★★★★★★★

Baked Mashed Potatoes

4 large potatoes (about 2 pounds),
  peeled and quartered
¼ cup milk
½ teaspoon salt
2 tablespoons margarine, melted,
  divided

1 egg, beaten
1 cup sour cream
1 cup small-curd cottage cheese
5 green onions, finely chopped
½ cup crushed butter-flavored
  crackers

Cook potatoes until tender; drain. Place in large bowl. Add milk, salt, and 1 tablespoon margarine. Beat until light and fluffy. Fold in egg, sour cream, cottage cheese, and onions. Place in a greased 1½-quart baking dish. Combine the cracker crumbs and remaining margarine. Sprinkle over potato mixture. Bake uncovered at 350° for 20–30 minutes or until crumbs are lightly browned. Serves 4–6.

Note: This can be made ahead and refrigerated. Sprinkle crumbs on top just before baking.

Country Classics II (Colorado)

Potato Puffs

We serve this recipe at our banquets. They hold well, are different, and good.

4 pounds potatoes
¾–1¼ cups milk
¼ cup butter
1½ teaspoons salt
2 teaspoons sugar

1 cup grated Cheddar cheese
2 egg yolks
1 cup crushed cornflakes
3 tablespoons toasted sesame seeds

Peel potatoes. Boil until soft; drain and mash. Heat milk, butter, salt, and sugar together. Gradually whip in until potatoes are smooth and fluffy. Add cheese and egg yolks and chill. Form into balls. Roll in mixture of cornflakes and sesame seeds. Can serve, or freeze. To freeze, place puffs on baking sheet, freeze, then package. To serve, brush lightly with melted butter. Bake in hot oven at 400° for 20 minutes for small puffs, or 30 minutes for medium puffs. Makes 48 small.

The Fifth Generation Cookbook (Ohio)

★★★★★★★★★★★ ★★★★★★★★★★★

Cattle King Potatoes

3 pounds potatoes
1 clove garlic
Salt to taste
1/2 pound mushrooms
1/3 cup butter, divided

2 egg yolks
1/2 cup cream
1/4 cup minced parsley
Pepper to taste

Peel potatoes and cut in uniform size; boil with garlic and salt until tender.

Meanwhile, slice and sauté the mushrooms in 1 tablespoon of the butter. Mash potatoes with remaining butter. Beat egg yolks with cream, and mix into the potatoes along with the mushrooms and parsley. Add more salt, if necessary, and pepper to taste. Pile in a buttered baking dish and bake at 375° until brown. Serves 8–10.

The Best from New Mexico Kitchens (New Mexico)

Block Island Potatoes

3 pounds small or new red potatoes
6 tablespoons unsalted butter
3 tablespoons olive oil
3 large garlic cloves, crushed or minced
1 tablespoon crushed fresh thyme, or 1/2 teaspoon dried

1 1/2 teaspoons crushed fresh or dried rosemary
1 1/2 teaspoons paprika
Dash of cayenne pepper
1/2 teaspoon salt
1/4 teaspoon fresh ground pepper
1/2 cup chopped parsley

Preheat oven to 375°. Scrub and dry potatoes. Melt butter in oil over moderate heat in roasting pan or casserole. Add the next 8 ingredients. Stir to mix. Add potatoes and roll them in butter mix to coat well. Bake, basting potatoes occasionally, for about 40 minutes, or until tender.

A Taste of Salt Air & Island Kitchens (New England/Rhode Island)

★★★★★★★★★★★ ★★★★★★★★★★★

Sweet Potato and Pineapple

Sweet potatoes team with pineapple for a good old Southern flavor.

3 pounds sweet potatoes	**Salt**
1 stick butter	**Pepper**
3 eggs	**$1/3$ cup brown sugar**
$1^1/2$ teaspoons cinnamon	**1 large can crushed pineapple**
1 teaspoon nutmeg	**Small marshmallows**

Boil sweet potatoes in skins. Peel while warm. Beat with electric beater (do not pull strings from beater blades). Add butter. Add eggs, cinnamon, nutmeg, salt and pepper. Add brown sugar. Lift beater and remove strings. Add crushed pineapple (including juice). Pour into buttered casserole. Cover with small marshmallows. Bake at 350° for 5 minutes, or until thoroughly heated.

Gourmet Cooking (Florida)

Sweet Potatoes and Apples

This is a good "fix ahead" dish to serve with pork or fowl. When your oven is going, bake 3 or 4 sweet potatoes, or pierce and cook in the microwave, then peel, cube, and refrigerate a day or two until ready to use.

2 tablespoons margarine	**2 teaspoons lemon juice**
4 apples, peeled and cubed	**$1/4$ teaspoon cinnamon**
$1/4$ cup minced onion	**Dash of allspice**
2 tablespoons firmly packed brown sugar	**3 or 4 cooked sweet potatoes, cut in cubes**

Heat margarine in skillet; add apples and onion. Cook 4 or 5 minutes until apples are soft. Stir in sugar, juice, cinnamon, and allspice, stirring until sugar is melted; add the sweet potatoes and cook until thoroughly heated.

Apples, Apples, Apples (Missouri)

Apple-Carrot Casserole

This is a not-too-sweet and colorful casserole. Pretty any time, but especially on a buffet table.

2 tablespoons flour
1/4 cup sugar
1 pound carrots, cut diagonally
1/2 teaspoon salt
1/2 cup water
4 medium cooking apples, peeled,
  cored and cut into 1/4-inch slices,
  divided

1/4 cup butter or margarine, thinly
  sliced, divided
1/4 cup frozen orange juice mixed
  with 1/2 cup water

Mix flour and sugar together in a small bowl. Set aside. Combine carrots, salt, and water in small saucepan. Cover and bring to a boil; reduce heat and simmer just until crisp-tender. Drain and set aside. Layer 1/2 of the carrots, then 1/2 of the apples in a lightly greased shallow 2-quart baking dish. (I use 10 x 6 x 2-inch Pyrex dish.) Sprinkle with 1/2 of the flour mixture and dot with 1/2 of the butter. Repeat layers. Drizzle with orange juice. Bake at 350° for about 35 minutes or until apples are tender, gently pressing apples down into syrup midway of cooking. Yields 8 servings.

Raleigh House Cookbook II (Texas II)

★ **Editor's Extra:** Okay to use 3/4 cup already-mixed orange juice if you don't have frozen.

Apricot Glazed Carrots

2 pounds carrots, cut on the diagonal
3 tablespoons butter
1/3 cup apricot preserves
1/4 teaspoon ground nutmeg

1/4 teaspoon salt
1 teaspoon grated fresh orange peel
2 teaspoons fresh lemon juice
Parsley for garnish

Cook carrots in salt water until tender. Drain. Melt butter; stir in apricot preserves until well blended. Add nutmeg, salt, orange peel, and lemon juice. Toss the carrots with the apricot mixture until well coated. Sprinkle with chopped parsley. Serves 6–8.

Entertaining at Aldredge House (Texas)

★★★★★★★★★★★   ★★★★★★★★★★★

Zesty Carrots

A Shaker recipe.

6 carrots
2 tablespoons horseradish
2 tablespoons grated onion
1/2 cup mayonnaise
1 teaspoon salt

1/4 teaspoon pepper
1/4 cup water
1/4 cup bread crumbs
1 tablespoon butter, melted

Scrape carrots and cut into thin strips. Cook in water to cover in saucepan until tender; drain. Place in greased 6x10-inch baking dish. Combine horseradish, onion, mayonnaise, salt, pepper, and water in bowl; mix well. Pour over carrots. Sprinkle with mixture of bread crumbs and butter. Bake at 375° for 15 minutes.

Laurels to the Cook (Pennsylvania)

Cabbage and Onion Casserole

8 cups chopped cabbage
3 cups chopped onion
4 tablespoons butter
4 tablespoons flour
1/4 teaspoon pepper

1 1/2 cups milk
1 pound Velveeta cheese, cubed
2 cups croutons, divided
1 pound sausage, browned and
    drained, divided

Boil cabbage and onion on stove for 7 minutes; drain. Melt butter; add flour and pepper, then milk and cheese. Cook until melted. Layer 1/2 cabbage and onion mixture, 1/2 croutons, 1/2 sausage, 1/2 cheese. Layer again in same order. Let stand 5 minutes. Bake in 3-quart dish at 350° for 1/2 hour.

Treasures and Pleasures (Ohio)

★★★★★★★★★★ ★★★★★★★★★★

Broccoli-Cheese Casserole

2 packages frozen chopped broccoli
4 tablespoons butter
$\frac{1}{2}$ cup chopped celery (optional)
$\frac{1}{2}$ cup chopped onion (optional)

1 can mushroom soup
1 roll bacon or garlic cheese
Bread crumbs, cracker crumbs, or
  onion rings (optional)

Cook broccoli according to directions on package; drain well. Melt butter in skillet; sauté celery and onion, if desired. Stir in soup and cheese until melted and well blended; add broccoli. Pour into greased casserole. Top with bread crumbs, cracker crumbs, or onion rings, if desired. Bake at 350° for 20 minutes. Serves 6–8.

Koinonia Cooking (Tennessee)

Snow-Capped Broccoli Spears

Impressive and delicious.

2 (10-ounce) packages frozen
  broccoli spears
1 tablespoon butter or margarine,
  melted

2 egg whites
$\frac{1}{4}$ teaspoon salt
$\frac{1}{2}$ cup mayonnaise or salad dressing
Parmesan cheese, grated

Preheat oven to 350°. Cook broccoli according to package directions and drain well. Arrange stem ends toward center of an ovenproof platter or 9-inch pie plate. Brush with butter. In a small bowl, beat egg whites and salt until stiff peaks form. Gently fold in mayonnaise. Spoon mixture in center of broccoli and sprinkle with Parmesan cheese. Bake at 350° for 12–15 minutes. Yields 6 servings. (Pictured on cover.)

Market to Market (North Carolina)

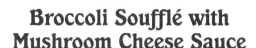

★★★★★★★★★★★   ★★★★★★★★★★★

Broccoli Soufflé with Mushroom Cheese Sauce

SOUFFLÉ:

3 tablespoons margarine
3 tablespoons flour
1 cup milk
1 teaspoon salt
1 tablespoon lemon juice

$1^{1}/_{2}$ teaspoons grated onion
1 cup finely chopped, cooked
   broccoli, well drained
4 eggs, separated

Melt margarine; blend in flour. Gradually add milk. Cook over medium heat, stirring constantly, until mixture thickens. Stir in salt, lemon juice, onion, and broccoli. Beat egg whites until stiff, but not dry. In separate bowl, beat egg yolks until thick; add broccoli mixture. Mix thoroughly. Fold in egg whites. Pour into $1^{1}/_{2}$-quart casserole; place in pan of hot water. Bake in moderate oven (350°) for 40 minutes, or until knife inserted halfway between edge and center comes out clean. Serve at once with Mushroom Sauce.

MUSHROOM SAUCE:

2 tablespoons margarine
2 tablespoons flour
$1/_{4}$ teaspoon salt
Dash of pepper

1 cup milk
1 (3- to 4-ounce) can sliced
   mushrooms, drained
$1/_{2}$ cup grated sharp cheese

Melt margarine; blend in flour, salt, and pepper. Gradually add milk. Cook, stirring constantly, until mixture thickens. Add mushrooms and cheese; heat until cheese melts. Makes 6 servings.

256 calories per serving.

From our Kitchens with Love (Michigan)

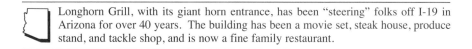

Longhorn Grill, with its giant horn entrance, has been "steering" folks off I-19 in Arizona for over 40 years. The building has been a movie set, steak house, produce stand, and tackle shop, and is now a fine family restaurant.

Pot-Luck Peas

Cornbread is a must with Pot-Luck Peas! Happy New Year!

1/2 pound bacon
2 cups finely chopped celery
2 cups finely chopped onion
2 cups finely chopped bell pepper
1 (16-ounce) can stewed tomatoes,
  undrained

1 (16-ounce) can tomatoes,
  undrained
3–4 (16-ounce) cans black-eyed
  peas, drained
Salt and pepper to taste

Fry bacon in skillet; remove, drain and crumble, then set aside. In a small amount of the bacon grease, sauté the celery, onion, and bell pepper until tender. Add all tomatoes and cook together 15–20 minutes on low heat. Add drained peas, salt and pepper. Cook 10 more minutes on low heat. Add crumbled bacon just before serving.

Ready to Serve (Texas)

Green Bean Casserole

This is excellent to make ahead and freeze. It is a delicious casserole.

4 (10-ounce) boxes frozen
  French-style green beans, or
  2 (16-ounce) cans, drained
1/2 pound mushrooms, sliced
1 large onion, chopped
1 stick margarine
1/4 cup flour
1 pint half-and-half
3/4 pound sharp Cheddar cheese,
  grated

1/8 teaspoon Tabasco
2 teaspoons soy sauce
1 tablespoon Worcestershire sauce
Salt and pepper to taste
1 can water chestnuts, chopped
Chopped almonds or cracker
  crumbs
1–2 tablespoons butter, melted

Cook beans; drain well. Cook mushrooms and onions in butter until done, but do not let onions brown. Add flour; mix well, then add cream and let thicken. Add cheese and stir until smooth. Add seasonings. Mix in beans and water chestnuts. Sprinkle top with either chopped almonds or cracker crumbs; drizzle with butter. Bake at 350° until thoroughly heated, about 20 minutes. Serves 14.

Eufaula's Favorite Recipes (Alabama)

★★★★★★★★★★ ★★★★★★★★★★

Husband Pleasin' Baked Beans

Great for a barbecue dinner.

1 pound ground beef
2 medium onions, chopped
1/2 stick margarine
3 (15-ounce) cans Ranch Style beans
2 (16-ounce) cans pork and beans

1/4 cup prepared mustard
1/4 cup maple syrup
1/2 cup brown sugar
1 cup catsup

Brown beef and onions in margarine and combine with remaining ingredients. (This can be refrigerated overnight or popped in the oven.) Bake at 300° for 1 1/2 hours. Serves 12 generously.

Variation: For a delicious one-dish meal, increase beef to 2 pounds.

Cooking with Mr. "G" and Friends (Louisiana II)

Indian-Style Pinto Beans

Ah, beans! A New Mexican loves pinto beans! He may eat the kidney, navy, and stringed varieties, but when it comes to a showdown in the kitchen, the pinto bean will always win. Slow-simmering with just the right spices, a little bacon fat, and stirred lovingly by "Mamacita," the pinto bean has long been the foundation upon which many a New Mexican meal is built.

1 pound dried pinto beans
3 quarts water
1/2 pound bacon, cut into pieces
1 medium-size yellow onion, finely
  chopped

1 teaspoon garlic salt
1 teaspoon salt
1 teaspoon ground black pepper
2 teaspoons dried red chile powder

Wash the beans thoroughly, removing any stones or bad beans. Soak overnight in cold water, changing the water at least once. Cook the bacon for a few minutes, add onion, and cook until transparent. Put the beans into a large pot with the bacon and onion; cover with water and simmer, covered, for 4 hours or until beans start to soften. Add garlic salt, salt, pepper, and chile powder, and cook for 30 minutes. Serve hot. Serves 6–8.

New Mexico Cook Book (New Mexico)

★★★★★★★★★★★ ★★★★★★★★★★★

South of the Border Casserole

1½ pounds summer squash (yellow
  or zucchini)
1 medium onion, chopped
2 tablespoons butter or margarine
1 (4-ounce) can diced green chiles
2 tablespoons flour
1 teaspoon salt

¼–½ teaspoon pepper
1½ cups Monterey Jack or
  mozzarella cheese
1 egg
1 cup cottage cheese
2 tablespoons parsley
½ cup Parmesan cheese

Dice squash; sauté with onion in butter until tender-crisp. Fold in chiles, flour, salt and pepper. Place in 2-quart greased baking dish. Sprinkle with cheese. Combine egg, cottage cheese, and parsley. Layer over cheese; sprinkle with Parmesan. Bake, uncovered, at 400° for 25–30 minutes, until heated through.

More Goodies and Guess-Whats (Colorado)

Green and Gold Squash

1 medium onion, chopped
2 tablespoons salad oil
¾ pound zucchini, shredded coarsely
¾ pound yellow squash, shredded
  coarsely
2 tablespoons chopped parsley
½ teaspoon salt

½ teaspoon basil
¼ teaspoon pepper
3 eggs, slightly beaten
½ cup milk
1 cup shredded sharp cheese,
  divided
½ cup saltine crumbs, divided

In large frying pan, sauté onion in oil until golden. Remove from heat. Stir in next 6 ingredients. Add eggs and milk. Spoon ½ of mixture in 1½-quart casserole. Sprinkle with ½ of cheese and ½ of crumbs. Repeat. Bake, uncovered, at 325° for 45 minutes.

Dixie Delights (Tennessee)

Ever wondered where the center of North America is? In January 1931, a U.S. Geological Survey determined the center of North America to be in Pierce County, North Dakota, or more specifically, in the town of Rugby. The location is marked by a rock monument which is about 21 feet high, and 6 feet wide at its base.

★★★★★★★★★★★★ ★★★★★★★★★★★★

Eden's Flower

1 head cauliflower, separated into
  flowerets
1 cup water
1½ teaspoons salt, divided
1 stick butter
¼ teaspoon coarse-ground black
  pepper

1 generous teaspoon basil
1 generous teaspoon oregano
2 cloves garlic, pressed
Juice of ¼ lemon
3 medium zucchini, sliced ½ inch
  thick
½ cup grated Parmesan cheese

In skillet, poach cauliflower in water with ½ teaspoon salt, about 5 minutes. Pour off water; remove flowerets. Melt butter in skillet; stir in seasonings (do not forget other 1 teaspoon of salt). Add zucchini first, then cauliflower. Cover. Cook on low heat for 20 minutes, stirring occasionally. Toss with ½ cup Parmesan cheese before serving.

A Taste of South Carolina (South Carolina)

Spinach Stuffed Squash

8 large or 10 small yellow squash
2 sticks butter
1 large stalk celery, chopped
1 small onion, chopped
1 small bunch green onions, chopped
⅓ cup chopped parsley
2 cloves garlic, minced
1 egg, beaten
1 cup Italian bread crumbs
⅓ cup grated Parmesan

½ teaspoon thyme
1 teaspoon black pepper
1 teaspoon onion salt
½ teaspoon Beau Monde Seasoning
3 boxes frozen chopped spinach,
  thawed, liquid squeezed out
Salt to taste
½ cup bread crumbs
½ stick butter

Cut squash in half, lengthwise, and steam until just half cooked with about 1½ inches water in the pot. Remove from pot and set aside to cool.

Melt 2 sticks butter in a saucepan and sauté the celery, onion, green onions, and parsley until wilted. Stir in the next 9 ingredients, then the spinach. Scoop out the seeds from the squash and discard. Stuff the squash halves with the spinach mixture; sprinkle each one with salt and extra bread crumbs, then dot each one with butter. Bake at 350° for 20–25 minutes. Serves 8–10. The stuffing freezes well, and is good stuffing for mushrooms.

La Bonne Louisiane (Louisiana)

★★★★★★★★★★★★ ★★★★★★★★★★★★

Spinach and Bacon Bake

2 slices bacon, fried crisp and
  crumbled, drippings reserved
1/2 cup chopped onion
1/2 cup chopped celery
1 can cream of mushroom soup
1 (3-ounce) package cream cheese,
  softened

2 (10-ounce) packages spinach,
  thawed and drained
1/2 cup croutons
1 tablespoon margarine, melted

Cook onion and celery in bacon drippings. Stir in soup and cream cheese; heat until cheese melts. Stir in spinach and bacon. Pour into casserole. Toss croutons with margarine; sprinkle over all. Bake, uncovered, at 325° for 45–50 minutes. Can be mixed ahead and baked later. Serves 10.

Cookin' with the Stars (West Virginia)

Jalapeño Spinach

This is better if made the day before. It also freezes beautifully.

4 packages frozen chopped spinach
1 stick butter
4 tablespoons flour
1 small onion, finely chopped
1 cup evaporated milk
1 cup vegetable liquor
1 teaspoon pepper
Dash cayenne

2 teaspoons celery salt
2 teaspoons garlic salt
1 teaspoon salt
2 teaspoons Worcestershire
2 tablespoons lemon juice
2 (6-ounce) rolls jalapeño cheese
Buttered bread crumbs

Cook spinach. Drain well and reserve liquor. Melt butter; add onions and sauté until tender. Add flour and mix until smooth. Add milk and vegetable broth slowly, stirring constantly to avoid lumping. Cook until it thickens. Add seasonings and cheese. Stir until cheese is melted. Combine with spinach and place in casserole. Top with buttered bread crumbs. Before serving, heat until bubbly. Serves 12.

Cuckoo Too (Texas)

Chile Relleno Casserole

1 (7-ounce) can whole green chiles
2 cups grated Monterey Jack cheese
2 eggs

1 cup milk
Salt and pepper to taste

Carefully split green chiles lengthwise and open flat. Remove seeds.
Divide 1½ cups cheese among chiles. Place on center of chiles and roll
them up starting at pointed end. Place seam-side-down in greased
9x5x3-inch loaf pan. Beat eggs, milk, salt and pepper. Pour over chiles
and sprinkle with remaining cheese. Bake at 375° for 40 minutes or until
puffed and brown.

Rehoboth Christian School Cookbook (New Mexico)

Pop's Pepper Poppers

Great as an appetizer, too!

Hot banana peppers (or your choice)
Cream cheese

Sharp Cheddar cheese
Bacon or bacon bits

Wash and cut stem end off peppers; remove seeds and cut in half, lengthwise. Lay on foil-lined pan (for easy cleanup) and stuff with cream
cheese or Cheddar cheese (or mixture). Put in 350° oven for 20 minutes.
Meanwhile, fry bacon and crumble. Sprinkle on peppers and serve while
hot.

Note: Because hot peppers contain oils that can burn your eyes, lips,
and skin, protect yourself when working with the peppers by covering
one or both hands with plastic gloves or plastic bags. Be sure to wash
your hands thoroughly before touching your eyes or face.

Sisters Two II (Great Plains/Kansas)

Eggplant Parmigiana

1 large eggplant, unpeeled
Salt and pepper
1 cup dry bread crumbs
2 eggs
Cooking oil to fry (olive oil preferred)
1½ cups tomato sauce, divided
  (heat to spread evenly)

½ pound cheese of your choice
  (sliced mozzarella is the classic
  cheese for this dish), divided
1 teaspoon crumbled dried basil,
  divided
½ cup grated Parmesan cheese

Wipe eggplant clean and cut in ¼-inch circular slices. Season with salt and pepper. Dip into bread crumbs, then in lightly beaten eggs, and again into bread crumbs. Place individually on cookie sheet and refrigerate for 30 minutes.

Heat lightly oiled skillet and fry slices until brown and tender. Drain on absorbent paper towels. Next, lightly butter baking dish; pour in some of the tomato sauce, spreading evenly. Arrange eggplant slices over the sauce. Cover with a layer of mozzarella cheese, more sauce, and a sprinkling of basil. Repeat procedure until dish is filled. Top with Parmesan. Bake in preheated 350° oven for 25–30 minutes.

Southern Vegetable Cooking (South Carolina)

★ **Editor's Extra:** I added a pat of butter to the frying oil. This is *very* enjoyable.

Company Vegetable Casserole

1 bag frozen California blend
  vegetables (cauliflower, broccoli,
  and carrot slices)
1 (8-ounce) box Brussels sprouts
  (optional)
½ cup minute rice

1 small can mushrooms, drained
1 can cream of mushroom soup
1 small jar Cheez Whiz
1 tablespoon onion flakes
1 teaspoon seasoned salt
¾ cup milk

Place frozen vegetables in 2½-quart casserole. (Do not cook.) Mix rice (uncooked) and mushrooms with vegetables. Combine mushroom soup, Cheez Whiz, onion flakes, seasoned salt, and milk. Place in saucepan and heat until cheese melts. Pour cheese sauce over vegetables (may not cover completely). Bake at 350° for 1 hour. Serves 10.

Blue Ridge Christian Church Cookbook (Missouri)

Corn Casserole

2 tablespoons chopped onion
2 tablespoons flour
½ teaspoon salt
2 tablespoons margarine or butter

1 cup sour cream
2 (15-ounce) cans whole-kernel corn
6 slices bacon, fried and crumbled

Sauté onion, flour, and salt together in butter. Mix sour cream and corn. Blend and bring to a boil. Add to onion mixture and pour in greased baking dish. Sprinkle with crumbled bacon. Bake at 350° for 30–45 minutes. Serves 6–8.

Cooking...Done the Baptist Way (South Carolina)

Corn Relish

2 quarts corn kernels
1 quart chopped cabbage
1 cup chopped sweet red peppers
1 cup chopped sweet green peppers
1 cup diced onions
2 cups granulated sugar
4 cups apple cider vinegar

1 cup water
1 teaspoon celery seed
1 teaspoon mustard seed
1 tablespoon salt
1 teaspoon turmeric
1 teaspoon dry mustard

Cook corn on cobs submerged in boiling water for 5 minutes. Plunge into cold water to stop cooking and preserve color. Drain, then cut from cobs. Mix gently with other vegetables. Combine sugar, vinegar, water, and spices (making sure sugar is dissolved). Pour over vegetables and simmer for 20 minutes or until vegetables are tender, but not mushy.

The Best of Amish Cooking (Pennsylvania)

Mitchell, South Dakota, boasts the nation's only Corn Palace. No, the building is not made of corn, but each year the exterior is adorned with thousands of bushels of corn, grain, grasses, wild oats, brome grass, blue grass, rye, straw and wheat. The yearly tradition of decorating the Corn Palace was begun by early settlers who wanted to uniquely display the fertility of South Dakota soil.

★★★★★★★★★★★   ★★★★★★★★★★★★

Tomato Pie

12 slices bacon
3 large tomatoes, seeded and sliced
   (enough to fill shell)

1 (9-inch) deep-dish pastry shell,
   baked
8 green onions, chopped

Fry bacon; drain and crumble. Arrange tomato slices in pastry shell; place chopped onions and crumbled bacon on top. Add Topping. Bake at 350° for 30 minutes. Yields 6 servings.

TOPPING:
1½ cups grated extra sharp
   Cheddar cheese

1½ cups Hellmann's mayonnaise

Mix cheese and mayonnaise together. Spread Topping evenly over top of pie. Yields 3 cups.

Quail Country (Georgia)

Greenback Tomatoes

This is a good vegetable dish for a buffet supper because it is colorful, tasty, and arranged in individual servings.

2 (10-ounce) packages frozen
   chopped spinach
2 cups Progresso Bread Crumbs
6 green onions and tops, chopped
6 eggs, slightly beaten
½ cup butter, melted
¼ cup Parmesan cheese

¼ teaspoon Worcestershire
1 teaspoon salt
½ teaspoon pepper
1 teaspoon thyme
¼ teaspoon Tabasco
12 large thick slices of tomato

Cook spinach and drain well. In large mixing bowl, combine crumbs, onions, eggs, butter, Parmesan, Worcestershire, salt, pepper, thyme, and Tabasco. Arrange tomato slices in buttered shallow baking dish. Mound spinach mixture on top of each tomato slice. Bake at 350° about 15 minutes. Serves 12.

Variation: Great for hors d'oeuvres. You may use it to stuff little cherry tomatoes. Reduce cooking time accordingly.

The Texas Experience (Texas II)

★★★★★★★★★★★ ★★★★★★★★★★★

Fried Green Tomatoes

Green tomatoes (about 4)
Salt and pepper
1 egg, beaten
3 tablespoons milk

Flour
$^1/_2$ cup bread crumbs
$^1/_2$ cup cornmeal
4 tablespoons oil

Slice tomatoes in $^1/_4$-inch slices. Salt and pepper tomatoes. Mix egg and milk together. Dip tomatoes in flour, then in egg mixture and then into mixture of bread crumbs and cornmeal. Then fry in heated oil in cast-iron skillet until brown on both sides.

Oklahoma Cookin' (Oklahoma)

Crispy Fried Okra

1 pound fresh okra, stemmed and
  cut into $^1/_2$-inch slices, or 1
  (10-ounce) package frozen cut okra,
  thawed and dried
1 or 2 egg whites, slightly beaten
$^1/_2$ heaping cup white cornmeal

$^1/_2$–$^3/_4$ teaspoon onion powder
$^1/_2$ teaspoon salt, or to taste
$^1/_4$ teaspoon freshly ground pepper,
  or to taste
Corn oil

Add okra slices to egg whites and toss until well coated. Combine cornmeal, onion powder, salt and pepper in a plastic bag. Add okra slices a handful at a time to the cornmeal mixture, shaking until thoroughly coated. Remove from the bag and place on a baking sheet. Okra can be refrigerated at this point.

Heat oil and fry a small batch of okra at a time. (If too much is added at one time, okra will smother rather than fry.) Remove from oil; drain on a paper towel and place in a warm oven until all okra is prepared. Serve immediately. Serves 3–4.

Taste of the South (Mississippi)

SPAM fans worldwide can now pay homage to their luncheon meat of choice in Austin, Minnesota, at a 16,500 square-foot SPAM Museum opened in September 2001. The museum houses 4,752 cans of SPAM luncheon meat from all over the world and from throughout the 64-year history of SPAM.

★★★★★★★★★★★ ★★★★★★★★★★★

Greens and Ham Hocks

2 ham hocks
1½ quarts water
1 teaspoon crushed red pepper
Salt to taste

1 onion, chopped
4 pounds fresh collard greens
1 teaspoon sugar

Place hocks in Dutch oven or large saucepan. Add water, pepper, salt, and onion; cover. Bring to a boil until hocks are tender. Break off stems of greens. Wash leaves thoroughly. Slice leaves into bite-size pieces. Add greens and sugar to hocks. Cook 30–40 minutes, or until greens are done. Makes 8–10 servings.

Great Grandmother's Goodies (Pennsylvania)

*The Old Arsenal Powder Magazine in Baton Rouge, Louisiana,
on the Mississippi River, is just a lovely historic walk away from the
state capitol building. Since the land in South Louisiana is so flat,
kids love to climb up this rare hill to play on the cannons.*

Don't-Cook-The-Pasta-Manicotti

1 pound lean ground beef
1/2 cup chopped onion
2 cloves garlic, minced
4 cups tomato juice, divided
1 (6-ounce) can tomato paste
1 teaspoon sugar
2 teaspoons oregano
1 teaspoon salt
1/8 teaspoon pepper
3 cups shredded mozzarella cheese,
  divided

2 cups ricotta cheese, or cottage
  cheese
1 (10-ounce) package frozen,
  chopped spinach, thawed, drained
2 eggs, slightly beaten
1/2 cup grated Parmesan or
  Romano cheese
1 (8-ounce) package manicotti shells

In a large skillet, brown meat with onion and garlic; drain well. Stir in 2 cups tomato juice, tomato paste, sugar, and seasonings; simmer while preparing filling.

In a large bowl, combine 2 cups mozzarella cheese, ricotta cheese, spinach, eggs, and grated cheese; mix well. Stuff dry pasta shells with cheese mixture; arrange in a greased 9x13-inch baking dish. Spoon meat sauce evenly over shells; pour remaining tomato juice on top. Cover with foil; place pan on a baking sheet; bake at 350° for 1 hour. Remove from oven; remove foil and top with remaining mozzarella cheese. Let stand 15 minutes before serving.

Celebration (Arkansas)

★★★★★★★★★★★★ ★★★★★★★★★★★★

Inside Out Ravioli

No stuffing . . . it's on the outside!

1 (7-ounce) package shell or elbow
  macaroni
1 pound ground beef
1 medium onion, chopped
1 clove garlic, minced
1 tablespoon salad oil
1 (10-ounce) package frozen
  chopped spinach
1 (1-pound) can spaghetti sauce
  with mushrooms

1 (8-ounce) can tomato sauce
1 (6-ounce) can tomato paste
1/2 teaspoon salt
1/4 teaspoon pepper
1 cup shredded sharp cheese
1/2 cup soft bread crumbs
2 eggs, well beaten
1/4 cup salad oil

Boil and drain macaroni; set aside.

Brown beef, onion, and garlic in the 1 tablespoon salad oil. Cook spinach according to package directions. Drain, reserving liquid; add water to make 1 cup. Stir spinach liquid, spaghetti sauce, tomato sauce, tomato paste, salt and pepper into meat mixture. Simmer 10 minutes. Combine spinach with pasta and remaining ingredients. Spread spinach mixture in a greased 9x13x2-inch baking dish. Top with meat sauce. Bake at 350° for 30 minutes. Let stand 10 minutes before serving. Serves 8–10.

The Mississippi Cookbook (Mississippi)

Italian Stuffed Shells

12 ounces jumbo pasta shells
8 ounces part-skim mozzarella
  cheese, shredded, divided
12 ounces herb-seasoned spaghetti
  sauce, divided

1 (10-ounce) package chopped
  spinach, thawed and drained
8 ounces skinless chicken breasts,
  cooked and chopped

Bring 3 quarts of water to a boil. Cook pasta shells for 18–20 minutes, stirring frequently. Spray a 9x13x2-inch baking dish with vegetable oil cooking spray. Place drained shells in dish. Mix together 1/2 of the mozzarella, 1/2 of the spaghetti sauce, the spinach, and the chicken in a bowl. Stuff mixture into the shells and cover with the remainder of the sauce. Sprinkle with the remainder of the mozzarella. Bake at 350° for 15–20 minutes, or until cheese is bubbly and slightly browned.

Lowfat, Homestyle Cookbook (Colorado)

★★★★★★★★★★★★   ★★★★★★★★★★★★

Scallops and Green Noodles

This recipe was the Grand Prize Winner of a recipe contest held by The Pocono Record *newspaper, Stroudsburg, Pennsylvania, in 1983—won a microwave oven!*

2 carrots, peeled
1 large pepper
8 green onions
1/2 cup butter, divided
2/3 cup dry white wine
1 pound scallops, cut into 1/4-inch
  slices

1 cup whipping cream
8 ounces spinach noodles
Salt and pepper
Freshly grated nutmeg
Parsley

Cut carrots, pepper, and onions (with greens) in slivers about 1/8 inch thick and 2 inches long. Melt 2 tablespoons butter in skillet. Add carrots, pepper, and onions. Remove vegetables after sautéing briefly. Into pan, add wine and bring to a boil. Add scallops; cover and cook until opaque (about 3 minutes). Lift scallops from liquid and set aside. Add cream to pan liquid and bring to a boil. Turn heat to low and stir in remaining butter until it melts.

Meanwhile, cook noodles; drain and rinse. Add to cream. Mix by lifting with 2 forks. Add scallops and vegetables. Mix gently. Season to taste with salt, pepper, and nutmeg. Garnish with parsley. Serves 4–6.

Chefs and Artists (Pennsylvania)

Italian Shrimp and Pasta Toss

1 cup sliced fresh mushrooms
1/2 cup chopped onion
2 cloves garlic, minced
1 teaspoon ground basil leaves
2 tablespoons olive oil
1/2 cup water
2 tablespoons lemon juice
2 teaspoons chicken bouillon

1 pound medium, raw shrimp,
  peeled, and deveined
1 cup chopped green pepper
1 large tomato, seeded and chopped
8 ounces angel hair pasta, cooked
2 tablespoons grated Parmesan
  cheese

In large skillet, cook mushrooms, onion, garlic, and basil in oil until tender. Add water, lemon juice, and bouillon; bring to a boil. Reduce heat; add shrimp and green pepper. Simmer, uncovered, 5–8 minutes or until shrimp are pink. Stir in tomato. In large bowl, toss shrimp mixture with hot pasta and cheese. Serve with additional cheese, if desired.

Cook, Line and Sinker (Ohio)

Seafood Fettuccine

1 (12-ounce) package fettuccine
  noodles
2 tablespoons butter
1 small onion, finely chopped
2 or 3 cloves garlic, finely chopped

1 pound fresh seafood (shrimp,
  scallops, crab, or a combination)
2 cups whipping cream
$^1/_2$ cup grated Romano cheese
$^1/_2$ cup grated Parmesan cheese

Cook fettuccine to al dente stage (just done—not overcooked) in boiling salted water. Rinse well and set aside. In a heavy large sauté pan, melt butter. Sauté onion and garlic until onion is transparent (do not brown). Stir all the time. Add seafood and sauté. Add whipping cream and stir until cream is warm. Add grated cheeses and heat over low heat until cheese melts and sauce thickens. You can increase heat a little, but you must stir all the time. Add cooked fettuccine and lift and toss until noodles are coated with the sauce. Serve to 4 or 5 lucky people.

It's About Thyme (Indiana)

Angel Hair Pasta Primavera

1 (16-ounce) package angel hair
  pasta or vermicelli
$^1/_4$ cup vegetable oil
1 medium-size yellow squash, sliced
  (about 1 cup)
1 medium-size onion, diced
1 cup sliced fresh mushrooms

4 ounces fresh or 6 ounces frozen
  Chinese pea pods, thawed
1 large clove garlic, minced
2 large ripe tomatoes, chopped
$1^1/_2$ teaspoons salt (optional)
1 teaspoon dried basil
$^1/_4$ cup grated Parmesan cheese

In a deep 4-quart saucepan, bring 2 quarts of water to a boil. Cook angel hair pasta according to package directions. In a 12-inch skillet over medium heat, heat oil, adding squash, onion, mushrooms, pea pods, and garlic. Cook 5 minutes, stirring occasionally until vegetables are crisp-tender. Add tomatoes, salt, and basil to vegetables; cook 2 minutes until heated through. Drain pasta. Add vegetables to pasta in saucepan along with $^1/_4$ cup Parmesan cheese. Stir to mix. Serve with additional cheese. Serves 6.

The Parkview Way to Vegetarian Cooking (New England/Maine)

★ **Editor's Extra:** If your tomatoes are not big and juicy enough to make it nice and moist, add an extra tomato or can of chopped tomatoes. This is a delightful low-cal, vitamin-rich dish.

Chicken Spaghetti
"Carole Curlee Special"

This is super!

BROTH:

1 (3- to 4-pound) chicken
1 onion
2 stalks celery

Salt to taste
Water to cover

Combine ingredients for Broth and boil till chicken is tender. Cool to handle; bone chicken, reserving broth. Cut into bite-size pieces.

1 large onion, chopped
3 ribs celery, sliced
1 carrot, grated
3 tablespoons margarine
2 cans cream of chicken soup
1 can or more saved broth or evaporated milk
1¾ cups grated Cheddar cheese, divided
1 teaspoon chili powder

Salt and pepper to taste
½ teaspoon garlic salt
1 small jar pimientos, chopped
1 small can sliced mushrooms (optional)
3–4 chicken bouillon cubes (optional)
1 (12-ounce) package spaghetti, cooked

Sauté onion, celery, and carrot in margarine. Add soup and broth (or evaporated milk). You can add a little more if you want thinner sauce. Add 1 cup grated cheese to the sauce mixture and heat. Also, add chili powder, salt, pepper, garlic salt, pimientos, and mushrooms. Add the chicken. Taste for seasoning; can add chicken bouillon cubes for more flavor. Toss the sauce with cooked spaghetti, saving a ladle of extra sauce to put on top for eye appeal, and sprinkle ¾ cup grated cheese on top. Either refrigerate until later, or cook at 325° for 25 minutes, or until bubbly and hot. Serves 8.

A Casually Catered Affair (Texas II)

★ **Editor's Extra:** To add a little color and pizzazz, add a can of diced green chiles. This makes a lot, so sometimes I freeze half in a casserole dish before baking, then thaw, and bake at a later date.

Chicken, anyone? The world's largest frying pan, measuring 10 feet in diameter, can hold up to 800 chicken quarters! Check it out at the annual Delmarva Chicken Festival, held each year in different communities near Wilmington, Delaware.

Macaroni and Cheese

Everyone loves my macaroni and cheese. It is creamy and easy to make. A terrific potluck casserole. Very rich and yummy!

1 (7-ounce) package elbow macaroni	3 cups grated Cheddar cheese,
6 tablespoons butter, divided	divided
3 tablespoons flour	1/2 teaspoon salt
2 1/2 cups milk (can use part canned	1/2 teaspoon pepper
milk)	1 cup dry bread crumbs
1 (8-ounce) package cream cheese	

Cook macaroni until tender, as directed on package. Melt 4 tablespoons butter in saucepan. Stir in flour until smooth. Gradually add milk. Add cream cheese, 2 cups Cheddar cheese, salt and pepper. Stir over low heat until cheeses are melted and mixture is smooth. Drain and rinse macaroni and mix cheese mixture into macaroni. Transfer to a greased casserole dish or 9x13-inch pan. Sprinkle remaining 1 cup Cheddar cheese on top. Melt remaining 2 tablespoons butter and add bread crumbs. Spread on top of cheese. Bake uncovered at 400° for 20–25 minutes or until golden brown.

Bounteous Blessings (Washington)

Lower-Fat Pesto

Toss some with warm pasta—nice!

1 cup firmly packed fresh basil leaves	2 cloves garlic, quartered
1/2 cup torn fresh spinach leaves	1/4 teaspoon salt
1/4 cup grated Parmesan cheese	2 tablespoons olive oil or cooking oil
1/4 cup pine nuts, walnuts, or almonds	2 tablespoons water

In a blender container or food processor bowl, combine basil, spinach, cheese, nuts, garlic, and salt. Cover; blend or process with several on-off turns till paste forms, stopping the machine several times and scraping sides. With the machine running slowly, gradually add the oil and water and blend or process to the consistency of soft butter. Transfer to a storage container. Cover and refrigerate up to 2 days or freeze up to 1 month. Makes 3/4 cup.

Spinach Pesto: Prepare pesto as directed, except substitute fresh torn spinach for all the fresh basil and add 1 teaspoon dried crushed basil.

Favorite Herbal Recipes Volume III (Illinois)

★ ★ ★ ★ ★ ★ ★ ★ ★ ★ ★   ★ ★ ★ ★ ★ ★ ★ ★ ★ ★ ★ ★

Three Cheese Baked Rice

You won't believe how good this is!

1 small onion, chopped
1 small red pepper, diced
1 small green pepper, diced
1 rib celery, diced
3 tablespoons butter
1 cup uncooked rice
1¾ cups chicken broth

¾ cup white wine
1 small green chile pepper, diced
¾ teaspoon salt
1½ cups sour cream
2½ ounces Gruyére cheese, cubed
2½ ounces grated Cheddar cheese
2½ ounces grated mozzarella cheese

Preheat oven to 350°. In Dutch oven or oven-safe pan, sauté onion, peppers, and celery in butter for 3 minutes. Add rice, chicken broth, wine, chile pepper, and salt. Bring to boil, cover, and place in oven. Bake 15–20 minutes or until all liquid has been absorbed. Remove from oven and transfer to large bowl. Let cool slightly.

Stir sour cream and cheeses into cooled rice mixture and transfer to a buttered 9x13-inch pan. Bake at 400° for 20 minutes or until lightly browned. Serves 6–10.

It's Our Serve (New York)

★ **Editor's Extra:** The rice is so delicious even before you add the cheese, you'd best hide it till you do!

Rice Pilaf

PLAIN PILAF:
1 large onion, sliced
4 tablespoons butter

1 cup uncooked rice
2 cups bouillon (beef or chicken)

Brown sliced onion in butter. Add rice. Cook in butter and onion mixture over low heat for 4–5 minutes, stirring often. Rice will be lightly colored. Heat liquid bouillon to boiling point and pour over rice. Cover dish or pan tightly and bake in 350° oven for 25–30 minutes or until liquid is absorbed. Yields 8 servings.

Variations: Add 1 (16-ounce) can of drained mushrooms; add sliced green peppers; add chopped water chestnuts.

Nothing Could Be Finer (North Carolina)

★ **Editor's Extra:** I sometimes like slivered almonds, too.

★★★★★★★★★★★ ★★★★★★★★★★★

Pizza Rice Casserole

3 cups cooked rice
2 cups spaghetti or pizza sauce
1 pound ground beef, browned
1 cup sliced mushrooms
12–15 slices pepperoni

1/2 cup diced green onions
1/4 cup diced green pepper
Other pizza toppings, if desired
1 teaspoon dried basil
2 cups mozzarella cheese

In a 9x13-inch baking dish which has been sprayed with cooking spray, press the cooked rice. Pour sauce over rice. Layer ground beef, mushrooms, pepperoni, onions, and pepper as well as any additional toppings. Sprinkle with basil. Cover with cheese. Bake at 350° for 25–30 minutes.

Our Favorite Recipes (West Virginia)

★ **Editor's Extra:** You can also use chopped chicken instead of ground meat. I love this recipe!

Wild Rice Casserole

The cheese adds the zip!

3/4 cup uncooked wild rice
1 teaspoon salt
Dash of pepper
1 cup fresh mushrooms, sliced
1 onion, chopped
1 green pepper, chopped

2 teaspoons butter
1 can of cream of mushroom soup
1/2 soup can of milk
1 cup grated Cheddar cheese
3/4 cup fresh parsley (optional)

Cook wild rice (according to package directions) with salt and pepper. Sauté mushrooms, onion, and green pepper in butter. Heat soup and milk, adding cheese so it melts. Add to rice. Stir in parsley, mushrooms, onion, and green pepper. Put in greased casserole and cover. Bake at 325° for 1 hour, or until rice is tender. Serves 4.

Our Favorite Recipes (Minnesota)

★★★★★★★★★★★★ ★★★★★★★★★★★★

Shrimp in Wild Rice

Everyone goes wild over this! Out of this world!

1/2 cup flour
1 cup butter or margarine, melted, divided
4 cups chicken broth
1/4 teaspoon white pepper
1 cup thinly sliced onion
1/2 cup thinly sliced green pepper

1 cup thinly sliced mushrooms
2 pounds cooked, peeled, and deveined shrimp
2 tablespoons Worcestershire sauce
Few drops hot sauce
4 cups cooked wild rice

Gradually add flour to 1/2 cup melted butter and stir constantly over low heat until bubbly. Gradually add broth and stir until smooth and thickened. Add white pepper and simmer 2–3 minutes. Sauté onion, green pepper, and mushrooms in remaining 1/2 cup butter. Drain. Combine white sauce, sautéed vegetables, and remaining ingredients. Spoon into casserole and bake at 300° for 45–50 minutes. Freezes well.

Encore (Georgia)

Chicken and Wild Rice

3/4 cup Uncle Ben's Wild Rice, uncooked
4 cups chopped, cooked chicken
1/2–1 cup sherry
1 cup chicken broth
1 small onion, chopped
1 (8-ounce) can mushroom slices, drained
1/4 cup butter or margarine, melted

1 (10 3/4-ounce) can condensed cream of mushroom soup
1 (10 3/4-ounce) can condensed cream of chicken soup
2 (10-ounce) packages frozen broccoli or asparagus spears, cooked and drained
1 cup (4 ounces) shredded Cheddar cheese

Cook wild rice according to package directions. Combine rice with chicken, sherry, broth, onion, mushroom slices, margarine, mushroom soup, and chicken soup. Spread half the rice mixture in a 9x13-inch pan. Top with broccoli. Evenly spread remaining rice mixture over all. Bake, uncovered, at 350° for 45 minutes, or until heated through. Sprinkle with cheese and bake an additional 5 minutes, or until cheese is melted.

The Eagle's Kitchen (New Mexico)

Creole Jambalaya

2 tablespoons margarine or butter
3/4 cup chopped onion
1/2 cup chopped celery
1/4 cup chopped green pepper
1 tablespoon chopped parsley
1 clove garlic, minced
2 cups fully cooked, cubed ham
1 (28-ounce) can tomatoes,
 undrained, cut up
1 cup uncooked long grain rice

1 (10 1/2-ounce) can beef broth plus
 1 can water
1 teaspoon sugar
1/2 teaspoon dried thyme leaves,
 crushed
1/2 teaspoon chili powder
1/4 teaspoon pepper
1 1/2 pounds raw, peeled, and
 deveined shrimp

Melt margarine in Dutch oven. Add onion, celery, green pepper, parsley, and garlic. Cover and cook until tender. Add remaining ingredients, except shrimp. Cover and simmer 25 minutes or until rice is tender. Add shrimp and simmer uncovered to desired consistency and until shrimp are cooked, about 5 or 10 minutes. Makes 6–8 servings.

Editor's Note: Jambalaya, a traditional Louisiana dish, grew out of early French and Spanish Louisiana. The word jambalaya comes from the French "jamb" which means ham, and "paella," a Spanish rice dish. Jambalaya was cooked in a big black iron pot—originally for boiling syrup from sugar cane—and cooked over an open wood fire outdoors, and boat oars were used for stirring. Don't let that deter you, jambalaya can be cooked at home on the range . . . it's a lot easier.

Louisiana Largesse (Louisiana)

★ **Editor's Extra:** Paddle-stirrin' black-iron-pot jambalaya is often cooked right outside the stadium at LSU football tailgating parties.

Almond Topped Crab Quiche

Pastry for 9-inch pie shell
1 cup shredded Swiss cheese
1/2 pound fresh crabmeat
2 green onions, sliced
3 eggs
1 cup half-and-half

1/2 teaspoon salt
1/2 teaspoon grated lemon rind
Dash of dry mustard
Dash of pepper
1/4 cup sliced almonds

Line a 9-inch quiche dish with pastry. Trim excess from edges. Bake at 400° for 3 minutes; remove from oven, then gently prick with fork. Bake 5 minutes longer. Cool on rack.

Sprinkle cheese in pastry shell. Remove cartilage from crabmeat and place crabmeat on top of cheese. Sprinkle with green onions. Beat eggs until foamy; stir in half-and-half, salt, lemon rind, dry mustard, and pepper. Pour into pastry shell. Sprinkle with almonds. Bake at 325° for 1 hour. Let stand 10 minutes before serving.

Hospitality Heirlooms (Mississippi)

Fabulous Easy Quiche

16 slices white bread, crusts
   removed, cubed, divided
1 pound ham, cubed
1 pound Cheddar cheese, grated
1 1/2 cups cubed Swiss cheese

6 eggs
3 cups milk
1/2 teaspoon onion salt
Pepper

Spread 1/2 of bread cubes in a 9x13-inch baking dish. Sprinkle evenly with ham and both cheeses. Cover with remaining bread cubes. In a bowl, mix eggs, milk, onion salt, and pepper. Pour over bread. Refrigerate overnight.

TOPPING:

3 cups cornflakes   1/2 cup butter, melted

Combine and spread evenly over quiche. Bake, uncovered, at 375° for 40 minutes. Let stand a few minutes before serving. Makes 4–5 servings.

Recipes from Minnesota with Love (Minnesota)

Southwestern Quiche

1 (9-inch) pie shell, unbaked
4 eggs, separated
1 teaspoon salt
1 teaspoon onion salt, or ½ cup
  minced onion
1 teaspoon red chile powder

1 teaspoon black pepper
1 cup chopped mushrooms
1 cup chopped green chiles
2 cups heavy cream, or 1 cup
  evaporated milk
1 cup grated Swiss cheese

Prepare pie crust and set aside.

Separate eggs; beat egg yolks, then whip egg whites until foamy. Fold egg whites into yolks along with salt, onion salt or onion, red chile powder, black pepper, chopped mushrooms, and green chiles. Add cream or evaporated milk to mixture and blend well. Layer cheese over bottom of pie crust; pour egg mixture into pie crust. Bake at 425° for 25–30 minutes or until quiche is browned and solid. Serve hot. Makes 6–8 wedges.

Variation: Crumble ½ pound cooked pork sausage or 1 cup cooked crumbled bacon over top of egg mixture before baking.

Comida Sabrosa (New Mexico)

Almost Pizza

This meal-in-a-dish is big on flavor.

STEP 1:

7 cups raw potatoes (sliced or diced)
1 pound ground beef
1 can nacho cheese soup
1 cup milk

Butter
Dash of salt
Dash of pepper

Place raw potatoes in greased 9x13-inch pan. Brown ground beef and cover potatoes. Heat nacho cheese soup and milk. Pour over hamburger. Dot with butter; sprinkle with salt and pepper.

STEP 2:

1 can tomato soup
$^1/_2$ teaspoon oregano
1 teaspoon sugar
$^1/_2$ cup chopped onion

2 cups sliced pepperoni
Parmesan cheese to sprinkle
1–2 cups shredded mozzarella
  cheese

Mix tomato soup, oregano, sugar, and onion. Pour this over nacho cheese soup. Place the pepperoni on top. Cover with foil and bake at 400° for 15 minutes. Turn oven down to 350° for 1 hour or until potatoes are done. Take out and sprinkle with Parmesan cheese and mozzarella cheese. Place in oven to melt cheese. Serves 8–10.

Variation: Canadian bacon, green pepper, olives, or any other toppings may be added.

Red River Valley Potato Growers Auxiliary Cookbook
(Great Plains/North Dakota)

No, we're not riding them, but merely pausing to think it would be a neat way to take in all the scenery around Granbury, Texas.

Oven-Fried Chicken
with Honey Butter Sauce

HONEY BUTTER SAUCE:

$^1/_4$ cup butter, melted $\qquad$ $^1/_4$ cup honey
$^1/_4$ cup lemon juice

Melt butter in a saucepan; blend in honey and lemon juice. Do not boil.

$^1/_2$ cup butter or margarine $\qquad$ $^1/_4$ teaspoon pepper
1 cup flour $\qquad$ 2 teaspoons paprika
2 teaspoons salt $\qquad$ 1 frying chicken, cut up

Melt butter in a shallow baking pan. Combine flour, salt, pepper, and paprika; dip chicken into flour mix and then in the butter, turning each piece. Arrange, skin-side-down, in a single layer; bake at 400° for 30 minutes. Turn and pour Honey Butter Sauce over all; bake another 30 minutes at 350°, until chicken is tender.

Neighboring on the Air (Iowa)

Oven Barbecued Chicken

Everyone wants this recipe.

5–6 pounds chicken thighs $\qquad$ 1 cup pineapple juice
Garlic powder $\qquad$ $1^1/_2$ cups catsup
3 eggs, beaten $\qquad$ 1 cup white vinegar
2 cups granulated sugar $\qquad$ 2 teaspoons soy sauce

Wash chicken thighs and pat dry. Sprinkle with garlic powder and let set for about 5 minutes. Dip chicken in beaten eggs. Fry until nearly done. Spray large oven pan with nonstick spray. Mix together the granulated sugar, juice, catsup, vinegar, and soy sauce. Put chicken in pan and pour the sauce over chicken. Cover pan with aluminum foil and bake 30–45 minutes in 300° oven, or until sauce is thick. Put chicken on platter and spoon remaining sauce over top.

In the Kitchen with Kate (Great Plains/Kansas)

Monterey Chicken

¼ cup flour
1 (1¼-ounce) package taco
  seasoning mix
4 skinned chicken breasts
¼ cup (½ stick) margarine
1 cup crushed tortilla chips

Combine flour and taco seasoning in a bag. Add chicken and shake to coat. Roll each piece in crushed chips and return to baking pan. Bake at 375° about 30 minutes.

CHEESE SAUCE:

2 tablespoons chopped onion
1 tablespoon vegetable oil
2 tablespoons flour
¼ teaspoon salt
1 (13-ounce) can evaporated milk
¼ teaspoon hot pepper sauce
1 cup (4 ounces) grated Monterey
  Jack cheese
¼ cup sliced olives
1 teaspoon lemon juice
Shredded lettuce

Cook onion in oil until tender but not brown. Stir in flour and salt. Add milk and hot pepper sauce. Heat, stirring constantly, until bubbly. Cook an additional 1–2 minutes. Stir in cheese, olives, and lemon juice; cook until cheese melts. Serve chicken on shredded lettuce, and pour Cheese Sauce over top. Serves 4.

Coastal Cuisine, Texas Style (Texas II)

Crispy Sesame Chicken

1¼ cups cornflake crumbs
¼ cup sesame seeds
¾ teaspoon paprika
¼ teaspoon salt
¼ teaspoon ground ginger
½ cup plain nonfat yogurt
2 tablespoons honey
8 skinned chicken breast halves
Vegetable cooking spray
2 tablespoons melted margarine

Combine first 5 ingredients in a large zip-lock plastic bag; set aside. Combine yogurt and honey in a shallow dish; stir well. Coat chicken pieces with yogurt mixture. Place chicken in zip-lock bag and shake to coat. Remove chicken from bag and place on baking sheet coated with vegetable spray. Drizzle with melted margarine. Bake at 400° for 45 minutes or until done.

Applause Applause (Iowa)

Breast of Chicken Veronique

9 tablespoons butter, divided
3 large chicken breasts, split
18 medium mushrooms, quartered
  (caps only)
3 tablespoons flour

$1\frac{1}{2}$ cups half-and-half
$\frac{3}{4}$ cup white wine
1 cup diced ham
Salt and pepper to taste
$1\frac{1}{2}$ cups seedless grapes

Melt 6 tablespoons butter in large heavy pan and brown chicken breasts. Remove to casserole. Melt 3 tablespoons butter in same pan and sauté mushrooms over high heat for 3 minutes. Remove with slotted spoon and scatter over chicken. Reduce heat and stir flour into skillet. Cook the roux 1 minute. Gradually add half-and-half and wine, stirring constantly. Cook until thick. Add diced ham. Season with salt and pepper and pour sauce over chicken. Bake covered in a 350° oven for 35–40 minutes. Uncover and scatter grapes over chicken and bake another 10 minutes. Yields 6 servings.

Treat Yourself to the Best Cookbook (West Virginia)

Chicken à la Bethany

4–6 chicken breasts (boneless)
1 egg, beaten
Flour for dredging
Butter
Salt and pepper to taste
1 can chicken broth
$\frac{1}{4}$ cup vinegar

1 cup sugar
1 red pepper, sliced
1 green pepper, sliced
1 onion, sliced
1 small can crushed pineapple
2 tablespoons flour

Lightly dip chicken breasts in egg and then in flour. Sauté in buttered skillet until done. Add salt and pepper to taste. In a separate saucepan, mix chicken broth, vinegar, and sugar. Add sliced peppers, onion, and pineapple. Simmer until vegetables are cooked.

To thicken sauce, mix small amount of hot water with 2 tablespoons flour; stir until smooth and add to sauce. Serve chicken topped with sauce. Accompany with rice.

South Coastal Cuisine (Mid-Atlantic/Delaware)

★★★★★★★★★★★ ★★★★★★★★★★★

Chicken Bundles

An impressive bundle of deliciousness!

³/₄ cup chopped green onions
³/₄ cup mayonnaise
3 tablespoons lemon juice
3 cloves garlic, minced, divided
³/₄ teaspoon dry tarragon
²/₃ cup margarine, melted

12 sheets phyllo
6 chicken breast halves, boned and
  skinned
Salt and pepper to taste
2 tablespoons grated Parmesan
  cheese

Mix together onion, mayonnaise, lemon juice, 2 cloves garlic, and tarragon. Set aside. Combine remaining garlic and butter. For each bundle, place 2 sheets of phyllo on a board and brush with garlic butter. Spread one side of chicken breast with about 1½ tablespoons mayonnaise mixture. Turn over onto corner of phyllo sheets and top with 1½ tablespoons more of mixture.

Wrap breast in phyllo as follows: Flip corner of phyllo over chicken. Roll once. Fold side over top and roll again. Fold opposite over, then roll up. Folds like an envelope. Place bundles slightly apart on an ungreased baking sheet. Brush with remaining garlic butter. Sprinkle with cheese. Bake at 375° for 20–25 minutes or until golden. Serves 6.

Note: May be frozen—but thaw completely, covered, before baking.

The Steinbeck House Cookbook (California)

Crab-Stuffed Chicken Breasts

May be prepared the night before serving.

4 whole chicken breasts, boned,
  skinned, halved
1/4 cup butter
1/2 cup thinly sliced green onions
1/4 cup thinly sliced mushrooms
6 tablespoons flour
1/2 teaspoon thyme
1 cup chicken broth

1 cup milk
1 cup dry white wine
Salt and pepper
8 ounces crabmeat
1/3 cup chopped parsley
1/3 cup dry bread crumbs
1 cup shredded Swiss cheese

Pound chicken between 2 sheets of plastic wrap until 1/4 inch thick. Set aside.

Melt butter in large skillet; sauté onions and mushrooms. Add flour and thyme. Blend in broth, milk, and wine; cook and stir until thickened. Add salt and pepper to taste. Remove 1/4 cup sauce.

Make stuffing of 1/4 cup sauce, crabmeat, parsley, and dry bread crumbs. Spoon crab mixture evenly on chicken breasts. Roll meat around filling and place seam-side-down in greased 8x12-inch baking dish.

Pour remaining sauce over chicken breasts. Sprinkle with cheese. Cover and bake at 400° for 35 minutes; uncover and bake 10 minutes. Serves 8.

Brunch Basket (Illinois)

★★★★★★★★★★★   ★★★★★★★★★★★

Provolone Chicken

An impressive dish for a buffet dinner.

5 boneless, skinless, chicken
  breasts, cut in medium bite-size
  pieces, flattened
3 eggs, beaten
Seasoned bread crumbs
Butter ($^{1}/_{4}$ cup)

8 ounces fresh or canned
  mushrooms, sliced
1 cup chicken broth
6 ounces white wine
$^{1}/_{2}$ pound provolone cheese, grated

Marinate chicken in eggs while getting the rest of recipe together; drain each piece of chicken and roll in bread crumbs. Brown in butter until lightly brown on both sides. Transfer into a 9x13-inch casserole, layering in rows, overlapping pieces.

    Sauté mushrooms and arrange over chicken. Add chicken broth and wine. Cover with grated cheese. Bake, covered, at 350° for 30 minutes. Uncover and bake 15 minutes longer. Serve immediately. Serves 8.

Note: You can freeze, but add chicken broth, wine and cheese just before baking.

Angels and Friends Cookbook II (Ohio)

Eddy's Chicken Kiev

An easier, different approach to this ever-popular entrée...so good that it starred in the menu for "Dinner for Ten," an Overlake School auction item.

4 whole chicken breasts, boned and
  skinned
$^{1}/_{2}$ pound butter
$^{1}/_{2}$ cup chopped parsley
$^{1}/_{2}$ cup green onions

4 ounces Monterey Jack cheese
8 thin slices ham
2 eggs, beaten
$1^{1}/_{2}$ cups fine bread crumbs

Preheat oven to 350°. Cut chicken pieces in half and place between 2 sheets of wax paper. Pound with a mallet until uniformly $^{1}/_{4}$ inch thick. Melt butter over low heat, adding parsley and green onions. Cut cheese into $3x^{1}/_{2}$-inch sticks. With breasts smooth-side-down, top each with a ham slice and piece of cheese. Roll up, tucking in ends, and secure with toothpicks.

    Dip breasts in beaten eggs and roll in crumbs. Place, seam-side-down, in ungreased shallow 8x12-inch casserole. Pour butter mixture over all. Bake, uncovered, at 350° for 45 minutes, basting several times. Serves 4–6.

The Overlake School Cookbook (Washington)

★★★★★★★★★★★★   ★★★★★★★★★★★★

Santa Fe Chicken

This is quick, easy, and delicious!

4 boneless, skinless chicken breasts	1 garlic clove, minced
1 teaspoon paprika	1 (10-ounce) can tomatoes
1 teaspoon salt	with green chiles
1/4 teaspoon pepper	Chicken broth
2 teaspoons olive oil or margarine	1 1/2 cups converted Instant Rice
1 small onion, chopped	3/4 cup (3 ounces) shredded
1 small bell pepper, chopped	Monterey Jack cheese

Cut cooked chicken into strips or chunks. Sprinkle with paprika, salt, and pepper. Heat oil in 10-inch skillet over medium-high heat. Cook chicken in oil for 2 minutes. Add onion, bell pepper, and garlic; cook until tender (about 4 minutes), stirring frequently. Drain tomatoes, reserving liquid. Add chicken broth to tomato liquid to equal 1 1/2 cups of liquid. Add liquid to skillet; bring to boil. Stir in rice and reserved tomatoes. Cover and remove from heat. Let stand until liquid is absorbed (about 5 minutes). Sprinkle with cheese. Yields 4 servings.

From Cajun Roots to Texas Boots (Texas II)

Fiesta Chicken

1 stick margarine, divided	5 green onions (tops, too) chopped
1 3/4 cups finely crushed Cheddar	1 (4-ounce) can chopped green chiles
cheese crackers	2 cups heavy cream
2 tablespoons taco seasoning mix	1 teaspoon instant chicken bouillon
8 chicken breasts, boned, skinned,	2 cups grated Monterey Jack cheese
and flattened	

Melt margarine in a 9x13-inch baking dish and set aside. Combine cracker crumbs and taco mix. Dredge chicken in this mixture—pat this on so you get plenty of crumbs to stick on chicken. Place chicken in baking dish with margarine.

In a medium-size saucepan, take out a couple tablespoons of the melted margarine and place in saucepan. To the melted margarine in saucepan, add chopped onions and sauté. Then add the green chiles, heavy cream, instant chicken bouillon and the Monterey Jack cheese; mix well. Pour this mixture over chicken breasts. Bake uncovered at 350° for 50–55 minutes. Serves 6–8.

Great Tastes of Texas (Texas II)

Herbed Parmesan Chicken

This is a low-fat recipe that can be prepared ahead, frozen, and reheated in the microwave.

3 pounds chicken breasts, skinned
   and boned
$1/4$ teaspoon garlic powder
$1/4$ teaspoon paprika
$1/8$ teaspoon dried thyme
$1/4$ cup freshly grated Parmesan
   cheese

1 tablespoon minced fresh parsley
$1/3$ cup fine bread crumbs
1 tablespoon vegetable oil
2 tablespoons margarine
$1/3$ cup Marsala wine

Cut chicken breasts into pieces $1^1/2$–2 inches wide. Combine next 6 ingredients in a paper bag. Coat chicken with mixture a few pieces at a time by shaking the bag. Place chicken in a baking dish and press any remaining seasonings into chicken. Sprinkle chicken with oil and melted margarine. Bake, uncovered, at 350° for 30 minutes.

Pour wine over chicken and cover with foil. Reduce heat to 325°; bake 15 additional minutes. Remove foil, raise heat to 350°, and bake 10 minutes longer. Serves 6–8.

Gateways (Missouri)

Dandy Chicken

4 whole boneless chicken breasts,
   split in half for 8 pieces
Salt, pepper, paprika, garlic
   powder to taste
$1^1/2$ cups sour cream

2 tablespoons lemon juice
2 tablespoons Worcestershire sauce
1 package herbed dressing mix
$3/4$ stick margarine, melted

Sprinkle chicken breasts with salt, pepper, paprika, and garlic powder to taste. Mix sour cream, lemon juice, and Worcestershire sauce. Dip each piece of chicken in sour cream mixture. Marinate at least 4 hours (or overnight). Roll in dressing mix and place in a 9x13-inch baking dish. Drizzle with margarine. Bake at 325° for 1 hour and 15 minutes. Makes 8 servings.

Cooking...Done the Baptist Way (South Carolina)

Chicken Alfredo

An Italian chicken delight...can be made in advance.

3 chicken breasts, boned and cut in
  half
1/2 cup flour
2 eggs, beaten
1 cup seasoned Italian-style bread
  crumbs
1/2 cup plus 2 tablespoons grated
  Italian cheese, divided

2 tablespoons oil
1/2 teaspoon parsley
Salt to taste
Pepper to taste
4 tablespoons sweet butter
1 pint heavy cream
4 ounces mozzarella cheese, sliced

Coat chicken with flour, then dip in beaten eggs, and roll in bread crumbs flavored with 2 tablespoons grated cheese. In a little oil, fry on both sides to brown. Put in a baking dish or pan, and season with salt, pepper, and parsley. Melt sweet butter, then add heavy cream and 1/2 cup Italian cheese; pour over chicken. Put 1 slice mozzarella cheese on each piece of chicken. Cover and bake at 350° for 30–40 minutes. Yields 6 servings.

The Eater's Digest (Pennsylvania)

Swiss Chicken

4 whole chicken breasts, split,
  boned, and skinned
8 sandwich slices Swiss cheese,
  divided
5 tablespoons butter, divided
2 tablespoons flour

1/2 cup milk
1/2 cup chicken broth
Salt
Freshly ground black pepper
1/4 cup white wine
1 cup dry stuffing mix

Place chicken breasts in buttered baking dish. Cover each breast with 1 slice of cheese. Melt 2 tablespoons butter over low heat. Add flour and blend over heat until smooth and bubbling. Slowly stir in milk and chicken broth. Season with salt and pepper to taste. Add white wine. Pour over chicken. Mix stuffing mix with 3 tablespoons melted butter. Spread over top of chicken. Bake at 350° for 45–60 minutes. Makes 8 servings.

Honest to Goodness (Illinois)

★★★★★★★★★★★ ★★★★★★★★★★★

Sweet and Sour Baked Chicken

Incredibly good . . . just try it!

1 (3-pound) broiler-fryer, cut up
$1/2$ cup chopped onion
$1/2$ cup coarsely chopped green
  pepper
$1/2$ cup coarsely chopped carrots
$1/4$ cup butter or margarine
$3/4$ cup ketchup
1 cup pineapple juice
2 tablespoons vinegar

$1/4$ cup firmly packed brown sugar
1 tablespoon soy sauce
$1/2$ teaspoon garlic salt
1 teaspoon salt
$1/4$ teaspoon pepper
Dash ground red pepper
Dash ground ginger
1 cup pineapple chunks

Preheat oven to 400°. In medium skillet, cook onion, green pepper, and carrots in butter for 5 minutes, stirring. Stir in ketchup, pineapple juice, vinegar, sugar, soy sauce, garlic salt, salt, peppers, and ginger. Cook, stirring constantly, until mixture boils. Add pineapple chunks. Arrange chicken pieces, skin-side-up, in a 9x13-inch baking pan. Pour sweet and sour sauce over all. Bake covered for 45 minutes. Uncover and bake about 30 minutes longer, or until chicken tests done.

Our Favorite Recipes (Illinois)

 The Big Duck, in Long Island, New York, is a wood frame, wire mesh, concrete surfaced building designed in the shape of a Peking duck. It measures 15 feet wide across the front, 30 feet from breast to tail, and 20 feet to the top of the head. The eyes are Ford Model "T" tail lights. The interior is approximately 11 by 15 feet. Originally home to a retail poultry store built in 1931 by duck farmer Martin Maurer, it now houses a retail gift shop operated by the Friends for Long Island Heritage.

★★★★★★★★★★★★ ★★★★★★★★★★★★

Moo Goo Gai Pan
(Stir-Fried Chicken and Mushrooms)

1 cup regular long grain rice
2 large whole chicken breasts,
  boned and skinned
2 tablespoons soy sauce
2 tablespoons cooking or dry sherry
2 teaspoons cornstarch
1 teaspoon minced ginger root, or
  $1/4$ teaspoon ground ginger

$1/4$ teaspoon sugar
$1/8$ teaspoon garlic powder
1 pound medium mushrooms
2 cups chopped broccoli
4 green onions
$1/4$ cup sliced water chestnuts
3–4 tablespoons oil
1 cup snow peas, thawed

Prepare rice as package directs; keep warm. Cut each chicken breast into 1-inch-thick slices. In medium bowl, mix chicken, soy sauce, sherry, cornstarch, ginger root, sugar, and garlic powder; set aside. Thinly slice mushrooms and broccoli; cut each green onion crosswise into 3-inch pieces.

In 12-inch skillet or wok, over medium-high heat, in oil, cook mushrooms, green onions, broccoli, and water chestnuts, stirring quickly and frequently until mushrooms are tender, about 3 or 4 minutes. With spoon, remove mushrooms and broccoli mixture to bowl. In same skillet or wok, over high heat, in 3 tablespoons hot oil, cook chicken mixture, stirring quickly and frequently until chicken is tender, about 4–5 minutes. Return mushroom mixture to skillet; add peas and heat through. Serve with rice. Yields 4 servings.

Mountain Laurel Encore (Kentucky)

Crispy Parmesan Chicken Strips

A great appetizer, too.

$1^1/2$ cups seasoned croutons,
  crushed
$1^1/2$ ounces ($1/3$ cup) fresh
  Parmesan cheese, grated
1 teaspoon dried parsley
$1/4$ teaspoon garlic salt

2 egg whites
1 tablespoon water
1 pound boneless, skinless chicken
  breasts, cut into 1-inch pieces
$1/4$ cup ranch dressing

Preheat oven to 450°. Combine croutons, cheese, parsley, and salt. Whisk egg whites and water. Dip chicken pieces into egg mixture, then into crumb mixture. Place on baking sheet. Bake 14–16 minutes, or until chicken is no longer pink inside. Serve with ranch dressing.

Taste of Balboa (Washington)

Fantastic Chicken Fajitas

1 pound boneless chicken breast or
  thigh meat
1 teaspoon each garlic powder,
  oregano, ground cumin, and
  seasoned salt
2 tablespoons orange juice

2 tablespoons vinegar
$1/2$ teaspoon hot pepper sauce
1 tablespoon cooking oil
1 medium onion, peeled and sliced
1 green pepper, seeded and sliced
4 flour tortillas

Slice chicken into $1/4$-inch strips. Mix together garlic powder, oregano, cumin, salt, orange juice, vinegar, and hot pepper sauce. Marinate chicken strips in mixture for 10 minutes. Heat oil in heavy skillet until hot. Stir-fry chicken strips, onion, and green pepper until chicken is no longer pink, about 3–5 minutes. Serve with flour tortillas and accompany with sliced green onion, shredded lettuce, and salsa, if desired. Serves 4.

Heavenly Recipes (Great Plains/North Dakota)

Mini Chicken Pies

Everybody will love these.

1 (3-ounce) package cream cheese,
  softened
2 tablespoons mayonnaise
$3/4$ cup cooked and chopped chicken
$1/8$ cup finely chopped green bell
  pepper
$1/8$ cup finely chopped red bell pepper

$1/4$ cup chopped onion
$1/2$ cup shredded Cheddar cheese
1 (7-ounce) can Mexican-style corn,
  drained
1 can refrigerated large, flaky
  biscuits
Sesame seeds

Heat oven to 375°. Lightly grease 8 muffin cups. In a medium bowl, blend cream cheese and mayonnaise until smooth. Stir in chicken, green and red bell peppers, onion, Cheddar cheese, and corn. Separate biscuits and then divide into 2 parts by removing the top $1/3$ of each biscuit. Place bottom $2/3$ of biscuit into greased muffin cups. Firmly press in bottom and up the sides forming a $1/4$-inch rim. Spoon $1/3$ cup of chicken mixture into each cup. Top each with remaining $1/3$ biscuit, stretching slightly to fit. Press edges to seal. Sprinkle with sesame seeds. Bake for 15–20 minutes or until golden brown.

Feeding the Flock—HCCLA (West Virginia)

★★★★★★★★★★★★ ★★★★★★★★★★★★

Heavenly Chicken Casserole

Filled with such goodies as almonds, mushrooms, and wild rice, and it serves 10!

1 (4-ounce) box wild rice
½ cup (1 stick) margarine
½ cup chopped onion
½ cup chopped green pepper
½ cup chopped celery
2 (10¾-ounce) cans cream of
  mushroom soup
1 cup sliced almonds, toasted

2 cups shredded Cheddar cheese,
  divided
4 cups diced, cooked chicken
1 (4-ounce) jar chopped pimiento,
  drained
1 (4-ounce) can sliced mushrooms,
  drained
Salt to taste

Heat oven to 350°. Cook wild rice according to package directions until nearly done; drain. Melt margarine in Dutch oven; add onion, green pepper, and celery. Cook until tender; remove from heat.

Add soup, almonds, 1½ cups cheese, chicken, pimiento, mushrooms, and cooked wild rice. Blend well and add salt, if necessary. Pour mixture into a greased 9x13-inch baking dish. Bake for 20 minutes; sprinkle remaining ½ cup cheese over top. Continue to bake for an additional 10–15 minutes or until hot and bubbly. Serves 10.

Lasting Impressions (Georgia)

★★★★★★★★★★★   ★★★★★★★★★★★

Favorite Chicken Casserole

A real favorite of everyone and so easy to prepare.

2 cups diced, cooked chicken
1 can cream of chicken soup
$^1/_2$ cup milk
1–1$^1/_4$ cups chicken broth
$^1/_2$ cup chopped celery
$^1/_4$ cup chopped onion

1 egg, beaten
$^1/_2$ bag (2 cups) herb stuffing mix
1 tablespoon parsley flakes
  (optional)
Paprika

Spread chicken in bottom of a 2-quart flat casserole dish. Dilute soup with milk. Pour over top of chicken. Cook celery and onion in broth until tender (if you don't have broth, substitute 1 cup water with $^1/_2$ stick butter and 1 chicken bouillon cube). Make dressing by combining broth, celery, onion, egg, stuffing, and parsley flakes. Spread dressing on top of soup. Sprinkle with paprika. Bake at 350° for 35–40 minutes or until bubbly and brown.

Granny's Kitchen (Virginia)

First Place Chicken Casserole

Superlatives are definitely in order for this make-ahead dish which came to us already aptly named. We suggest cooking the rice in the broth left from the chicken. We promise rave notices to you, too!

2–3 cups diced, cooked chicken
4 hard-boiled eggs, chopped
2 cups cooked rice
1$^1/_2$ cups chopped celery
1 small onion, chopped
1 cup mayonnaise
2 cans mushroom soup

1 (3-ounce) package slivered
  almonds
1 teaspoon salt
2 tablespoons lemon juice
1 cup bread crumbs
2 tablespoons margarine

Mix all ingredients except bread crumbs and margarine. Place mixture in buttered 9x12-inch pan or casserole. Brown bread crumbs lightly in margarine. Sprinkle over casserole; refrigerate overnight. Remove from refrigerator 1 hour before cooking. Bake 40–45 minutes at 350°.

Cotton Country Cooking (Alabama)

Chicken and Spinach Casserole

2 packages frozen chopped spinach,
  defrosted and drained
4 whole chicken breasts, halved,
  skinned, boned, and cooked
1 cup mayonnaise
2 (10¾-ounce) cans cream of
  chicken soup

1 tablespoon lemon juice
1 cup shredded sharp Cheddar
  cheese
½ cup buttered bread crumbs

Place drained spinach in a 9x13-inch ungreased dish. Place chicken breasts on top. Combine and mix mayonnaise, soup, and lemon juice. Spread over chicken. Sprinkle with cheese. Top with buttered crumbs. Bake at 350° for 30–40 minutes. Makes 8 servings.

Historic Lexington Cooks (Virginia)

Crescent Chicken Casserole

A sure-to-please favorite.

½ cup chopped celery
½ cup chopped onion
2 tablespoons butter
4 cups chicken breast, skinned or 3
  cups chopped cooked chicken
1 (8-ounce) can water chestnuts,
  drained

1 can cream of chicken soup
1 (4-ounce) can sliced mushrooms,
  drained
⅔ cup mayonnaise
½ cup commercial sour cream
1 (8-ounce) package crescent rolls

Sauté celery and onion in butter until softened. Heat next 6 items until bubbly, then mix with celery-onion mixture. Put in a greased 9x13-inch pan, then separate crescent rolls into 2 rectangles. Lay over mixture.

TOPPING:
½ cup slivered almonds
1 cup shredded cheese

2–3 tablespoons butter, melted

Mix ingredients and sprinkle over top. Bake at 350° for 45 minutes.

Potluck Volume II (Minnesota)

Chicken and Spinach Enchilada Casserole

This is a great entrée for a casual dinner party.

2 pounds boneless chicken breasts
4 tablespoons ($^1/_2$ stick) unsalted
  butter
1 large onion, chopped
1 (10-ounce) box frozen chopped
  spinach, thawed and drained
3 cups sour cream
1 teaspoon ground cumin

1 (4-ounce) can chopped green
  chiles (or more to taste)
$^1/_4$ cup milk
Salt and freshly ground pepper to
  taste
12 flour tortillas
8 ounces shredded Monterey Jack
  cheese

Place chicken breasts in a skillet and add water to just cover. Poach on medium-low heat until cooked through, approximately 15–20 minutes. Remove from water and cool. Shred or cut into bite-size pieces and place in a mixing bowl.

Preheat oven to 350°. Grease a 9x13-inch baking dish. In a small skillet, melt the butter and sauté the onion until tender, about 5 minutes. In a large bowl, combine cooked onion, spinach, sour cream, cumin, chiles, and milk. Season with salt and pepper. Add half the sauce to the shredded chicken and mix well. Layer 3 tortillas in bottom of casserole dish. Cover with $^1/_3$ of the chicken mixture. Repeat process 3 times, ending with a layer or tortillas. Cover casserole with remaining sauce, spreading evenly with a spatula. Top with grated cheese. Bake casserole approximately 40 minutes, or until heated through and bubbly and cheese begins to brown. Serve hot. Serves 6–8.

In the Kitchen with Kendi (Mid-Atlantic/Maryland)

Three cities vie for the title of Spinach Capital of the World celebrating with a yearly Spinach Festival. Crystal City, Texas, is home to a large Del Monte packing plant; their Spinach Festival is held the second weekend of November, and attracts about 60,000 people. Alma, Arkansas, has a spinach-green water tower in the center of town and is near the Allen Company's huge cannery. Their festival, held the fourth Saturday in April, is the smallest of the three. Lenexa, Kansas, celebrates the earliest claim to fame. Their first Spinach Festival was in 1937, and to celebrate, they put a statue of Popeye in the town center.

Almond Turkey Casserole

1 cup Cheddar cheese, divided
1 tablespoon flour
3 cups chopped, cooked turkey
1½ cups sliced celery
⅔ cup slivered almonds, divided
1 cup mayonnaise
1 tablespoon lemon juice

½ teaspoon dried oregano leaves
¼ teaspoon salt
¼ teaspoon pepper
1 large can Mandarin oranges,
    drained
Pastry for 2-crust (9-inch) pie

Preheat oven to 400°. Toss ¾ cup cheese with flour. Mix cheese mixture, turkey, celery, ⅓ cup almonds, mayonnaise, juice, seasonings, and oranges. Roll pastry to 11x15-inch square on lightly floured surface. Place in a buttered 9x13-inch baking dish; turn 1 inch beyond edge. Turn under edge; flute. Fill with turkey mixture. Top with remaining cheese and almonds. Bake 30–35 minutes. Serves 6–8.

A Taste of Fishers (Indiana)

Southern Corn Bread Dressing

The secret is in the liquid.

1 large onion, chopped
1 cup chopped celery
⅓ cup butter
2–2½ cups crumbled day-old
    bread (be sure it is dry)

3 cups crumbled corn bread
2–3 eggs
4–5 cups turkey or chicken broth
½ teaspoon pepper
½ teaspoon salt

Sauté onion and celery in butter. Preheat oven to 400°. Mix breads; add eggs and other ingredients and mix well. Have dressing soft, about the consistency of cake batter or thick soup. (The secret of good dressing is to have it really soupy, as it will cook dry.) Bake in greased 9x13-inch baking dish for about 40 minutes. Serves 10–12.

If you wish, you may stuff your bird with this dressing. If bird is stuffed, allow 5 minutes more cooking per pound.

Variation: You may make Chestnut Dressing by adding 1 cup chopped, roasted chestnuts; or make Oyster Dressing with the addition of 1 cup chopped oysters.

Sawgrass and Pines (Florida)

Seafood

The sailing is easy in the picturesque harbor of Perkins Cove in Ogunquit, Maine, where one of the only draw-footbridges in the country spans its entrance. Nearby there are beaches and coastline paths as well as quaint village shops.

Catfish Fillets Meuniere

Soak catfish fillets for 1 hour or more in a mixture of egg and milk, seasoned with salt, pepper, and a dash of hot sauce. Shake fillets in seasoned flour and fry until golden brown. Serve fillets on a warm platter with a generous amount of Sauce Meuniere spooned over them.

SAUCE MEUNIERE:

$\frac{1}{2}$ **cup butter**
1 tablespoon chopped green
  onion tops
1 tablespoon chopped fresh parsley
2 tablespoons Worcestershire sauce

3 tablespoons lemon juice
$\frac{1}{2}$ **teaspoon salt**
$\frac{1}{2}$ **teaspoon pepper**
Few drops of bottled brown
  bouquet sauce

Simmer all ingredients at least 15 minutes. Serve over fish.

Festival (Mississippi)

Grilled Citrus Salmon

1½ tablespoons freshly squeezed
  lemon juice
2 tablespoons olive oil
1 tablespoon butter
1 tablespoon Dijon mustard
4 garlic cloves, minced

2 dashes cayenne pepper
2 dashes salt
1 teaspoon dried basil
1 teaspoon dried dill
2 teaspoons capers
3 pounds fresh salmon fillets

In a small sauté pan over medium heat, combine lemon juice, olive oil, butter, mustard, garlic, pepper, salt, basil, dill, and capers. While stirring, bring to a boil. Reduce heat and simmer for 5 minutes.

While sauce is hot, brush on fish. Place salmon fillets skin-side-down on a piece of heavy-duty foil with edges folded up to make a pan. Pour remaining sauce evenly over fish. Place fish on grill and cover with a lid. Barbecue over medium-hot coals for 10–12 minutes, depending on thickness of fillets. Fish will be flaky and light pink in color when cooked. Yields 6 servings.

Note: May wrap fish in foil and bake in 350° oven for 15–20 minutes.

From Portland's Palate (Oregon)

Baked Dijon Salmon

This is a wonderful way to prepare fresh salmon fillets in the oven. Be sure to make extra; your family will be begging for more.

¼ cup butter, melted
3 tablespoons prepared Dijon
  mustard
1½ tablespoons honey
¼ cup dry bread crumbs

¼ cup finely chopped pecans
4 teaspoons chopped fresh parsley
4 (4-ounce) salmon fillets
Salt and pepper to taste
1 lemon for garnish

Preheat oven to 400°. In a small bowl, stir together butter, mustard, and honey. Set aside. In another bowl, mix together bread crumbs, pecans, and parsley.

Brush each salmon fillet lightly with honey-mustard mixture, and sprinkle top of fillets with bread crumb mixture. Bake salmon in preheated oven until it flakes easily with a fork, approximately 10–15 minutes. Season with salt and pepper, and garnish with a wedge of lemon. Makes 4 servings.

Allrecipes Tried & True Favorites (Washington)

Salmon Cakes

1 (16-ounce) can pink salmon
1 egg, beaten
1 (5.3-ounce) can evaporated milk
1 small onion, minced
½ cup minced green pepper

½ teaspoon salt
¼ teaspoon black pepper
3–4 slices fresh bread, torn into
    small bits
1 cup all-purpose flour

Drain and pick over salmon, removing skin and bones. In a large bowl, mix together all ingredients except flour. Shape into hamburger-sized patties, about ½ inch thick; dip into flour and fry in oil in a 10-inch skillet over medium heat until lightly browned. Drain on paper towels. Yields 4–6 servings.

Seafood Sorcery (North Carolina)

Pan-Fried Fish Parmesana

Trader Vic's restaurant, a local tradition as well as a tourist favorite, suggested this tasty and unusual way to prepare fish.

1 tablespoon lemon juice
1 tablespoon Worcestershire sauce
2 pounds rock cod or red snapper
    fillets, cut into 6 pieces
Salt and freshly ground pepper to
    taste

½ cup flour
3 eggs, lightly beaten
1 cup grated Parmesan cheese
3 tablespoons butter
2 tablespoons vegetable oil

Preheat oven to 400°. Combine lemon juice and Worcestershire sauce, and sprinkle on fish pieces. Salt and pepper fish, then dredge lightly in flour. Dip fish in eggs, then coat generously with grated cheese. In a heavy skillet, sauté fish in a mixture of butter and oil over medium heat for 3–4 minutes to brown. Turn and brown other side. Place skillet in oven for 4–5 minutes to heat through. Serve immediately. Serves 6.

San Francisco à la Carte (California)

Rockfish Chesapeake

1 pound rockfish fillets
1/4 teaspoon Worcestershire sauce
1/2 teaspoon lemon juice
1/2 teaspoon seafood seasoning
1 teaspoon white wine
2 tablespoons mayonnaise

Heat oven to 450°. Place fillets on foil-lined baking dish. Mix remaining ingredients. Spread mayonnaise mixture thinly and evenly over the fillets. Bake at 450° for 6–8 minutes. Fish is done when it flakes. Makes 4 servings.

More Favorites from the Melting Pot (Mid-Atlantic/Maryland)

Dilled Haddock Parmesan

1 cup sour cream
1/4 cup freshly grated Parmesan
1/4 cup grated Swiss cheese
1 teaspoon minced fresh dill, or 1/2 teaspoon dried
1/4 cup very soft butter
Salt and pepper to taste
3 pounds haddock fillets
Sprinkle of sweet Hungarian paprika
6 sprigs of dill for garnish
6 lemon wedges

In a small bowl, mix the sour cream, cheeses, minced dill, and butter. Add salt and pepper to taste. Set aside.

   Preheat oven to 375°. Cut fillets into 6 individual servings and place them on a buttered baking sheet. Top each piece with cheese mixture and bake for 15–20 minutes. Sprinkle lightly with paprika, garnish with dill sprig, and serve with a lemon wedge. Serves 6.

Recipes from a New England Inn (New England/Maine)

Measuring 4,260 feet long, Verrazano-Narrows Bridge, in New York, is the longest bridge span in America. The bridge has two levels, each holding six traffic lanes, linking the boroughs of Brooklyn and Staten Island.

Trout Almondine

6 large trout or redfish fillets
Juice of 2 lemons, divided
24 saltine crackers, crushed
2 sticks (1 cup) butter, divided

Garlic salt to taste
Pepper to taste
¾ cup sliced almonds
1 (4-ounce) can mushrooms, drained

Marinate fish in juice of 1 lemon for 5 minutes. Coat fish with crackers and sauté in 1 stick butter for 3–5 minutes on each side. Place fish in a baking pan, sprinkle lightly with garlic salt and pepper, and top with remaining lemon juice. Sauté almonds and mushrooms in remaining butter and pour over fish. Bake at 300° for 30 minutes. Serve immediately. Serves 6.

Flavors (Texas)

Baked Flounder with Crabmeat

STUFFING:
1 medium onion, chopped
2 cloves garlic, crushed
2 tablespoons chopped celery
2 tablespoons chopped green pepper
2 tablespoons bacon drippings
1 teaspoon salt

½ teaspoon pepper
⅛ teaspoon thyme
1 tablespoon chopped parsley
1 egg
¾ cup bread crumbs
1 cup crabmeat

Sauté vegetables in bacon drippings, then mix with remaining ingredients.

1 (3- to 4-pound) flounder
Salt to taste

1 stick butter, melted

Cut big pocket in cleaned fish. Season to taste. Place generous amount of Stuffing in pocket. Pour melted butter in a baking dish and place fish, dark-side-down, in butter. Bake at 375° for 30 minutes, covered. Uncover for the last 5–10 minutes. Serves 4.

The Crowning Recipes of Kentucky (Kentucky)

Barbecued Fish

This recipe came from an old fish camp on the Florida Keys.

½ pound (1 cup) butter
1½ cups brown sugar
¾ cup fresh lemon juice

⅓ cup soy sauce
3–5 pounds white meat fish
   (dolphin, snapper, grouper)

Melt butter and add sugar, lemon juice, and soy sauce. Bring to a boil, stirring constantly, then remove from heat and set aside to cool. Skin and bone fish. Marinate in sauce 1 hour before grilling. Cook fish on a grill over low fire, basting often with remaining marinade. For additional flavor, add wet hickory chips to the fire. Serves 10.

Seasons in the Sun (Florida)

Friday Night Fish

1½ pounds fish fillets (saltwater
   recommended)
3 tablespoons butter, softened
1 tablespoon lemon juice
1 teaspoon dried tarragon
½ teaspoon grated lemon peel or
   lemon pepper seasoning

⅓ cup dry white wine or vermouth
3 tablespoons minced fresh parsley
1 teaspoon dried chives, or 1
   tablespoon minced fresh
½ cup crumbled round, buttery
   crackers (optional)

Preheat oven to 425°. Place fish in lightly buttered baking dish. Mix together butter, lemon juice, tarragon, and lemon peel or lemon pepper seasoning. Spread on top of fish fillets. Pour wine over fish. Sprinkle parsley, chives, and crumbs over fish. Cover dish with foil and bake for 15–20 minutes until fish flakes with a fork. Transfer to a serving platter and pour pan juices over fish. Yields 4 portions.

Hospitality (New England/Massachusetts)

★ **Editor's Extra:** Also good to remove the foil last few minutes—or broil—if you like the top crispy.

Crabmeat Au Gratin

1 cup chopped onion	2 egg yolks
½ cup finely chopped celery	1 teaspoon salt
1 stick butter	¼ teaspoon red pepper
½ cup flour	1 pound lump crabmeat
1 (14-ounce) can evaporated milk	8 ounces grated Cheddar cheese

Sauté onion and celery in butter until soft. Add flour to this mixture. Add milk gradually, stirring constantly. Add egg yolks, salt, and red pepper. Cook for 10 minutes. Put crabmeat in a bowl and pour sauce over the crabmeat. Blend well and place in a lightly greased casserole and sprinkle with grated cheese. Bake at 375° until browned, approximately 15 minutes. Serves 4–6.

Paul Naquin's French Collection I—Louisiana Seafood (Louisiana)

Deviled Crabs

4 teaspoons butter	3 tablespoons chopped onion
3 teaspoons flour	1 teaspoon salt
1 cup milk	2 hard-boiled eggs, peeled and
2 cups cooked crabmeat	chopped
Juice of 1 lemon	½ cup toasted bread crumbs
1 teaspoon pepper (red or black)	4 teaspoons butter, melted
1 teaspoon dry mustard	

Melt 4 teaspoons butter; stir in flour and gradually add milk. Cook until thick. Remove from heat; add crabmeat, all seasonings, and eggs. Place mixture in crab shells, if available, or in a greased baking dish. Sprinkle with bread crumbs and melted butter. Bake at 400° for 15 minutes.

Inverness Cook Book (Mississippi)

Scallops and Crabmeat

1 stick plus 7 tablespoons butter,
  divided
1 pound fresh bay scallops
Fresh lemon juice
Salt to taste
3 tablespoons chopped bell pepper
3 tablespoons finely chopped onion
$\frac{1}{4}$ pound fresh mushrooms, sliced
$\frac{3}{4}$ cup flour
1 cup half-and-half
1 cup milk
$\frac{1}{4}$ teaspoon salt
$\frac{1}{4}$ cup dry white wine
Generous dash nutmeg
Dash cayenne pepper
3 tablespoons chopped pimiento
1 pound lump crabmeat
$1\frac{1}{2}$ cups whipping cream

Melt 4 tablespoons butter in heavy skillet over medium heat and sauté scallops, one-half at a time, until slightly brown. Remove with slotted spoon, sprinkling with lemon juice and a touch of salt. Add bell pepper and onion; simmer until tender. Add mushrooms; simmer 3 minutes, adding butter as needed. Remove from heat.

Melt 1 stick butter in double boiler over low heat; add flour, stirring until smooth. Pour in half-and-half and milk, stirring occasionally until sauce thickens. Add salt, wine, nutmeg, cayenne, pimiento, whipping cream, and 3 tablespoons butter. Pour vegetable-mushroom mixture into sauce; add scallops and gently fold in crabmeat. Heat and serve in patty shells or on toasted bread. Serves 6–8 as an entrée.

Note: If bay scallops are not available, substitute sea scallops, cut in half. May be served from a chafing dish as an appetizer.

Accent One (Mississippi)

Best Maryland Crab Cakes

Best tasting crab cakes ever!

**4 slices white bread with crusts
    trimmed, or ¹/₂ cup dry bread
    crumbs, or 6 saltines, crumbled**
¹/₂ teaspoon dry mustard
**¹/₂ teaspoon Chesapeake-style
    seafood seasoning**
¹/₄ teaspoon Acćent (optional)

1 egg, beaten
¹/₂ cup mayonnaise
¹/₂ teaspoon lemon juice
¹/₂ teaspoon Worcestershire sauce
**1 pound crabmeat, shell and
    cartilage removed**

Mix bread crumbs, mustard, seafood seasoning, and Acćent together and set aside.

In another bowl, gently fold together egg, mayonnaise, lemon juice, Worcestershire sauce, and bread crumb mixture. Add crabmeat, and shape into individual cakes. Refrigerate for at least 2 hours to avoid breaking apart when cooked.

Place under broiler and broil until brown, or fry in oil until brown and drain on paper towels before serving. Serves 4–6.

Of Tide & Thyme (Mid-Atlantic/Maryland)

Succulent Shrimp Cakes

**1 pound small raw prawns (shrimp),
    peeled, deveined, and cut into
    2 or 3 pieces**
**1 large stalk celery, chopped in
    small pieces**
**¹/₂ onion, chopped in small pieces
    (can use green onions)**
**¹/₄ cup chopped green pepper
    (optional)**

¹/₂ teaspoon salt
¹/₄ teaspoon pepper
**¹/₂ teaspoon Lawry's Seasoned
    Salt**
1 tablespoon lemon juice
1 teaspoon Worcestershire sauce
2 tablespoons cocktail sauce
3 eggs, slightly beaten
³/₄ cup cracker meal/crumbs

Mix all ingredients in a mixing bowl. Heat skillet over medium heat and spray or coat bottom of pan with olive oil. Drop spoonfuls of mixture into skillet and shape into 4-inch patties. Cook approximately 5 minutes on each side or until brown and center is done. Serve with Shrimp Dipping Sauce (or with hot Knorr's Newberg Sauce). Serves 4 people.

SHRIMP DIPPING SAUCE:

¹/₂ cup mayonnaise or salad dressing
¹/₄ cup ketchup

1 teaspoon lemon juice
1 teaspoon Worcestershire sauce

Combine ingredients. Serve cold or room temperature with seafood.

A Taste of Tillamook (Oregon)

★★★★★★★★★★★★ ★★★★★★★★★★★★

Fisherman's Wharf Garlic Prawns

4 garlic cloves, crushed
1 teaspoon salt
2 teaspoons black peppercorns,
  crushed coarsely
2 teaspoons lemon juice
1 tablespoon brandy

1 pound (16–20) shrimp (prawns),
  peeled, deveined, butterflied
3 tablespoons olive oil
½ cup heavy whipping cream
Freshly chopped parsley

Combine crushed garlic with salt; add crushed peppercorns, lemon juice, and brandy. Mix well. Place prawns in saucepan or in heavy-duty, cast-iron skillet. Add garlic mixture and olive oil. Cover and cook quickly until prawns change color. Stir in cream. Serve hot and sizzling in small bowls garnished with chopped parsley. Serves 2.

Little Dave's Seafood Cookbook (California)

Shrimp Scampi Sensation

The sauce is excellent over chicken breasts and all fish.

4 pounds jumbo shrimp, shelled
4 ounces butter, melted

1 cup fresh bread crumbs

Split shrimp down the middle, and arrange on a baking tray. Brush with butter, and sprinkle with bread crumbs. Broil 5 minutes. Arrange on a platter and pour the Sauce over.

SAUCE:
4 scallions
1 clove garlic
1 tablespoon Worcestershire sauce
1 cup lemon juice

Salt
¾ cup cream sherry
¾ pound butter (12 ounces)
¾ cup Dijon mustard

Chop the scallions finely, and press garlic. Add Worcestershire sauce, lemon juice, salt, and sherry. Mix the butter with the mustard until soft and smooth. Add to the rest of the sauce. Boil for 5 minutes, stirring constantly. Serves 8.

Ship to Shore II (North Carolina)

Tequila-Lime Shrimp

$1/2$ stick margarine
2 tablespoons olive oil
2 garlic cloves, minced
$1^1/2$ pounds medium shrimp,
  shelled, deveined
3 tablespoons tequila
$1^1/2$ tablespoons lime juice

$1/2$ teaspoon salt
$1/2$ teaspoon chili powder
4 tablespoons coarsely chopped
  fresh cilantro
Hot cooked rice
Lime wedges for garnish

Pat shrimp dry with paper towels. Heat margarine and oil in a large skillet over medium heat. Add garlic and shrimp; cook about 2 minutes, stirring occasionally. Stir in tequila, lime juice, salt, and chili powder. Cook 2 minutes more or until most of liquid is evaporated and shrimp are pink and glazed. Add cilantro. Serve over hot cooked rice, garnished with lime wedges.

Southwest Ole! (Texas II)

Capt'n 'Fuskie's Lowcountry Boil

Plenty of paper towels will be needed, as this boil is drippin'-lickin'-good!

6 pounds smoked sausage, cut in
  pieces
20 ears of corn, broken in half
1 pound butter
4 large onions, cut in chunks
4 bell peppers, cut in quarters

6 pods garlic
3 pounds Irish potatoes, scrubbed
  and left in their jackets
Salt and pepper to taste
6 pounds shrimp, headed and
  washed

In huge pot of water, cook sausage for about 20 minutes. Add remaining ingredients except headed shrimp. Cook until potatoes are almost done. Add shrimp and cook until just tender.

Drain off water. Cover table(s) with newspaper. Take pot of boil and throw it out on the table(s) as though you were throwing out a bucket of water. Let everyone help himself, using paper plates. Have plenty of iced tea on hand, and if you like, some slices of Vienna or French bread smeared with garlic butter.

Stirrin' the Pots on Daufuskie (South Carolina)

★★★★★★★★★★★★   ★★★★★★★★★★★★

Sweet and Sour Shrimp

These deep-fried shrimp, when combined with green pepper, pineapple, and tomato, provide an eye as well as a taste pleaser. The Sweet and Sour Sauce is especially good.

SWEET AND SOUR SAUCE:

$\frac{1}{2}$ cup sugar
1 tablespoon cornstarch
2 teaspoons salt
$\frac{1}{2}$ cup red wine vinegar

$\frac{1}{4}$ cup orange juice
$\frac{1}{4}$ cup pineapple juice
3 ounces tomato paste

Blend sugar, cornstarch, and salt. Stir in vinegar, fruit juices, and tomato paste. Cook, stirring constantly, until thickened. Set aside.

$1\frac{1}{2}$ pounds shrimp, cleaned and
  deveined
1 tablespoon soy sauce
$\frac{1}{2}$ teaspoon salt
$\frac{1}{2}$ cup cornstarch
Peanut oil

2 onions, cut in wedges
2 green peppers, cut in chunks
$1\frac{1}{2}$ cups Sweet and Sour Sauce
1 (11-ounce) can pineapple chunks
  (save juice for sauce)
2 tomatoes, cut in wedges

Combine shrimp, soy sauce, and salt. Coat shrimp with cornstarch. Deep-fry shrimp about 3 minutes. Drain on paper towels.

In wok or large fry pan, heat 1 tablespoon oil. Add onions and peppers. Cook 1 minute. Add Sweet and Sour Sauce and drained pineapple. Add shrimp and tomato wedges. Cook until heated. Place on serving dish.

Gourmet Cooking (Florida)

★★★★★★★★★★★★ ★★★★★★★★★★★★

Bob's Barbecued Shrimp

5 pounds medium to large shrimp,
  headless
$1/2$ pound butter
$1/2$ pound margarine
$1/2$ teaspoon rosemary
3 ounces Worcestershire sauce

$2^1/2$ tablespoons black pepper
2 tablespoons salt
2 lemons, sliced thin
3 cloves garlic, minced
$1/2$ tablespoon Tabasco
1 ounce soy sauce

Wash shrimp and place in a large baking dish. Combine remaining ingredients; bring to a boil. Pour over shrimp. Bake at 400° for 20 minutes. Serve hot with plenty of garlic bread.

Hallmark's Collection of Home Tested Recipes (Alabama)

Shrimp Florentine

$1/4$ cup finely chopped onion
$1/4$ cup butter
$1/4$ cup flour
1 teaspoon salt
$1/2$ teaspoon dry mustard
2 cups milk
$1/2$ cup grated Swiss cheese
1 cup grated Parmesan cheese,
  divided

2 (10-ounce) packages frozen
  chopped spinach, cooked and
  drained
1 (8-ounce) can water chestnuts,
  drained and sliced
1 tablespoon lemon juice
$1^1/2$ pounds shrimp, boiled and
  peeled
Paprika

Preheat oven to 400°. Cook onion in butter until tender. Stir in flour, salt, and dry mustard. Add milk. Cook, stirring constantly, until thickened. Remove from heat. Add Swiss cheese and stir until melted. Fold in $1/2$ the Parmesan cheese.

Combine spinach and water chestnuts and spread in a greased, shallow $1^1/2$- to 2-quart baking dish. Drizzle lemon juice over spinach. Add shrimp, then sauce; top with remaining Parmesan cheese. Garnish with paprika. Bake for 15–20 minutes or until hot. Yields 6 servings.

Some Like It South! (Florida)

★★★★★★★★★★★★   ★★★★★★★★★★★★

Shrimp Etouffée

ROUX:
6 tablespoons oil   6 tablespoons flour

Stir oil and flour over medium heat in heavy skillet for 20 minutes, making Roux a medium brown.

2 cups chopped onions   1 teaspoon basil
1 cup chopped bell pepper   1 teaspoon chili powder
1 cup chopped celery   1/2 teaspoon cayenne
5 garlic cloves, crushed   1/4 teaspoon black pepper
1 small can stewed tomatoes   1 teaspoon seasoning salt
2 (10 1/2-ounce) cans chicken broth 3–4 pounds peeled shrimp
2 cups water   1 cup chopped green onions
2 bay leaves   2 tablespoons chopped parsley

Add to Roux the onions, bell pepper, celery, and garlic. Add canned tomatoes, mixing well. Add chicken broth and water. While simmering, add spices. Let simmer 1 hour. Now add shrimp, green onions, and parsley. Cook 20 minutes on very low heat until shrimp is done. Serve over rice.

Nibbles Cooks Cajun (Arkansas)

Shrimp Creole

4 tablespoons butter   1/2 cup hot water
1 tablespoon oil   Juice of 1 lemon
1 cup chopped onions   1/2 teaspoon sugar
1 cup chopped celery   4 bay leaves
1 cup chopped bell pepper   Salt and cayenne pepper to taste
6 cloves garlic, chopped   3 pounds peeled and deveined
6 tablespoons flour   medium shrimp
1 (16-ounce) can tomato sauce   1/2 cup chopped green onions

In a heavy pot, melt butter. Add oil. Sauté next 4 ingredients until done (approximately 5 minutes). Add flour and blend well. Add tomato sauce, hot water, juice, and sugar. Add bay leaf, salt, and cayenne. Cook over medium heat approximately 30 minutes. Season to taste. Add shrimp; cook 30 minutes longer. Add green onions last. Serve over rice.

The Encyclopedia of Cajun and Creole Cuisine (Louisiana)

★★★★★★★★★★★★ ★★★★★★★★★★★★

Cajun Peppered Shrimp and Grits

A delightful combination of flavors straight from the South! Try serving this impressive dish for brunch.

GRITS:

6 cups water
2 teaspoons salt
1½ cups quick grits
2 tablespoons butter

1 roll garlic cheese
1 cup grated Cheddar cheese
1 teaspoon Worcestershire

Preheat oven to 350°. Grease a large saucepan with cooking spray; add water, and bring to a boil over high heat. Stir in salt and grits. Lower heat and cook, stirring occasionally, until water is absorbed and grits thicken. Add butter, cheeses, and Worcestershire. Cook until cheese melts. Pour in a greased casserole dish and bake for about 20 minutes to set.

SHRIMP:

½ cup butter or margarine
¼ cup olive oil
3 pounds medium shrimp, peeled
1 clove garlic, minced
1 cup chopped green onions
1 cup sliced mushrooms
½ cup chopped parsley

½ teaspoon salt
1 teaspoon pepper
¼ teaspoon cayenne pepper
½ teaspoon paprika
¼ teaspoon each: basil, thyme, and
  oregano
1 tablespoon lemon juice

In a large saucepan, melt butter and oil over medium heat. Add shrimp and sauté just until pink. Stir in all ingredients and seasonings. Simmer about 10 minutes. Mixture will be very saucy.

Serve a scoop of grits surrounded with shrimp and sauce. Serve with hot French bread for dipping. Serves 8.

Kay Ewing's Cooking School Cookbook (Louisiana II)

 The Highway 127 Corridor Sale claims to be the world's longest outdoor sale with more than 2,000 vendors. The sale, held in August, stretches for 450 miles on Highway 127 from North Covington, Kentucky, extending through Jamestown, Tennessee, and continuing all the way to Gadsden, Alabama.

Shrimp and Scallops Gruyére

Delicious—worth the time spent in preparation. Sauce may be made ahead and shrimp and scallops added on the serving day.

³⁄₄ cup plus 2 tablespoons butter, divided
³⁄₄ cup flour
3 cups milk
12 ounces Gruyére cheese
¹⁄₄ teaspoon garlic powder
3 teaspoons salt, divided
Pepper to taste

¹⁄₄ teaspoon dry mustard
2 teaspoons tomato paste
3 teaspoons lemon juice, divided
1 pound raw scallops
1 pound shrimp, cooked and cleaned
¹⁄₂ pound mushrooms, sliced
3 tablespoons diced green pepper

Make a cream sauce in the top of a double boiler with ³⁄₄ cup butter, flour, and milk. Cut the cheese into small pieces and add to the sauce. Stir until cheese melts. Add garlic powder, 2¹⁄₂ teaspoons salt, pepper, mustard, tomato paste, and 2 teaspoons of the lemon juice.

Poach scallops for 10 minutes in water to which the remaining 1 teaspoon lemon juice and ¹⁄₂ teaspoon salt have been added. If cream sauce is too thick, add a little scallop broth. Drain scallops and add scallops and shrimp to the sauce. Sauté mushrooms in remaining 2 tablespoons butter. Add to the sauce. Heat for 15 minutes. Sauté green pepper in a little butter and add to sauce. Put all in chafing dish. Serve with rice or in patty shells. Serves 8–10.

Winterthur's Culinary Collection (Mid-Atlantic/Delaware)

Blend of the Bayou Seafood Casserole

1 (8-ounce) package cream cheese
1 stick margarine or butter
1 pound shrimp, peeled
1 large onion, chopped
1 bell pepper, chopped
2 ribs celery, chopped
2 tablespoons butter
1 can mushroom soup

1 can mushrooms, drained
1 tablespoon garlic salt
1 teaspoon Tabasco
¹⁄₂ teaspoon red pepper
1 pint crabmeat
³⁄₄ cup cooked rice
Sharp cheese, grated
Cracker crumbs

Melt cream cheese and 1 stick butter using double boiler. Sauté shrimp, onion, pepper, and celery in 2 tablespoons butter. Add to the first mixture. Add soup, mushrooms, seasonings, crabmeat, and rice. Mix well, place in 2-quart casserole, and top with cheese and cracker crumbs. Bake at 350° for 20–30 minutes, until bubbly. Freezes. Serves 8.

Pirate's Pantry (Louisiana)

Merrymount Lobster

Can be prepared ahead of time. Excellent for large buffets.

3 cups cut-up lobster, crab, shrimp,
  or sea legs
1 tablespoon lemon juice
2 eggs, slightly beaten
2 cups light cream
2 tablespoons butter
1 cup soft bread crumbs
1 heaping teaspoon prepared
  mustard

Dash of cayenne pepper
1/4 teaspoon freshly ground black
  pepper
Salt to taste
1 cup cracker crumbs (preferably
  buttered)

Lobster may be frozen, canned, or fresh. Sprinkle lemon juice and beaten eggs over lobster in buttered casserole dish. Bring cream, butter, and bread crumbs just to a boil; stir together well and pour over lobster. Stir mustard, cayenne pepper, black pepper, and salt carefully into lobster mixture. Top with cracker crumbs. Bake, uncovered, in a preheated oven at 350° until crumbs are brown and lobster is bubbly—no more. Serves 8.

Sandy Hook Volunteer Fire Company Ladies Auxiliary Cookbook
(New England)

Oysters Parmesan

1/2 pint oysters, drained
1 tablespoon chopped onion
1 cup milk, divided
1 1/2 tablespoons butter
2 tablespoons flour
1/4 teaspoon salt

Dash pepper
1/4 teaspoon celery salt
1/4 cup Parmesan cheese
1 teaspoon chopped parsley
3 English muffins, split, or toast
  points, or patty shells

Combine oysters, onion, and 1/2 cup milk and cook over medium heat 15 minutes. (Do NOT overcook oysters.) Melt butter and blend in flour and seasonings and remaining milk; cook until thick, stirring constantly. Add Parmesan and parsley and stir well. Add oyster mixture and cook 5 minutes. Serve over lightly toasted and buttered muffins, toast points, or patty shells. You may also serve oysters in a chafing dish for added elegance.

A Taste of History (North Carolina)

Meats

★★★★ ★★★★

"Up a lazy river by the old mill stream" are old song lyrics that might have been inspired by this lovely setting on the Brandywine River. It is behind the Brandywine Museum that was a 19th-century grist mill, and now displays artworks of the Wyeth family who live in this Chadds Ford area of Pennsylvania.

Shrimp and Beef Filet Brochettes with Sesame Marinade

This is a delicious combination. The beef and shrimp marinate for only 5 minutes, long enough to give them a hint of Asian flavor, but not so long that the shrimp become tough. Perfect!

1 cup peanut oil
½ cup soy sauce
3 tablespoons honey
3 tablespoons cider vinegar
2 tablespoons sesame seeds, toasted
2 cloves garlic, minced

1 teaspoon minced fresh ginger
3 pounds beef filet, cut into 1-inch cubes
45 medium shrimp, shelled and, if desired, deveined
16 bamboo skewers

In a bowl, whisk together the oil, soy sauce, honey, vinegar, sesame seeds, garlic, and ginger. Set aside. On each skewer, alternate 4 pieces of beef with 2 or 3 shrimp. Place in a roasting pan in 1 layer. Pour marinade over and let sit for 5 minutes. Grill over medium-hot coals for 4 minutes on each side or until the shrimp turn pink. Makes 6–8 servings.

The Long Island Holiday Cookbook (New York)

Swiss Bliss Round Steak

Easy, make ahead, tender . . . delicious!

2 pounds round steak, cut in serving-size portions	**1 (1-pound) can tomatoes, chopped, drained (save juice)**
1 envelope onion soup mix	**¹⁄₂ cup juice from tomatoes**
1 small can mushrooms, drained	**1 tablespoon A-1 Steak Sauce**
¹⁄₂ green pepper, sliced	**1 tablespoon cornstarch**

Use a 20-inch piece of aluminum foil. Butter middle. Arrange raw meat, overlapping, down the middle. Sprinkle with onion soup mix, mushrooms, green pepper, and tomatoes. Mix juice, A-1 Sauce, and cornstarch. Pour over meat and seal foil. Bake at 350° for 2 hours.

We Love Country Cookin' (Great Plains/North Dakota)

★ **Editor's Extra:** Try making individual packets (4–6), dividing all ingredients on foil squares. Everybody likes to open their own steamy packet. Fun to add carrot and potato chunks, too.

Italian Spiedini

This is a delicious one-dish meal certain to become a family favorite. It is also great for parties and company dinners. It freezes well, also.

2 pounds round steak	**Salt and pepper**
Oil	**8–10 potatoes, thinly sliced**
Italian bread crumbs (or add oregano and grated cheese to regular bread crumbs)	**1 large green pepper, cut in strips**
	1 large onion, thinly sliced
	Butter or margarine

Pound steak until tender. Brush with oil and cover both sides with bread crumbs which have been mixed with salt and pepper. Cut into 4-inch squares; roll and insert toothpicks.

In large baking pan, apply oil to bottom; then in layers, insert potatoes, green pepper, onion, and dots of butter or margarine. (Season to taste.) Continue doing this, layer upon layer, until at last you top it off with round steak rolls. Cover with tin foil and bake at 350° for 1¹⁄₂ hours. Uncover and brown for 10 minutes.

Simply Sensational (Michigan)

Nana's Swiss Steak

This was the Swiss steak contest winner!

6 tablespoons flour
2 teaspoons salt
$1/4$ teaspoon pepper
2 pounds round steak, cut 1 inch
  thick
4 medium onions

6 tablespoons shortening, divided
$1/2$ cup chopped celery (about 2 ribs)
1 clove garlic, minced
$3/4$ cup chili sauce
$3/4$ cup water
1 green pepper (optional)

Combine flour, salt, and pepper; rub into both sides of steak, or pound in with meat mallet. Cut into 8 portions. Peel and slice onions. Preheat skillet and add half of shortening, then onions; brown lightly. Remove from skillet. Add remaining shortening. Brown steak on both sides. Reduce heat. Add celery, garlic, chili sauce, and water; cover and simmer 1 hour. Cut green pepper into slices. Add pepper and onions to meat and cover with foil and bake at 350° for 2–2$1/2$ hours. Makes 8 servings.

Return Engagement (Iowa)

Skillet Supper

Not fancy, but fine.

1$1/2$ pounds lean ground meat
1 large onion, chopped
1 teaspoon seasoned salt
$1/2$ teaspoon salt

$1/2$ teaspoon pepper
1 can tomatoes and green chiles
$1/2$ cabbage, chopped
Soy sauce (optional)

Brown ground meat and chopped onion in a large skillet. Season with seasoned salt, salt, and pepper. Add tomatoes; stir and cover with cabbage. Cover with a tight fitting lid and cook on medium heat until cabbage is tender. May season with soy sauce. Serve this with a salad and don't forget the cornbread.

More Calf Fries to Caviar (Texas II)

★ **Editor's Extra:** Tastes like hard-to-make cabbage rolls, but much quicker. Delicious!

Black-Iron Skillet One Dish Meal

The title says it all!

1 pound hamburger (or ¹/₂ pound
   ground beef and ¹/₂ pound ground
   turkey)
1¹/₂ pounds zucchini squash, thinly
   sliced
1 medium onion, sliced

1 green pepper, chopped
1 (1-pound) can stewed tomatoes
Seasoned bread crumbs
¹/₈–¹/₄ pound (2–4 ounces) grated
   cheese

In skillet that can go in the oven, brown meat. Top with 4 layers of vegetables and cover. Simmer 10 minutes. Uncover and top with bread crumbs, then cheese. Put skillet in oven and bake at 350° for 25 minutes.

225 Years in Pennington & Still Cooking (Mid-Atlantic/New Jersey)

Taste of the Rockies Casserole

1 pound ground beef
1 tablespoon oil
1 tablespoon chili powder
2 cloves garlic, minced
Salt and pepper to taste
1 large onion, chopped
1 green bell pepper, chopped
1 can tomatoes with green chiles

1 (14¹/₂-ounce) can whole tomatoes
1 (15¹/₂-ounce) can kidney or pinto
   beans
³/₄ cup raw rice
1 (14¹/₂-ounce) can beef bouillon
¹/₄ cup sliced ripe olives
1 cup grated Cheddar cheese

Brown meat in oil. Add chili powder, garlic, salt, pepper, onion, and bell pepper. Cook 3 minutes. Add tomatoes with juice, breaking up; then add beans and rice. Turn into greased 2-quart baking dish; pour beef broth over meat and rice mixture and bake, covered, at 350° for 45 minutes. Sprinkle olives and cheese on top, and bake, uncovered, until cheese is melted. Serves 6–8.

Colorado Foods and More... (Colorado)

Hamburger-Spinach Casserole

1 (10-ounce) package frozen
  chopped spinach
1 (8-ounce) package cream cheese,
  softened
¹/₂ cup sour cream
3 tablespoons milk
3 tablespoons finely chopped onion

4 ounces wide noodles
1 pound ground beef
1 (15-ounce) can tomato sauce
2 teaspoons sugar
Salt, pepper and garlic powder, to
  taste
Cheddar cheese, shredded

Cook spinach according to directions; drain well, then set aside. Mix cream cheese, sour cream, milk, and onion in a separate bowl and let sit to continue softening. Cook noodles in boiling salted water for 10 minutes. Drain well; set aside. Brown ground beef and drain well. Add tomato sauce, sugar, salt, pepper, garlic powder, and noodles. Heat thoroughly.

In a 2-quart casserole, place a layer of hamburger-noodle mixture (use ¹/₂). Top with ¹/₂ of cream cheese mixture. Top with spinach and finish with remainder of hamburger-noodle mixture. Bake in covered casserole at 350° for 40 minutes.

Remove from oven and top with remaining cream cheese mixture. Cover completely with shredded Cheddar cheese. Return to oven uncovered for approximately 10 minutes or until cheese melts completely. Serves 4.

Seminole Savorings (Florida)

Sour Cream Meat Loaf

When all is said and done, what most home cooks are looking for is a good meat loaf. This is my favorite.

2 pounds ground chuck
2 slices good bread, crumbled
2 eggs
¹/₂ cup sour cream
¹/₂ cup chili sauce
1 medium onion, chopped

4 tablespoons butter
1 teaspoon salt
Freshly ground pepper
4 slices bacon
2 Idaho baking potatoes, cut in
    thick, lengthwise slices

Combine meat with bread crumbs, eggs, sour cream, and chili sauce. Sauté onion in butter until just wilted and add to mixture. Mix in salt and pepper and form into a round or loaf shape. Place in a greased baking dish and cover top with bacon slices. Surround with potato slices. Bake in a 350° oven 1 hour or until juices run clear. Baste potato slices from time to time with pan juices. Serves 4–6.

The New Gourmets & Groundhogs (Pennsylvania)

Glazed Meatloaf

2 eggs, beaten
²/₃ cup milk
2 teaspoons salt
¹/₄ teaspoon pepper
3 slices bread, cut into small pieces
²/₃ cup shredded carrots

²/₃ cup chopped onion
1¹/₂ cups shredded Cheddar cheese
2 pounds hamburger
¹/₄ cup brown sugar
¹/₄ cup catsup
1 tablespoon mustard

Stir together eggs, milk, salt, pepper, and bread. Add carrots, onion, cheese, and hamburger. Mix well. Form into a loaf. Bake at 350° for 1 hour and 15 minutes. Combine brown sugar, catsup, and mustard. Spread over meatloaf and bake 15 minutes longer. About 10 servings.

Amish Country Cookbook III (Indiana)

The world's largest catsup bottle, which also doubles as a water tower, stands just south of downtown Collinsville, Illinois. The 170-foot-tall water tower was built in 1949 for the G.S. Suppiger Company's catsup bottling plant. The diameter of the bottle is 25 feet and the diameter of the cap is 8 feet.

★★★★★★★★★★★ ★★★★★★★★★★★

Strombolis

Italian Sloppy Joes. Great to make and take.

GARLIC SPREAD:

2 tablespoons butter, softened
¼ teaspoon garlic powder

¼ teaspoon paprika

Combine butter, garlic powder, and paprika; mix well.

1 pound ground beef
1 tablespoon chopped onion (or
  more to taste)
½ cup ketchup
3 tablespoons grated Parmesan
  cheese
⅓ teaspoon garlic powder

¼ teaspoon fennel seed, crushed (a
  must ingredient)
¼ teaspoon dried oregano
6–8 hamburger buns
Garlic Spread
6–8 slices mozzarella cheese

Brown meat; drain fat. Add onion, ketchup, Parmesan cheese, garlic powder, fennel seed, and oregano. Simmer for 20 minutes.

Split hamburger buns. Spread about 1 teaspoon Garlic Spread on each bun top. Divide meat mixture evenly on bun bottoms. Top meat mixture with a cheese slice. Top with bun top. Wrap each sandwich in a square of foil. Bake in 350° oven for 15 minutes, or until heated through. Yields 6–8 sandwiches.

Note: These can be frozen for up to 1 month. Partly thaw, then bake.

Herrin's Favorite Italian Recipes Cookbook (Illinois)

Popover Pizza

A bit of a twist on the old favorite.

1 pound ground beef
1 (15-ounce) can tomato sauce
$^{1}/_{2}$ cup chopped green pepper
1 cup plus 2 tablespoons Bisquick,
　divided
1 tablespoon parsley

$^{1}/_{2}$ teaspoon pepper
2 cups shredded Cheddar cheese
$^{3}/_{4}$ cup water
$^{1}/_{4}$ cup butter or margarine
4 eggs
$^{1}/_{4}$ cup chopped green onions

Brown ground beef in a 10-inch skillet. Stir in tomato sauce, green pepper, 2 tablespoons Bisquick, parsley, and pepper. Heat to boiling. Boil and stir 1 minute. Pour into ungreased 9x13-inch baking pan. Sprinkle with cheese. Heat water and margarine to boiling in a 3-quart saucepan. Add 1 cup Bisquick all at once. Stir vigorously over low heat until mixture forms a ball, about $1^{1}/_{2}$ minutes. Remove from heat. Beat in eggs, one at a time; continue beating until smooth. Spread over beef mixture. Sprinkle with onions. Bake in 400° oven for about 25–30 minutes, until puffy and golden brown. Serve immediately. Serves 6.

What's Cookin' (Mid-Atlantic/Maryland)

Biscuit Pie

$1^{1}/_{2}$ cans Hungry Jack Biscuits
Parmesan cheese, grated
1 pound mozzarella cheese, sliced,
　divided
$1^{1}/_{2}$ pounds ground beef
1 medium onion, chopped
1 medium bell pepper, chopped

1 rib celery, chopped
3 garlic buds, minced
1 package spaghetti sauce mix
1 small can tomato paste
Salt and pepper to taste
$1^{1}/_{2}$–2 cans water

Use a 9x13-inch pan. Press biscuits in the bottom of pan to form a crust. Sprinkle with Parmesan cheese. Place $^{1}/_{2}$ of mozzarella cheese on top of Parmesan cheese. Brown ground beef, onion, pepper, celery, and garlic; drain fat. Add spaghetti sauce mix, tomato paste, seasonings, and water; cook until meat is cooked. Spoon meat mixture on top of cheese in pan. Top with remaining mozzarella cheese slices. Bake at 400° for 15 minutes.

Sisters' Secrets (Louisiana II)

★★★★★★★★★★★ ★★★★★★★★★★★

Impossible Cheeseburger Pie

1 pound ground beef	1½ cups milk
1½ cups chopped onion	¾ cup Bisquick
½ teaspoon salt	2 tomatoes, sliced
¼ teaspoon pepper	1 cup shredded Cheddar or
3 eggs	processed American cheese

Heat oven to 400°. Grease a 10-inch pie plate. In skillet, cook and stir ground beef and onion over medium heat until brown; drain. Add salt and pepper. Spread in plate. Beat eggs, milk, and baking mix until smooth. Pour into plate. Bake 25 minutes. Top with tomatoes; sprinkle with cheese. Bake until knife inserted in center comes out clean, 5–8 minutes. Cool 5 minutes. Serves 6–8.

Cooking with the Menno-Haven Auxiliary (Pennsylvania)

Sour Cream Enchiladas

2 pounds ground beef	4 drops hot sauce
1 onion, diced	½ cup chopped ripe olives
1 green pepper, diced	½ cup margarine, melted
1 teaspoon salt	¼ cup all-purpose flour
Pepper	1½ cups milk
2 tablespoons picante sauce	2 cups sour cream
1 tablespoon chili powder	18 corn tortillas
½ teaspoon cumin	2 cups grated Longhorn cheese
1 tablespoon garlic powder	

Brown beef in skillet; drain. Add onion and green pepper; cook until vegetables are soft. Add salt, pepper, picante sauce, seasonings, and olives; simmer 5 minutes and set aside.

Combine butter and flour in a saucepan; slowly add milk, stirring constantly. Cook and stir until thickened. Blend in sour cream; heat 1 minute. (Do not boil.)

Fill each tortilla with meat mixture; roll. Place in a greased 9x13x2-inch casserole. Cover with sour cream sauce; sprinkle with cheese. Bake at 375° for 25 minutes or until bubbly. Yields 18 servings.

Flavor Favorites (Texas)

Mexican Casserole

¼ cup chopped onion
½ pound ground beef
2 tablespoons vegetable oil
½ pound kidney beans, drained
1 can mild enchilada sauce

1 (8-ounce) can tomato sauce
1½ cups sour cream or plain
   yogurt
2 cups grated Cheddar cheese
10 ounces tortilla chips

Brown onion and beef in oil, then drain. Add beans and sauces. Place in a 2-quart casserole dish. Bake in 375° oven, uncovered, ½ hour. Cover top with sour cream, sprinkle with cheese and place chips around edge. Return casserole to the oven until cheese melts. Serves 4.

In Good Taste (North Carolina)

★ **Editor's Extra:** A meal in a dish, this can also be a heavy hors d'oeuvre.

Taco Smacho

You can add green onions to diversify the performance of this dish, which plays like a symphony to the taste buds.

1½ pounds ground beef
1 (3-ounce) package cream cheese,
  cubed and softened
2 teaspoons salt
2 teaspoons chili powder
18 jumbo pasta shells, cooked,
  rinsed, and drained

2 tablespoons butter, melted
1 cup taco sauce
2 cups shredded Cheddar cheese
1½ cups crushed tortilla chips
1 cup sour cream
3 green onions, chopped (optional)

Heat oven to 350°. In large skillet, brown ground beef; drain fat. Add cream cheese, salt, and chili powder; simmer for 10 minutes. Toss shells with butter; fill with meat mixture (use hands to fill pasta shells). Arrange shells in buttered 9x13-inch baking pan. Pour taco sauce over each shell. Cover with foil; bake for 15 minutes. Uncover; top with Cheddar cheese and tortilla chips. Bake for 15 minutes more or until bubbly. Garnish with sour cream and onions. Makes 6–8 servings.

Serving Up Oregon (Oregon)

Taco Bake

The crust makes the difference.

MEAT FILLING:

1 pound lean ground beef
½ cup chopped onions

1 package taco seasoning mix
¾ cup water

TACO CRUST:

1¾–2 cups all-purpose flour,
  divided
1 package rapid-rise yeast
1 tablespoon sugar
½ teaspoon dried minced onion

¾ teaspoon salt
⅔ cup warm water
2 tablespoons oil
½ cup crushed corn chips

TOPPING:

1 cup shredded Cheddar cheese
1 cup shredded lettuce

1½ cups chopped tomatoes
Taco sauce to taste

Brown ground beef with onions. Add taco seasoning mix and ¾ cup water; simmer for 25 minutes. In a medium bowl, combine 1 cup flour, yeast, sugar, onion, and salt. Add very warm water (120–130°) and oil to flour mixture. Mix by hand until almost smooth. Stir in crushed corn chips and enough remaining flour to make a stiff dough. Spread in 6 well-greased (4-inch) or 2 (8-inch) pie pans, forming rim around edge. Cover and let rise in a warm place, about 10–15 minutes.

Spread meat mixture over dough in pie pans and bake at 375° for 20–25 minutes, until edges are crisp and golden brown. Sprinkle cheese, lettuce, and tomatoes on top; add taco sauce to taste.

Fortsville UMC Cookbook (New York)

East of Raleigh, North Carolina, Vollis Simpson has covered a field with a series of huge, moving metal sculptures called whirligigs (wind-powered, windmill-type folk art). He started building his enormous whirligigs (some over 40 feet tall) in 1985.

One Step Tamale Pie

1 pound ground beef
1 cup chopped onion
2 cloves garlic, minced
1 (12-ounce) can whole-kernel corn,
  drained
2 (8-ounce) cans tomato sauce
1 cup milk

2 eggs, beaten
Few dashes of Tabasco sauce
$^3/_4$ cup yellow cornmeal
$1^1/_2$–2 teaspoons chili powder
2 teaspoons salt
1 cup grated Cheddar cheese

In large skillet, brown meat, onion, and garlic. Stir in remaining ingredients except cheese. Pour into a greased 12 x 7$^1/_2$ x 2-inch pan. Bake at 350° for 30 minutes. Add cheese over top. Bake an additional 15 minutes.

Recipes to Remember (Washington)

Frito Pie

1 pound ground beef
1 package taco seasoning
2 cans chili (hot or mild)
$^1/_4$ cup water
1 (10-ounce) package Fritos
  (dip size)

1 medium onion, chopped
3 cups grated cheese (Mexican
  three cheeses or Cheddar)

Preheat oven to 400°. Prepare meat according to directions on taco mix packet. Do not cook the meat too dry. Heat chili in saucepan. (Moisture is the key to this dish and a $^1/_4$ cup water in the chili will add enough moisture.) Spray a large casserole dish or stoneware dish with nonstick cooking spray, and layer ingredients in the following order: Layer fritos on bottom (lightly mashed to settle); layer prepared meat on top; sprinkle onion over meat; spoon chili over onion; cover chili with cheese. Repeat layering until all ingredients are added (usually 2 or 3 layers). The Fritos should be soaked, but firm and crisp at serving. Bake covered for 20 minutes. Serve with salad, avocados, and salsa.

Dishes from the Deep (Arizona)

Chimichangas

1 pound ground beef
1 (10-ounce) can tomatoes and green chiles
1 package taco seasoning mix
12 (8-inch) flour tortillas
3 cups shredded lettuce
3 cups grated Cheddar cheese
½ cup sliced green onions
1½ cups homemade or bottled red chile sauce

In a skillet, brown ground beef. Drain. Add tomatoes and green chiles and seasoning. Simmer 5 minutes. Spoon 3 tablespoons of meat near one edge of a tortilla. Fold nearest edge over meat; fold both ends in like an envelope. Roll tortilla and secure with toothpicks. Fry in 1-inch hot oil until golden on each side. Drain on paper towels and keep warm. To serve, top each Chimichanga with lettuce, cheese, onions, and chile sauce. Makes 12.

Note: Chimichangas can also be made with roast pork or cooked chicken.

License to Cook New Mexico Style (New Mexico)

Taco Ring

Great presentation!

½+ pound ground beef, cooked and drained
1 package taco seasoning mix
4 ounces Cheddar cheese, shredded
2 tablespoons water
2 (8-ounce) packages refrigerated crescent rolls
1 medium green pepper
1 cup salsa
½ head lettuce, shredded
1 medium tomato, cubed
1 small onion, chopped
½ cup whole black olives, sliced
Sour cream

Preheat oven to 375°. Mix together meat, taco seasoning, cheese and water. Arrange uncooked crescent roll triangles in a circle on a 13-inch baking sheet, overlapping in center, with point to the outside. (Leave at least a 5-inch hole in the center of the dough.) Arrange meat on dough and fold triangles over meat, tucking under at center. Bake 20–25 minutes until golden brown. Cut top off green pepper and remove seeds; fill with salsa. Arrange lettuce, tomato, onion, and olives in center of ring and nestle green pepper in center of lettuce. Garnish with sour cream.

Hospice Hospitality (Arizona)

★★★★★★★★★★★★ ★★★★★★★★★★★★

Chile Relleños Casserole

1 pound ground beef
1/2 cup chopped onion
1/2 teaspoon salt
1/2 teaspoon pepper
2 (4-ounce) cans green chiles, divided
2 1/2 cups shredded sharp Cheddar cheese, divided

1 1/2 cups milk
2 tablespoons flour
2/3 teaspoon salt
Pepper to taste
Hot sauce to taste
3 eggs, beaten

Cook beef, onion, salt, and pepper in a skillet until the meat begins to brown. Drain. Spread 1 can of the green chiles over bottom of a 9x13-inch baking dish. Sprinkle with 1/2 the cheese and top with all the meat mixture. Add remaining cheese and second can of chiles. Combine milk, flour, salt, pepper, hot sauce, and eggs. Pour over casserole and bake at 350° for 50 minutes or until knife inserted comes out clean. Cool 5 minutes. Cut in squares. May be frozen. Reheat at 400° while still frozen, until heated through. Serves 4–6.

The Texas Experience (Texas II)

Picadillo II

An all-time favorite.

2 medium onions
1 large green pepper (optional)
Olive oil
6 small tomatoes, chopped, or 2 small cans
2 teaspoons salt
1 teaspoon garlic powder
Pepper to taste
1 pound ground beef

1 pound ground pork
1 tablespoon brown sugar
1/4 cup vinegar
1/4 cup chopped, stuffed green olives
1/2 cup raisins
1 tablespoon capers
1/2 cup red wine or 1/2 cup tomato juice or bouillon

Chop onions and green pepper very fine, and brown in olive oil. Add chopped tomatoes, salt, garlic, pepper, and meat, stirring constantly to break in small bits. Add remaining ingredients slowly until meat is tender, about 1 hour.

Serve over rice, mashed potatoes, or split buttered and toasted hamburger buns. Serves 10.

The Gasparilla Cookbook (Florida)

Cajun Chow Mein

Especially good for church suppers, teen-age parties and potluck suppers.

1 pound ground pork
1 pound ground beef
2 tablespoons bacon drippings
1 green pepper, chopped
2 stalks celery, chopped
1 large onion, chopped
1 (4-ounce) can mushrooms

1 (20-ounce) can whole tomatoes
1 cup water
1 cup rice
Salt, pepper, garlic to taste
1 can bean sprouts
1 small can water chestnuts,
   chopped

Sauté meat in bacon drippings; add pepper, celery, onion, and mushrooms. Add tomatoes and water. Let come to boil and add rice. Add seasonings to taste. Turn to simmer and cook 25 minutes. Remove cover and add bean sprouts and water chestnuts. Let cook 10 more minutes with top on—until rice is no longer grainy. Serves 8.

Talk About Good! (Louisiana)

The Atchafalaya Basin, cutting a 15-mile-wide path across South Louisiana, is the largest active river delta on the continent. Remaining largely unpopulated by humans, the 860,000 acres of swamps, lakes and water prairies are home to a plethora of wildlife. The name is taken from the Choctaw hacha falaia, meaning "Long River."

Dry Rub

Use this spicy dry rub on chicken, ribs, or beef the night before grilling.

1 tablespoon ground black pepper	1 tablespoon garlic powder
1 tablespoon ground white pepper	1 tablespoon ground oregano
1 tablespoon sugar	4 tablespoons sweet paprika
1 tablespoon brown sugar	1 tablespoon celery salt
2 teaspoons ground cayenne chiles	1 tablespoon salt
2 tablespoons chili powder	1 teaspoon dry mustard
1 tablespoon cumin	

Thoroughly combine all ingredients. Rub mixture into the meat of your choice. Wrap coated meat tightly in plastic wrap and refrigerate overnight, or for at least 8 hours. Store remaining mixture in a jar in the refrigerator or freezer.

License to Cook Arizona Style (Arizona)

Bar-B-Que Brisket

A definite holiday favorite that leaves your mouth watering for more!

1½ teaspoons salt	2 teaspoons pepper
1 teaspoon garlic salt	2 teaspoons celery salt or seed
2 teaspoons Worcestershire sauce	1 (4–5 pound) brisket or chuck
1 teaspoon onion salt	roast

Mix all ingredients together and rub into both sides of brisket. Bake in a heavy, closed foil container on a baking sheet or pan. Bake at 225° for 8 hours or overnight. Pour off most of the liquid, saving about ¼ cup or less. Refrigerate to cool.

Slice thin (about ½-inch slices) and return to pan. Add 2 cups Brisket Sauce and bake at 325° for 45–60 minutes.

BRISKET SAUCE:

1 cup sugar	1 cup bottled Russian dressing
1 cup favorite barbecue sauce	

Mix together.

Sharing Our Best (California)

Crock Pot Ribs

They will melt in your mouth.

¾–1 cup vinegar
½ cup ketchup
2 tablespoons sugar
2 tablespoons Worcestershire sauce
1 garlic clove, minced
1 teaspoon dry mustard

1 teaspoon paprika
½–1 teaspoon salt
⅛ teaspoon pepper
2 pounds pork spareribs
1 tablespoon vegetable oil

Combine first 9 ingredients in a slow cooker. Cut ribs into serving-size pieces. Brown in skillet in oil. Add browned ribs to slow cooker and cook on LOW 4–6 hours, or until tender.

Country Chic's Home Cookin' (Mid-Atlantic/Maryland)

Blue Ribbon Barbecued Country Back Ribs

Detailed instructions to perfect ribs—even for those of us who say they don't grill.

2 slabs country back pork ribs
Teriyaki sauce (enough to cover ribs)
Morton Nature's Seasons
  Seasoning Blend, to taste

1 (12-ounce) can beer, room
  temperature
KC Masterpiece Barbecue Sauce
  (original)

Do not trim fat from ribs or parboil. Marinate overnight in the refrigerator in a mixture of teriyaki sauce and Morton's seasoning.

Prepare coals around sides of grill and let ash down, about 45 minutes. Stack slab of ribs, one on top of the other, in the center of the grill. Leave in this position for 10 minutes, with the lid closed, at 300°. Rotate the stack, putting top slab on bottom, and cook for 10 minutes more. Repeat the process on the other side of each slab of ribs. (This takes 40 minutes in all.) Allow heat to lower to 225° and continue rotating slabs, occasionally basting with beer to keep ribs moist on the outside. Turn every 20–30 minutes for about 2 hours. Baste with barbecue sauce for another hour, continuing to rotate ribs and letting fire die out naturally. Serves 4–6.

Wild About Kansas City Barbecue (Great Plains/Kansas)

★ ★

Special Indoor Barbecued Spare Ribs with Sauce

1 large onion, chopped
¼ cup Wesson oil
1 (6-ounce) can tomato paste
½ cup water
1 beef bouillon cube
¼ cup Worcestershire sauce
¼ cup soy sauce
¼ cup white vinegar

2 tablespoons honey
2 teaspoons Tabasco sauce
2 teaspoons salt
1½ teaspoons liquid smoke
1 large clove garlic, minced
1 teaspoon dry mustard
4–5 pounds pork spareribs

In small saucepan, sauté onion in oil until transparent. Add remaining ingredients, except spareribs; mix well. Simmer 15 minutes. Pour over spareribs in large glass baking dish; let stand 1 hour, turning occasionally. Arrange on shallow rack or broiler pan; bake at 350° for about 1½–2 hours. Turn ribs and baste with remaining barbecue sauce 2 or 3 times during baking. Cut into portions to serve. Makes 4 servings. (Pictured on cover.)

Down Memory Lane (West Virginia)

Boxcar Barbecue

1 (6-pound) Boston butt pork roast
1 (28-ounce) can whole peeled
   tomatoes, mashed
½ cup vinegar
1 (5-ounce) bottle soy sauce

1 (5-ounce) bottle Worcestershire
   sauce
½ cup brown sugar
4 medium onions, chopped

Place roast in roasting pan. Mix all other ingredients and pour over roast. Bake at 300° for 4–5 hours. Remove all bones and shred meat in sauce. Freezes well. Yields 8–10 servings.

Dinner on the Diner (Tennessee)

When Walter Scott began to offer prepared food from a converted horse-drawn freight wagon in Providence, Rhode Island in 1872, he unknowingly inspired the birth of what would become one of America's most recognized icons—the diner. The word "diner" is a derivative of "dining car" and reflects the styling that diner manufacturers borrowed from railroad cars. There are many of these original diners still in existence today.

Pork Loin Roulade

4 boneless center-cut pork loin
  slices, about 1 pound
$1/2$ red bell pepper, cut into strips
$1/2$ green pepper, cut into strips

1 tablespoon cooking oil
$2/3$ cup orange juice
$2/3$ cup bottled barbecue sauce
1 tablespoon Dijon mustard

Place cutlets between 2 pieces of clear plastic wrap. Pound with a mallet to about $1/4$-inch thickness. Place several red and green pepper strips crosswise on each pork portion; roll up jellyroll-style. Secure rolls with wooden toothpicks. In a large skillet, brown the pork rolls in hot cooking oil. Drain fat from pan. Combine remaining ingredients and add to skillet. Bring mixture to boiling; reduce heat. Cover and simmer 10–12 minutes or until pork is tender. Remove toothpicks. Serves 4.

License to Cook Iowa Style (Iowa)

★ **Editor's Extra:** Browns easier by adjusting or removing toothpicks. This is so good!

Pork Tenderloin with Orange Sauce

The sauce is superb.

2 pounds pork tenderloin
2 tablespoons butter
$1/2$ cup chopped onion
1 teaspoon grated orange peel
$2/3$ cup orange juice
$1/3$ cup dry sherry

2 tablespoons sugar
1 teaspoon salt
Dash of pepper
1 bay leaf
1 tablespoon cornstarch
1 tablespoon cold water

Brown meat on all sides in butter; remove meat. In same skillet, cook onion until tender. Stir in all remaining ingredients except cornstarch and water. Return meat to skillet and cover. Simmer 1 hour or until tender, turning occasionally.

Remove meat. In small bowl combine cornstarch and water. Stir into orange mixture and bring to boil. Cook 1 or 2 minutes. Serve meat with sauce. Serves 6.

More Than Delicious (Pennsylvania)

★★★★★★★★★★★ ★★★★★★★★★★★

Spiced Pineapple Pork Roast

If you think this sounds good, wait till you taste it!

1 (4-pound) pork loin roast
1 (12-ounce) jar pineapple preserves
2 tablespoons honey
2 tablespoons red wine vinegar
1 teaspoon prepared mustard

¼ teaspoon salt
¼ teaspoon cinnamon
¼ teaspoon ground cloves
1 (8-ounce) can pineapple slices, drained

Place roast in shallow roasting pan. Insert meat thermometer into thickest part of roast, not touching bone. Roast, uncovered, at 350° about 2½–3 hours, until meat thermometer registers 170°. Combine pineapple preserves, honey, vinegar, mustard, salt, cinnamon, and cloves in a small saucepan. During last 20 minutes of roasting time, garnish roast with pineapple slices and brush with pineapple glaze several times. Serve remaining warm glaze with roast. Yields 6 servings.

Bethel Food Bazaar II (South Carolina)

Mom's Stuffed Pork Chops

So easy and so good.

4–6 pork chops
3 cups bread crumbs
2 tablespoons chopped onion
½ teaspoon salt
½ teaspoon pepper
2 tablespoons parsley flakes

2 tablespoons chopped celery
¾ tablespoon sage
¼ cup milk
¼ cup broth
1 egg, beaten

Brown chops quickly. Place chops in single layer in casserole dish. Mix remaining ingredients together and mound the stuffing on top of each chop. Cover and bake at 350° for 1 hour. Serves 3–4.

Third Wednesday Homemakers (West Virginia)

Pork Chop Skillet

Great flavor in this skillet meal.

4 pork chops
1/2 teaspoon salt
1/8 teaspoon pepper
1/4 teaspoon garlic powder

2 cups chopped celery
1/2 cup sliced onion
1 medium apple, peeled and sliced
1 cup beef bouillon

Sprinkle chops with salt, pepper, and garlic powder. Brown chops and remove from pan. Add celery and onion slices and cook until slightly softened. Arrange chops over vegetables and top with apple slices and bouillon. Cover skillet and simmer 45 minutes or until chops are tender.

Just Plain Country (West Virginia)

Pork Chop 'n' Potato Bake

6 pork chops
Vegetable oil
Seasoned salt (or plain salt)
1 can cream of celery soup
1/2 cup milk
1/2 cup sour cream
1/4 teaspoon black pepper

1/2 teaspoon salt
1 (24-ounce) package O'Brien or
   hash brown potatoes (thawed)
1 cup (4 ounces) shredded Cheddar
   cheese, divided
1 can French-fried onions, divided

Brown pork chops in lightly greased skillet. Sprinkle with salt; set aside. Combine soup, milk, sour cream, pepper, and 1/2 teaspoon salt. Stir into potatoes. Last add 1/2 cup cheese, and 1/2 can French-fried onions. Spoon mixture into a 9x13-inch pan. Arrange pork chops over potatoes. Bake covered at 350° for 40 minutes. Top with remaining cheese and onions. Uncover; bake 5 minutes longer. Makes 6 servings.

Zion Lutheran Church Cookbook (Iowa)

Hearty Ham Pie

A great way to use leftover ham.

¹/₂ cup fresh broccoli
¹/₄ cup chopped green pepper
¹/₄ cup chopped fresh mushrooms
3 tablespoons chopped onion
1 garlic clove, minced
2 teaspoons vegetable oil

2 cups chopped cooked ham, divided
1¹/₂ cups (6 ounces) shredded Swiss
  cheese, divided
1 unbaked (9-inch) pastry shell
4 eggs, beaten
1 cup light cream

In a saucepan, sauté the broccoli, green pepper, mushrooms, onion, and garlic in oil until tender. Sprinkle half the ham and cheese in the pie crust and cover with vegetables. Cover with remaining ham and cheese. Combine eggs and cream and pour over ham and cheese. Bake at 350° for 45–50 minutes or until a knife inserted near center comes out clean. Makes 6 servings.

Note: It may be necessary to cover edge of crust with foil the last part of baking to prevent over-browning.

Then 'til Now (Oregon)

Festive Baked Ham

1 cup apple cider
¹/₂ cup water
1 (5-pound) uncooked ham half
12 whole cloves

1 cup firmly packed brown sugar
1 (21-ounce) can cherry pie filling
¹/₂ cup raisins
¹/₂ cup orange juice

Combine apple cider and water in saucepan; bring to a boil. Set aside. Remove skin from ham. Place ham, fat-side-up, on a cutting board; score fat in a diamond design, and stud with cloves. Place ham in a shallow baking pan, fat-side-up; coat top with brown sugar.

Insert meat thermometer, making sure it does not touch fat or bone. Bake, uncovered, at 325° for about 2 hours (22–25 minutes per pound) or until meat thermometer registers 160°, basting every 30 minutes with cider mixture.

Combine remaining ingredients in a saucepan; bring to a boil. Serve sauce with sliced ham. Serves 10.

Sawgrass and Pines (Florida)

Curried Lamb Chops

The following recipe is from Bruce and Heather Hebert, owners and chefs of the Patit Creek Restaurant in Dayton. Their restaurant has received many plaudits and awards and this recipe is a winner! Sheep farms are found throughout the state; several are in southeast Washington.

1 teaspoon olive oil
4–6 loin lamb chops
Salt and pepper
½ teaspoon minced garlic
2 tablespoons brandy
½ cup dry red wine
1 cup beef stock

1 teaspoon curry powder
½ teaspoon dried mint or 2
  teaspoons chopped fresh mint
2 tablespoons butter
Extra chopped fresh mint to
  sprinkle on top (optional)

Heat olive oil in a large frying pan. Add lamb chops and sauté over medium heat until done (about 5 minutes per side for medium). Remove chops from pan, add salt and pepper, and keep warm on heated platter. Cover loosely with foil.

Remove most of the oil from the pan and add garlic. Sauté garlic for a minute over medium heat, then add brandy and red wine. Bring to a boil over high heat then add beef stock, curry powder, and mint. Boil until thick and syrupy. Remove pan from heat and whisk in butter. Serve sauce with lamb chops. Sprinkle with minced fresh mint, if desired. Serves 2.

Wandering & Feasting (Washington)

Cakes

On State Road 119 near Napanee, Indiana, there is this amazing round barn that was built in 1911 and moved to its present site. It is still a great place to "play," having been transformed into the Round Barn Theatre at Amish Acres.

★★★★★★★★★★★ ★★★★★★★★★★★

Prize Winning Johnson Special
Chocolate Cake

Always won ribbons at the State Fairs. The best of the best!

2 cups sugar
1/2 cup butter or margarine
2 eggs
2 cups flour
1 teaspoon baking soda
1 teaspoon salt

1/2 cup cocoa
1/2 cup sour milk (1 teaspoon lemon
  juice or vinegar in milk), or
  buttermilk
1 teaspoon vanilla
1 cup hot water

Preheat oven to 350°. Sift sugar. Beat butter or margarine until soft. Add the sugar gradually. Blend these ingredients until they are creamy. Beat in eggs. Sift flour before measuring. Resift with baking soda, salt, and cocoa. Add the flour mixture in 3 parts to the butter mixture alternately with 1/3 of sour milk or buttermilk. Lightly beat the batter after each addition until it is smooth. Add vanilla and hot water. Grease 2 (8-inch) layer cake pans with Crisco and then flour lightly. Bake the layers in a 350° oven for about 45 minutes or until done. Top with Mocha Icing.

Variation: If you want a richer cake, use 3/4 cup butter instead of 1/2 cup, and use soured cream instead of soured milk.

Hint: After taking cake pans out of oven, put on damp cloth on counter for 5 minutes. Run knife around edges and put cake pans on wire rack for 5 minutes or more before removing cakes.

AWARD-WINNING MOCHA ICING:
The best chocolate icing you will ever taste!

1 box powdered sugar
1/2 cup cocoa
1 teaspoon vanilla
3 tablespoons cream (or milk)

3 tablespoons liquid coffee
2 tablespoon butter, melted
4 ounces cream cheese, softened

Combine powdered sugar and cocoa. Add slowly, stirring constantly, vanilla, cream, coffee, and melted butter. Add cream cheese. Mix until smooth. Use more coffee, if needed, to make Mocha Icing the right consistency to spread.

Four Generations of Johnson Family Favorites (Oklahoma)

Chocolate Upside-Down Cake

10 tablespoons butter, divided
1/4 cup packed brown sugar
2/3 cup Karo syrup
1/4 cup heavy cream
1 cup broken walnuts
1¾ cups sifted flour
2 teaspoons baking powder

1/4 teaspoon salt
1½ cups sugar
2 eggs, separated
3 squares unsweetened chocolate,
  melted
1 teaspoon vanilla
1 cup milk

Melt 4 tablespoons butter in small saucepan. Stir in brown sugar and heat until bubbly. Stir in Karo and cream; heat, stirring constantly, just until boiling. Add nuts and pour into buttered 10-inch tube pan.

Sift flour, baking powder, and salt and set aside. Beat remaining butter until soft. Gradually beat in sugar, egg yolks, chocolate, and vanilla. Add dry ingredients and mix alternately with milk. Beat egg whites until stiff and fold into cake batter. Spoon batter evenly over nut mixture in pan. Bake at 350° for 45 minutes. Invert and serve with cream or whipped cream.

Friend's Favorites (New York)

Whacky Cake

Easy, delicious, and only one pan to wash!

3 cups flour
2 teaspoons baking soda
1 teaspoon salt
2 cups sugar
4 tablespoons cocoa

1/2 cup oil
1 teaspoon vanilla
2 tablespoons vinegar
2 cups cold water

Mix dry ingredients in greased 9x13-inch pan. Make 3 holes in dry ingredients. Add oil, vanilla, and vinegar. Add cold water and mix well. Bake 30 minutes at 350°.

Pig Out (Oregon)

Carhenge, in Alliance, Nebraska, is an exact replica of Stonehenge made with junked cars. Thirty-eight automobiles assume the same proportions as Stonehenge (England's ancient mystical alignment of stones that chart the sun and moon phases) with the circle measuring approximately 96 feet in diameter. Some of the cars are held upright, trunk-end-down, buried five feet deep in the earth. The cars which form the arches are welded in place. All are covered with gray paint.

Milky Way Cake

A special occasion treat—rich, and expensive.

8 milky way bars, regular size
3 sticks butter or margarine, divided
4½ cups sugar, divided
4 eggs, beaten
2½ cups flour
½ teaspoon baking soda

1½ cups buttermilk
1 cup chopped pecans
1 (8-ounce) can evaporated milk
1 (6-ounce) package chocolate chips
1 cup marshmallow crème

Combine bars and 1 stick butter in saucepan. Cook over low heat, stirring constantly until melted. Set aside. Cream 2 cups sugar, and 1 stick butter in large bowl. Beat in eggs. Sift flour and baking soda and add to creamed mixture alternately with buttermilk. Stir in candy mixture. Add nuts and mix well. Pour into greased and floured 9x13-inch pan. Bake at 325° for 1 hour and 10 minutes.

Combine remaining 2½ cups sugar, evaporated milk, and remaining stick of butter in a saucepan and cook to soft-ball stage, stirring frequently. Remove from heat and add chocolate chips and marshmallow crème. Cool slightly. Beat until thick and spread over cake.

Culinary Arts & Crafts (Florida)

Chocolate Kahlúa Cake

Simple and simply delicious.

¹/₄ cup dried cherries (optional)
¹/₃ cup Kahlúa
1 box chocolate cake mix with
  pudding in the mix
12 ounces chocolate chips

2 cups sour cream
2 eggs
¹/₄ cup oil
Powdered sugar

Soak cherries a few minutes in Kahlúa. Combine cake mix, chocolate chips, sour cream, eggs, oil, Kahlúa, and cherries, if desired, and mix by hand. Pour into a greased Bundt pan. Bake at 350° for 45–50 minutes. Let stand 20 minutes, then turn onto cake plate. Sprinkle with powdered sugar. Serves 10–12.

Favorites for All Seasons (Arizona)

★ **Editor's Extra:** For perfect removal, melt 2 tablespoons shortening and brush onto entire inside of Bundt pan. Beautiful every time.

Black Russian Cake

This is a WOW!

1 Duncan Hines Deep Chocolate
  Cake Mix
¹/₂ cup salad oil
1 (4¹/₂-ounce) box instant chocolate
  pudding mix

4 eggs, room temperature
³/₄ cup strong coffee
³/₄ cup Kahlúa and crème de
  cacao, combined

Preheat oven to 350°. Combine cake mix, oil, pudding, eggs, coffee, Kahlúa, and crème de cacao in a large bowl. Beat 4 minutes on medium speed until smooth. Spoon into a well-greased Bundt pan. Bake for 45–50 minutes. Cool slightly before removing from pan.

TOPPING;
1 cup powdered sugar, sifted
2 tablespoons strong coffee

2 tablespoons Kahlúa
2 tablespoons crème de cacao

Combine all ingredients, beating well until smooth. Pour Topping over warm cake.

The Gathering (Texas II)

★★★★★★★★★★★ ★★★★★★★★★★★

Tunnelfudge Muffins

This recipe will have many fans—kids, chocolate lovers, and the chef!

½ cup butter	¼ teaspoon salt
⅓ cup water	1 egg
5 squares semisweet chocolate	½ cup milk
5 tablespoons cocoa	½ cup sour cream
⅔ cup granulated sugar	2 teaspoons vanilla extract
2 cups all-purpose flour	12 Hershey's Kisses candies
1 tablespoon baking powder	

Heat oven to 375°. In a small saucepan, melt the butter over low heat. Add the water and semisweet chocolate squares and stir until the chocolate is melted. Add the cocoa and sugar and cook 5 minutes, until the sugar is melted. Cool.

In a large bowl, sift together the flour, baking powder, and salt. In another bowl, combine the egg, milk, sour cream, and vanilla extract, and blend on low speed with an electric mixer. Make a well in the center of the dry ingredients, and pour in the egg mixture and the cooled chocolate mixture. Blend at medium speed.

Fill greased muffin tins. Take one Hershey's Kisses candy and push it down into the center of each cup of batter. Bake for 20 minutes or until a tester inserted into a muffin comes out clean. (Insert the tester off center to avoid the candy.) Cool. Makes 12 muffins.

Mad About Muffins (Illinois)

 At a length of 13,300 feet (about 2.5 miles), the Anton Anderson Memorial Tunnel on the Portage Glacier Highway in Alaska is the longest highway tunnel in North America. The tunnel is also the longest tunnel that accommodates both rail and highway use. Two sophisticated computer systems ensure that trains and cars are never in the tunnel at the same time.

★★★★★★★★★★★ ★★★★★★★★★★★

Candy Bar Pound Cake

A great favorite!

1 cup butter, softened
2 cups sugar
4 eggs
2¹/₂ cups cake flour
¹/₄ teaspoon baking soda

1 cup buttermilk
8 regular Hershey's bars
  (12 ounces total)
2 teaspoons vanilla
1 cup chopped pecans

Cream butter until light and fluffy, gradually adding the sugar. Add eggs, 1 at a time, beating well after each addition. Add sifted dry ingredients alternately with the buttermilk. Add melted Hershey's Bars, vanilla, and pecans, which have been rolled in a little flour until lightly coated. Grease and flour tube pan or Bundt pan and bake at 325° for 1¹/₂ hours, or until done.

Everyday Cakes (Georgia)

Buttery Pound Cake

So tasty, you won't believe it's low-fat.

³/₄ cup light margarine (Promise)
3 cups sugar
1¹/₃ cups egg substitute
1¹/₂ cups low-fat sour cream
1 teaspoon baking soda

4¹/₂ cups sifted cake flour
¹/₄ teaspoon salt
1 teaspoon liquid butter buds
1 teaspoon vanilla

Preheat oven to 350°. Spray a 10-inch tube pan with cooking spray. Cream together, on medium speed in mixer, the margarine and sugar until well combined. Gradually add egg substitute, beating well after each addition. In small bowl, combine sour cream and baking soda and set aside. Sift together flour and salt. Put mixer on slow speed, and beginning and ending with flour mixture, alternately add the sour cream and the flour to the mixer bowl. Stir in butter buds and vanilla. Spoon batter into tube pan and bake at 350° for 1 hour and 35 minutes, or until toothpick inserted in the center comes out clean. Cool in pan 10 minutes. Remove cake from pan and cool on a wire rack. Serves 18.

Per serving: 7g fat; 0mg cholesterol; 250 calories.

The Lucy Miele Too Good To Be Low-Fat Cookbook (Illinois)

Rave Review

A beautiful coconut cake . . . the name says it all!

CAKE:

1 package yellow cake mix	4 eggs
1 package instant coconut	¼ cup oil
pudding	2 cups coconut
1⅓ cups water	1 cup chopped nuts (toasted)

Combine and mix well. Put into 3 greased and floured (8- or 9-inch) round cake pans. Bake 30–35 minutes at 350°.

COCONUT ICING:

4 tablespoons butter	2 cups coconut
1 (8-ounce) package cream cheese	2 teaspoons milk
1 box powdered sugar	1 teaspoon vanilla

Cream butter and cream cheese. Add sugar, coconut, milk, and vanilla. Mix well and ice between layers.

Ship to Shore I (North Carolina)

Carolyn's Coconut Cake

Make-ahead, moist, marvelous . . . mmm . . .

2 cake layers, baked and cooled	16 ounces sour cream
(butter cake is good)	1 (12-ounce) package coconut (or
¼ cup coconut milk (optional)	fresh), divided
2 cups sugar	1 (8-ounce) container Cool Whip

Split cake layers. Sprinkle layers with coconut milk, if desired. Mix sugar, sour cream, and coconut (save ½ cup for topping). Chill. Keep 1 cup of this mixture for frosting. Spread remaining portion between layers. Combine Cool Whip with reserved 1 cup of frosting mixture. Pile frosting on top and sides of cake and sprinkle with reserved ½ cup coconut. Cover with cake saver and refrigerate 3 days. Yields 12 or more servings.

South Coastal Cuisine (Mid-Atlantic/Delaware)

Blue Ribbon Carrot Cake

An extremely moist, rich cake.

BUTTERMILK GLAZE:

1 cup granulated sugar
$\frac{1}{2}$ teaspoon baking soda
$\frac{1}{2}$ cup buttermilk

$\frac{1}{4}$ cup ($\frac{1}{2}$ stick) butter
1 tablespoon light corn syrup
1 teaspoon vanilla extract

In small saucepan over high heat, combine sugar, baking soda, buttermilk, butter, and corn syrup. Bring to a boil. Cook 5 minutes, stirring occasionally. Remove from heat and stir in vanilla. Set aside until Cake is baked.

CAKE:

2 cups all-purpose flour
2 teaspoons baking soda
2 teaspoons cinnamon
$\frac{1}{2}$ teaspoon salt
3 eggs
$\frac{3}{4}$ cup vegetable oil
$\frac{3}{4}$ cup buttermilk
2 cups granulated sugar

2 teaspoons vanilla extract
1 (8-ounce) can crushed pineapple, drained
2 cups grated carrots
$3\frac{1}{2}$ ounces shredded coconut
1 cup seedless raisins
1 cup coarsely chopped walnuts

Preheat oven to 350°. Generously grease a 9x13-inch baking pan or 2 (9-inch) cake pans. Sift flour, baking soda, cinnamon, and salt together; set aside. In a large bowl, beat eggs. Add oil, buttermilk, sugar, and vanilla and mix well. Add flour mixture, pineapple, carrots, coconut, raisins, and walnuts and stir well. Pour into prepared pan. Bake for 45–55 minutes or until toothpick inserted in the center comes out clean.

Remove Cake from oven and slowly pour Buttermilk Glaze over the hot Cake. Cool Cake in pan until Buttermilk Glaze is totally absorbed, about 15 minutes.

FROSTING:

$\frac{1}{4}$ cup ($\frac{1}{2}$ stick) butter, room temperature
1 (8-ounce) package cream cheese, room temperature
1 teaspoon vanilla extract

2 cups powdered sugar
1 teaspoon freshly squeezed orange juice
1 teaspoon grated orange peel

In a large bowl, cream butter and cream cheese until fluffy. Add vanilla, powdered sugar, orange juice, and orange peel. Mix until smooth. Frost Cake and refrigerate until Frosting is set. Serve Cake chilled. Yields 20–24 servings.

From Portland's Palate (Oregon)

Apple Dump Cake

So easy and so good.

1 cup chopped nuts
1 cup apple pie filling
2 eggs
1 teaspoon salt
1 cup corn oil

2 cups unsifted flour
1 teaspoon vanilla
2 cups sugar
1 teaspoon baking soda
1 teaspoon cinnamon

Dump all ingredients into large bowl and stir until mixed well (stir with spoon or fork, not mixer). Put into greased 9x13-inch pan. Bake at 350° for 35–45 minutes. When cool, top with icing made by mixing the following ingredients:

1 (8-ounce) package cream cheese
¾ stick margarine

½ box powdered sugar
1 teaspoon vanilla

Recipes from Jan's Cake & Candy Crafts (Indiana)

Apple Dapple Cake

3 eggs
1½ cups salad oil
2 cups sugar
3 cups flour
1 teaspoon salt

1 teaspoon baking soda
2 teaspoons vanilla
3 cups peeled and chopped apples
1½ cups chopped pecans

Mix eggs, oil, and sugar. Blend well. Add flour, salt, and baking soda. Mix well. Add vanilla, apples, and nuts. Bake in 350° oven for 1 hour in an 8- or 9-inch greased tube pan.

1 cup brown sugar
¼ cup milk

1 stick margarine

Combine brown sugar, milk, and margarine, and cook 2½ minutes. Pour over cake while still hot and in the pan. Let set until cool. Remove from pan when completely cold.

Home Cooking II (Indiana)

★★★★★★★★★★★   ★★★★★★★★★★★

Grant Wood's Strawberry Shortcake

Nostalgically delicious, this is the real thing.

1 quart fresh ripe strawberries,
  washed and hulled
$1/2$–1 cup granulated sugar
2 cups sifted all-purpose flour
3 teaspoons baking powder

$1/2$ teaspoon salt
6 tablespoons lard (or shortening)
$3/4$ cup milk
Butter (fresh homemade is best)
Rich country cream

Place strawberries in a bowl and bruise and chop with a silver spoon. Cover with sugar to suit and let stand at room temperature to bring out the juice.

Make a biscuit dough as follows: Preheat oven to 425°. Sift together flour, baking powder, and salt. Cut in lard. Add milk and mix lightly, the less the better. Spread out in a greased pie tin with a spoon. Bake in hot oven until done (12–20 minutes).

Carefully break biscuit dough into 2 layers, using a fork to separate them. Lay top layer to one side (remove with a pancake turner, if necessary). Butter the bottom layer and cover with crushed strawberries. Butter the top layer and put back on the strawberries. Top the cake with more strawberries. Cut in huge slices and serve with country cream. Makes 6–8 servings.

A Cook's Tour of Iowa (Iowa)

Strawberry Chocolate Mousse Cake

1 cup chocolate cookie crumbs
3 tablespoons butter, melted
2 pints strawberries, stemmed and
  halved lengthwise
12 ounces semisweet chocolate chips

2 tablespoons light corn syrup
$1/2$ cup orange liqueur
$2^1/2$ cups whipping cream, divided
1 tablespoon powdered sugar

Mix the cookie crumbs and butter thoroughly. Press evenly into the bottom of a 9-inch springform pan. Stand strawberry halves around pan, touching, side-by-side, pointed ends up, with cut sides against the side of pan, saving a few for top. Set aside.

Place chocolate chips, corn syrup, and orange liqueur in bowl. Microwave for 1 minute or until the mixture is smooth when stirred. Beat $1^1/2$ cups of cream until it forms stiff peaks. Fold the chocolate mixture into the cream. Pour into strawberry-lined bowl. Refrigerate. When ready to serve, unmold the dessert and whip the remaining cream. Arrange cream on top of dessert and top with the remaining strawberries.

Favorites for All Seasons (Arizona)

Cherry Walnut Delight

1¼ cups flour
¾ cup brown sugar
½ cup margarine
¾ cup coconut
¾ cup chopped walnuts
1 (8-ounce) package cream cheese
½ cup sugar

1 egg
1 teaspoon vanilla
1 (1-pound 5-ounce) can cherry pie
 filling
½ cup chopped walnuts (for
 topping)

Combine flour, brown sugar, and margarine; blend to fine crumbs. Add coconut and walnuts; mix. Reserve ⅓ cup crumb mixture and press the rest into bottom of a greased 9x13-inch pan. Bake at 350° for 12–15 minutes or until lightly browned.

Beat cream cheese until fluffy. Add sugar, egg, and vanilla. Spread over baked layer and bake 10 minutes. Put cherry filling over cream cheese. Sprinkle with walnuts and reserved crumb mixture. Bake for 15 minutes.

The Parkview Way to Vegetarian Cooking (New England/Maine)

Somersault Cake

As sent to me, Granny Nanny.

"Put fo' tablespoons er butter in a iron skillet, and when it melts up, add a generous cup er brown sugar. Pat it down smooth. Now sprinkle a cup er diced pineapple an a cup er pecans and a cup er raisins. Now po a cup of honey over this, a dribblin hit around.

Now po' yer favorite cake mix batter—white, yellow, spice or ginger. Bake in a 350° oven for 35 minutes. Turn out on plate before hit sets up. Serve it up with whipped cream. This'll sho' make'em foller they noses back ter the kitchen."

Kountry Kooking (Tennessee)

★ **Editor's Extra:** This really is a delicious cake. I use a 12-inch skillet or 2 (8-inch) skillets.

★★★★★★★★★★★ ★★★★★★★★★★★

Pineapple Cheese Torte

PAT-IN-THE-PAN-CRUST:

¹/₃ cup butter or margarine
1 cup flour

1¹/₄ cups powdered sugar
¹/₄ cup finely chopped almonds

Combine crust ingredients; pat into the bottom of a 12x8x2-inch baking dish. Bake at 350° for 20 minutes.

FILLING:

2 (8-ounce) packages cream cheese,
  softened
¹/₂ cup sugar

2 eggs
²/₃ cup unsweetened pineapple
  juice

Beat cream cheese in bowl until fluffy. Beat in sugar and eggs. Stir in juice. Pour Filling over crust. Bake at 350° for 20 minutes, or until center is set. Cool.

PINEAPPLE TOPPING:

¹/₄ cup flour
¹/₄ cup sugar
1 (20-ounce) can crushed pineapple,
  drained (save juice)

¹/₂ cup whipping cream

Combine flour and sugar in a saucepan. Stir in 1 cup of reserved pineapple juice. Bring to a boil, stirring constantly. Boil and stir 1 minute. Remove from heat; fold in pineapple. Cool. Whip cream until stiff peaks form; fold into topping. Spread carefully over dessert. Refrigerate 6 hours or overnight. Garnish with strawberries, if desired. Yields 12–16 servings.

Favorite Recipes (Ohio)

The Pineapple Garden Maze is the World's Largest Maze, according to *The Guinness Book of World Records*. You can spend half an hour or half a day among its 1.7 miles of paths. Located on Oahu at the Dole Plantation, it is about 10 minutes away from historic Haleiwa, Hawaii.

★★★★★★★★★★★ ★★★★★★★★★★★

Heavenly Dessert Torte

6 egg whites
2 teaspoons vanilla
1/2 teaspoon cream of tartar
Dash salt

2 cups sugar
2 cups whipping cream
6 ounces or more crushed Heath Bars

Combine egg whites, vanilla, cream of tartar, and salt. Beat to soft peaks. Gradually adding sugar, beat to stiff peaks. Cut 2 (9-inch) circles of brown paper. Place on cookie sheet and cover each with egg white mixture. Bake 1 hour at 275°. Let cool in oven.

Whip cream and combine with crushed Heath Bars. Spread half of mixture on one meringue circle (paper removed), top with second meringue circle (paper removed), and cover with remaining whipped cream. Chill in refrigerator at least 8 hours. Serves 10.

The Denton Woman's Club Cookbook (Texas II)

Southern Gingerbread with Caramel Sauce

1/2 cup sugar
1/2 cup butter and shortening, mixed
1 egg
1 cup dark syrup
1 teaspoon cinnamon
1/2 teaspoon salt

1 teaspoon ginger
1/2 teaspoon ground cloves
2 1/2 cups flour
1 1/2 teaspoons soda
1 cup hot water

Cream sugar into butter. Add egg and syrup. Sift remaining dry ingredients. Add alternately with water. Pour into greased 9-inch-square pan. Bake at 350° for 25–30 minutes. (Test for doneness with toothpick.)

CARAMEL SAUCE:
3 tablespoons butter
3 tablespoons flour

1 1/2 cups sugar
2 cups water

Cream butter and flour. Caramelize sugar by melting over low heat, stirring until browned. Add water slowly. Cook until bubbly. Add to butter and flour, mixing well. Pour over Southern Gingerbread to serve.

Betty Talmadge's Lovejoy Plantation Cookbook (Georgia)

Turtle Cheesecake

CRUST:

1 cup chocolate wafer crumbs

4 tablespoons butter or margarine, melted

Combine crumbs and butter. Press onto bottom of 9-inch springform pan.

FILLING:

4 (8-ounce) packages cream cheese, softened
1½ cups sugar

1 teaspoon vanilla
4 eggs

Beat cream cheese and sugar until light and fluffy. Add vanilla; beat in eggs, one at a time. Pour into crust. Bake at 300° for 1 hour and 40 minutes. Turn off heat; let cake cool in oven, with door ajar, for 1 hour. Remove from oven.

TOPPING:

20 caramels
3 tablespoons milk

1 cup chopped pecans

In small saucepan over low heat, melt caramels with milk. Stir until smooth. Pour over cake. Sprinkle with chopped pecans. Chill.

Cheesecakes et cetera (Colorado)

Mon Ami Oreo Cookie Cheesecake

C'est magnifique!

CRUST:

1¼ cups Oreo cookie crumbs   ¼ cup butter, melted

Mix cookie crumbs with melted butter; press in bottom of 9-inch spring-form pan and refrigerate ½ hour.

FILLING:

2 pounds cream cheese, room   2 large egg yolks
  temperature   ⅓ cup whipping cream
1½ cups sugar, divided   2 teaspoons vanilla, divided
2 tablespoons flour   1½ cups Oreo cookie crumbs
4 extra large eggs   2 cups sour cream

In large mixer bowl, beat cream cheese until fluffy. Add 1¼ cups sugar and flour, then blend in eggs and yolks until smooth. Stir in cream and 1 teaspoon vanilla. Pour half of this mixture into prepared pan; sprinkle with crumbs and pour in remaining batter. Bake 15 minutes at 425°; reduce temperature to 225° and bake 50 minutes. Cover loosely with foil if browning too quickly. Increase temperature to 350°; blend sour cream, ¼ cup sugar, and 1 teaspoon vanilla. Spread over cheesecake and bake 7 minutes. Refrigerate overnight. Top with Glaze and garnish.

GLAZE:

1 cup whipping cream, scalded   1 teaspoon vanilla
8 ounces semisweet chocolate

Combine scalded whipping cream with chocolate and vanilla, and stir 1 minute. Refrigerate 15 minutes before pouring over chilled cheesecake.

Mon Ami Restaurant and Historic Winery, Port Clinton, Ohio

Dining in Historic Ohio (Ohio)

Opened August 18, 1910, in Birmingham, Alabama, Rickwood Field now stands as the oldest baseball field in America, symbolizing the early days in American baseball. On opening day, the entire city of Birmingham was so "baseball-wild," businesses closed in honor of the event and 10,000 people packed the stands.

★★★★★★★★★★★ ★★★★★★★★★★★

Three Layered Cheesecake

Award-winning!

CRUST:

1 cup flour	**6 tablespoons brown sugar**
¹/₂ cup chopped nuts	**6 tablespoons butter, softened**

Combine ingredients in mixer and blend until smooth. Press into greased 9-inch springform pan. Bake at 375° for 10 minutes and set aside.

CAKE:

2 pounds cream cheese, softened	**³/₄ cup ground filberts**
1 teaspoon vanilla sugar	**¹/₈ teaspoon almond extract**
1¹/₂ cups sugar	**2 ounces bittersweet chocolate**
4 eggs	

Mix cream cheese until smooth, adding vanilla sugar, sugar, and eggs (one at a time). Remove 2 cups cheese batter; mix with ground filberts and almond extract. Pour onto Crust and level with metal beveled spatula. Freeze for 1 hour.

Melt chocolate. Remove another 2 cups cheese mixture and add to melted chocolate. Pour over filbert layer, leveling well. Freeze for 20 minutes. Pour remaining cheese mixture onto chocolate layer. Half fill 10x13-inch aluminum pan with water. Wrap bottom of springform pan with heavy-duty aluminum foil and place in water. Bake at 350° for 2 hours. Let cool for another 2 hours in oven without opening door. Refrigerate for at least 6 hours.

TOPPING:

1 (3¹/₂-ounce) bar white milk	**3 teaspoons water**
chocolate	**1 teaspoon light corn syrup**
1¹/₂ teaspoons coffee (liquid)	

Melt all ingredients over low heat until dissolved. Remove sides of springform pan. Pour Topping over Cake, allowing it to drizzle down sides. Decorate with chocolate curls.

Note: To make vanilla sugar, bury two vanilla beans in one pound of granulated or confectioners' sugar. Store in airtight container for about a week. (Pictured on cover.)

Culinary Creations (New York)

★ **Editor's Extra:** The vanilla sugar is a lovely plus, but can be omitted; and other ground nuts can be substituted for the filberts.

★★★★★★★★★★★★   ★★★★★★★★★★★★

Hugs and Chips Cheesecake

You'll get lots of hugs when you make this cheesecake.

2 (3-ounce) packages cream cheese,
  softened
1 (14-ounce) can sweetened
  condensed milk
1 egg
1 teaspoon vanilla extract

1 cup mini chocolate chips
1 teaspoon flour
1 (6-ounce) ready-made chocolate
  pie crust
Chocolate Glaze
Chocolate curls (optional)

Preheat oven to 350°. With a mixer, beat cheese until fluffy; gradually beat in condensed milk until smooth. Add egg and vanilla; mix well. Toss chips with flour; stir in cheese mixture, then pour into crust. Bake 35 minutes, or until center springs back when lightly touched. Cool and top with Chocolate Glaze and curls. Serve chilled. Refrigerate leftovers.

CHOCOLATE GLAZE:

½ cup mini chocolate chips   ¼ cup whipping cream

Melt chips and whipping cream. Cook and stir until thickened and smooth. Immediately spread over pie.

Fortsville UMC Cookbook (New York)

★★★★★★★★★★★ ★★★★★★★★★★★

Peanut Butter Chocolate Chip Cheesecake

Possibly the most unusual cheesecake ever.

CRUST:

1 (12-ounce) box vanilla wafers	1/3–1/2 cup unsalted butter, melted
1/2 cup granulated sugar	

Preheat oven to 350°. Make crust by combining wafers and sugar in processor to make uniform crumbs. Add butter and mix well. Press into bottom and halfway up side of 9-inch springform pan. Set aside.

FILLING:

1 pound cream cheese, softened	5 large eggs
1 1/2 cups granulated sugar	1/2 cup commercial sour cream
1 (6-ounce) jar creamy peanut	2 teaspoons fresh lemon juice
butter	3/4 cup chocolate chips

Combine cream cheese, sugar, peanut butter, eggs, sour cream, and lemon juice in processor and blend until smooth. Add chips and process for 10 seconds with on-off motion.

Pour Filling carefully into Crust. Bake 70–80 minutes until center is firm. Remove from oven but leave oven on, and let stand for 15 minutes before adding Topping.

TOPPING:

1 cup commercial sour cream	1/4 cup granulated sugar
3/4 cup chocolate chips, melted	

Blend sour cream, melted chocolate, and sugar, and spread over cake. Bake for an additional 10 minutes. Let cool, and chill for at least 3 hours or overnight. Unmold carefully and serve in thin wedges. Serves 16.

The Fine Art of Cooking (Pennsylvania)

Confused about chocolate? It comes in unsweetened, bittersweet, semisweet, milk chocolate and white chocolate. Unsweetened chocolate is pure chocolate liquor and 50% cocoa butter. Bittersweet contains at least 35% liquor, cocoa butter, sugar and vanilla; semisweet is the same, but with more sugar. Milk chocolate contains about 10% chocolate liquor with an additional 12% milk solids. White chocolate (which is not really chocolate) is made from cocoa butter, milk solids, sugar and vanilla. Cocoa powder is made by separating most of the cocoa butter out of the liquor.

Butter Pecan Cheesecake

1½ cups graham cracker crumbs
⅓ cup sugar
⅓ cup butter or margarine, melted
½ cup finely chopped pecans
3 (8-ounce) packages cream cheese, softened
1½ cups sugar

3 eggs
2 (8-ounce) cartons commercial sour cream
1 teaspoon vanilla extract
½ teaspoon butter flavoring
1 cup finely chopped pecans, toasted

Combine first 4 ingredients, mixing well. Reserve ⅓ cup mixture; press remaining mixture firmly onto bottom of a 9-inch springform pan.

Beat cream cheese with an electric mixer until light and fluffy; gradually add 1½ cups sugar, mixing well. Add eggs, one at a time, beating well after each addition. Add sour cream and flavorings; mix well. Stir in 1 cup pecans.

Spoon into prepared pan; sprinkle with reserved crumb mixture. Bake at 475° for 10 minutes; reduce temperature to 300° and bake an additional 50 minutes. Let cool to room temperature on a wire rack; chill. Before serving, spoon Praline Sauce over each piece.

PRALINE SAUCE:
1 cup light corn syrup
½ cup sugar
⅓ cup butter or margarine

1 egg, beaten
1 tablespoon vanilla extract
1 cup coarsely chopped pecans

Combine first four ingredients in a heavy saucepan; mix well. Bring to a boil over medium heat, stirring constantly. Boil 2 minutes without stirring. Remove from heat; stir in vanilla and pecans.

A Tasting Tour Through Washington County (Kentucky)

Old Lyme, Connecticut, is home to the nation's only Nut Museum. The museum houses a 35-pound double coconut which happens to be the world's largest nut, as well as nut crackers, nut art, nut music, and more.

Luscious Almond Amaretto Cheesecake

CRUST:

40 vanilla wafers
³⁄₄ cup toasted slivered almonds
¹⁄₃ cup sugar

¹⁄₄ cup plus 2 tablespoons butter,
   melted

Combine first 3 ingredients in processor and process until crushed. Add butter and process until blended. (If no processor, crush wafers by hand and mix all together.) Press into bottom and 1³⁄₄ inches up side of 9-inch springform or regular cake pan; set aside.

FILLING:

3 (8-ounce) packages cream cheese,
   softened
1 cup plus 1 tablespoon sugar,
   divided
4 eggs
¹⁄₄ cup plus 1 tablespoon amaretto,
   divided

¹⁄₃ cup heavy cream
2 teaspoons vanilla, divided
2 cups sour cream
Whipped cream, fresh raspberries,
   and toasted almonds for garnish

Beat cream cheese and 1 cup sugar. Add eggs 1 at a time. Beat in ¹⁄₄ cup amaretto, cream, and 1 teaspoon vanilla; beat well. Pour into Crust. Bake at 350° for 30 minutes, then reduce oven to 225° and bake 1 hour. Cool on rack 5 minutes.

Combine sour cream, 1 tablespoon sugar, 1 tablespoon amaretto, and 1 teaspoon vanilla. Spread evenly over cheesecake. Bake an additional 5 minutes. Remove from pan and cool 30 minutes. Cover and refrigerate overnight.

For garnish, at serving time, pipe rosette of whipped cream at intervals around edge. Place a raspberry on top of whipped cream. Sprinkle with almonds and serve. If you don't want to pipe the cream, just either spread it over the top, or drop in dollops by spoon over cheesecake.

Enjoy at Your Own Risk! Cookbook (West Virginia)

Autumn Cheesecake

This is a delicious apple cheesecake that I usually make in the fall.

CRUST:

1 cup graham cracker crumbs
$1/2$ cup finely chopped pecans
3 tablespoons sugar

$1/2$ teaspoon ground cinnamon
$1/4$ cup unsalted butter, melted

Preheat oven to 350°. In a large bowl, stir together graham cracker crumbs, pecans, sugar, cinnamon, and melted butter; press into bottom of 9-inch springform pan. Bake in preheated oven for 10 minutes.

CREAM CHEESE LAYER:

2 (8-ounce) packages cream cheese,
  softened
$1/2$ cup sugar

2 eggs
$1/2$ teaspoon vanilla extract

In large bowl, combine cream cheese and sugar. Mix at medium speed until smooth. Beat in eggs one at a time, mixing well after each addition. Blend in vanilla; pour filling into baked Crust.

APPLE LAYER:

$1/3$ cup sugar
$1/2$ teaspoon ground cinnamon
4 cups peeled, cored, and thinly
  sliced apples

$1/4$ cup chopped pecans

In small bowl, stir together sugar and cinnamon. Toss sugar-cinnamon mixture with apples to coat. Spoon Apple Layer over Cream Cheese Layer and sprinkle with chopped pecans. Bake in preheated oven for 60–70 minutes. With knife, loosen cake from rim of pan. Let cool, then remove rim of pan. Chill cake before serving. Makes 1 (9-inch) cheesecake.

Allrecipes Tried & True Favorites (Washington)

★ **Editor's Extra:** Don't wait till autumn—this is good any time of year.

Strawberry Glazed Cheesecake

This makes a beautiful presentation.

CRUST:

1 cup graham cracker crumbs
2 tablespoons sugar

¼ cup butter, melted

Combine Crust ingredients. Mix well with pastry blender. Press evenly over bottom and sides of 9-inch pie pan. Bake at 350° for 5 minutes.

FILLING:

1 (8-ounce) package cream cheese,
  softened
2 tablespoons milk or
  half-and-half
1 teaspoon lemon juice

1 teaspoon vanilla
¼ teaspoon salt
¼ cup sugar
2 eggs

Beat cream cheese, milk, lemon juice, vanilla, salt, and sugar until smooth and creamy. Add eggs, one at a time, beating well after each addition. Pour into Crust. Bake at 350° until Filling is firm, 20–25 minutes.

TOPPING:

1 package frozen strawberries,
  defrosted
¼ cup sugar

1 tablespoon cornstarch
1 pint fresh strawberries, cleaned
  and halved

Whiz defrosted strawberries and juice in blender until smooth or put strawberries through sieve. Combine sugar and cornstarch in saucepan. Stir in strawberry mixture. Cook over low heat, stirring constantly, until thick and clear. Cool slightly. Arrange strawberry halves on cheesecake. Spoon Topping over strawberries. Chill. Serves 8.

What's Cookin' in Melon Country (Colorado)

Cherry Cheesecake

1 box Deluxe II Duncan Hines
  Yellow Cake Mix
4 eggs, divided
2 tablespoons oil
2 (8-ounce) packages cream cheese
1/2 cup sugar

1 1/2 cups milk
3 tablespoons lemon juice
3 teaspoons vanilla
1 (1-pound 5-ounce) can cherry pie
  filling

Preheat oven to 300°. Reserve 1 cup of dry cake mix. In large mixing bowl, combine remaining cake mix, 1 egg, and oil. Mix well until crumbly. Press crust mixture evenly into bottom of greased 9x13x2-inch pan and 3/4 way up on sides. In same bowl, blend cream cheese and sugar. Add 3 eggs and reserved cake mix. Beat 1 minute at medium speed. At low speed, slowly add milk and flavorings. Mix until smooth. Pour into crust. Bake at 300° for 45–55 minutes until center is firm. When cool, top with pie filling. Store in refrigerator. To freeze, cover with foil.

Somethin's Cookin' at LG&E (Kentucky)

The Iao Valley in Maui, Hawaii, is a place of great nature, history and beauty. Gwen's daughter, Heather, and her husband, Arty, follow the path up to the Iao Needle, a volcanic monolith 2,250 feet high that soars nearly straight up from the valley floor.

Sugar Cookies (World's Best)

These are the world's best sugar cookies.

2 sticks margarine, softened
$1^1/2$ cups powdered sugar
1 egg
$^1/2$ teaspoon almond extract
1 teaspoon vanilla extract

$2^1/2$ cups flour
1 teaspoon baking soda
1 teaspoon cream of tartar
$^1/4$ teaspoon salt

Cream margarine and sugar; add egg and extracts. Sift dry ingredients and add to mixture. Roll into small balls and place on Pam-sprayed cookie sheets. Bake at 375° about 7–8 minutes. Yields $4^1/2$ dozen.

Betty is Still "Winking" at Cooking (Arkansas)

Sugar & Spice Cookies

A flavorful spice cookie with a delicious aftertaste.

$^3/4$ cup shortening
1 cup brown sugar
1 egg
$^1/4$ cup molasses
$2^1/4$ cups sifted flour
2 teaspoons baking soda

1 teaspoon cinnamon
$^1/2$ teaspoon ground ginger
$^1/4$ teaspoon ground cloves
$^1/4$ teaspoon salt
2 tablespoons sugar
3 dozen red cinnamon candies

Cream together shortening and sugar until fluffy. Add egg and molasses; blend well. Sift together next 6 ingredients. Stir into creamed mixture. Form balls using 1 teaspoon dough. Roll in sugar and place about 2 inches apart on a greased baking sheet. Bake at 375° for 10 minutes or until golden brown. Place a red cinnamon candy in middle of each cookie. Yields 3 dozen.

Cookies and Bars (Michigan)

Cream Cheese Cut-Out Cookies

1 cup sugar
1 cup (2 sticks) butter, softened
1 (3-ounce) package cream cheese,
   softened
1/4 teaspoon salt
1 teaspoon vanilla (or half almond
   or lemon) extract

1 egg yolk
2 1/4 cups flour
Confectioners' Sugar Glaze
Colored sugars (optional)

Cream sugar, butter, cream cheese, salt, extract, and egg yolk until light. Add flour, blending well. Chill dough several hours or overnight. When ready to bake, preheat oven to 375°.

Using a section at a time, roll dough to 1/8 inch on a floured cloth. Cut into desired shapes and bake on ungreased cookie sheets for 7–10 minutes or until light golden. Cool on a rack.

CONFECTIONERS' SUGAR GLAZE:
1 cup confectioners' sugar
2–3 tablespoons milk

1/4 teaspoon extract of choice

Brush cookies with Confectioners' Sugar Glaze and sprinkle with colored sugars, if desired. Yields 3–4 dozen.

Note: Cut-out cookie batter can also be rolled into logs, wrapped, and refrigerated to be sliced when needed. Saves time and fuss when you are not concerned about decorative shapes.

Christmas Memories Cookbook (New England/Connecticut)

★ **Editor's Extra:** Interesting to put colored or chocolate sprinkles on cookies before baking. Either way, they're cute and classy cut-outs!

★★★★★★★★★★★   ★★★★★★★★★★★

Melting Moments

1 cup butter or margarine, softened   1¼ cups unsifted all-purpose flour
½ cup powdered sugar   ¾ cup cornstarch

In large mixing bowl, cream butter and sugar until light and fluffy. Beat in flour and cornstarch until well mixed. Wrap and refrigerate dough at least 2 hours or overnight. Roll dough into 1-inch balls. Place on ungreased cookie sheet; bake at 325° for 10 minutes or until firm but golden. Cool slightly and remove from pan; cool completely. Top cookies with Glaze; let dry. Makes about 3½ dozen.

GLAZE:
1½ cups powdered sugar, sifted   3 tablespoons orange or lemon juice

In a small bowl, mix sugar and juice. Frost cookies.

Beyond the Bay (Florida)

Painted Cookies

A fun way to entertain kids.

½ cup margarine, softened   2 teaspoons baking powder
½ cup butter, softened   6 cups flour, divided
2 cups sugar   ½ cup buttermilk
2 eggs, beaten   1 teaspoon vanilla
½ teaspoon baking soda

Cream margarine, butter, and sugar. Add beaten eggs. Combine baking soda, baking powder, and 1 cup flour. Add dry ingredients alternately with buttermilk. Add vanilla to the butter mixture. Add enough of the remaining flour to make a soft dough. Turn out onto a floured board and knead until smooth. Chill dough if sticky. Roll out dough to ¼-inch thickness. Cut into shapes with a sharp knife (to make your own designs), or cookie cutters for the kids. Decorate before baking with Paint or sprinkles. Bake at 350° until golden. Makes 80–100 cookies.

EGG YOLK PAINT:
1 egg yolk   Food coloring
½ teaspoon water

Mix egg yolk with water; blend well. Divide liquid among small glass cups. Tint with food coloring. Use small paint brushes to paint designs on cookies before baking. Thin Paint, if necessary, with a few drops of water.

The Garden Patch (Arizona)

Cherry Winks

Ruth Derousseau's prize-winning recipe "The $5,000 Cooky"—reprinted with permission from Pillsbury, was shown on the back of a 1951 Kellogg's Corn Flakes cereal box.

2½ cups sifted Pillsbury's Best
  Enriched Flour
1 teaspoon double-acting baking
  powder
½ teaspoon baking soda
½ teaspoon salt
¾ cup shortening
1 cup sugar

2 eggs
2 tablespoons milk
1 teaspoon vanilla
1 cup chopped pecans
1 cup chopped dates
½ cup chopped maraschino cherries
2½ cups Kellogg's Corn Flakes
15 maraschino cherries, quartered

Sift together flour, baking powder, baking soda, and salt. Combine shortening and sugar; cream well. Blend in eggs; add milk and vanilla. Blend in sifted dry ingredients; mix well. Add pecans, dates, and chopped cherries. Mix well. Shape into balls using a level tablespoon of dough for each cooky. Crush corn flakes. Roll each ball of dough in corn flakes. Place on greased baking sheet. Top each cooky with ¼ maraschino cherry. Bake in moderate oven (375°) 10–12 minutes. Do not stack or store until cold. Makes about 5 dozen cookies.

Note: If you use Pillsbury's Best Enriched Self-Rising Flour, omit baking powder and salt; decrease baking soda to ¼ teaspoon.

Green Thumbs in the Kitchen (Wisconsin)

★ **Editor's Extra:** They may have spelled it differently a half century ago, but this "cooky" is equally delicious today.

Chocolate Covered Cherry Cookies

1½ cups flour
½ cup cocoa
¼ teaspoon salt
¼ baking powder
¼ teaspoon baking soda
1 cup sugar

½ cup butter or margarine,
  softened
1 egg
1½ teaspoons vanilla
1 (10-ounce) jar maraschino
  cherries

In a large bowl, stir together flour, cocoa, salt, baking powder, and baking soda; set aside. In mixing bowl, beat butter and sugar. Add egg and vanilla, mixing well; add dry ingredients. Shape dough into 1-inch balls. Place on ungreased cookie sheet. Press down center of dough with thumb and place a cherry in center. Spoon 1 teaspoon Frosting over each cherry, spreading to cover cherry. Bake at 350° for 10 minutes. Yields 48 cookies.

FROSTING:

1 (6-ounce) package semisweet
  chocolate morsels

½ cup sweetened condensed milk
4 teaspoons cherry juice

In small pan, combine chocolate chips and condensed milk and heat until chips are melted; stir in cherry juice.

Flaunting Our Finest (Tennessee)

Cherry Chip Cookies

¾ cup margarine, softened
1 cup brown sugar
1 egg
1 teaspoon vanilla
2¼ cups flour
1 teaspoon baking powder

½ teaspoon salt
½ cup maraschino cherries, cut
  small
1 cup miniature chocolate chips
½ cup coconut

Using mixer, cream together margarine and brown sugar. Add egg and vanilla; mix well. Mix flour, baking powder, and salt; add gradually to creamed mixture. Mixture will be stiff. Using spoon, stir in cherries, chocolate chips, and coconut. Chill in refrigerator about 2 hours. Roll chilled dough between hands into ½-inch small balls. Place balls on greased cookie sheets. Bake at 350° for 8 minutes or until light brown. Makes 85 small cookies.

College Avenue Presbyterian Church Cookbook (Illinois)

Mrs. Overlake's Cookies

*The secret is to overdose on chocolate chips and nuts, then underbake for a
chewy, moist, scrumptious cookie.*

1 cup butter, melted
3/4 cup sugar
3/4 cup brown sugar
2 eggs
1 overflowing teaspoon vanilla
2 1/2 cups unsifted flour

1 teaspoon baking soda
1 teaspoon salt
3–4 cups (18–24 ounces) chocolate
   chips
2 cups chopped pecans

Preheat oven to 325°. In a large bowl, cream together butter and sugars,
then beat in eggs and vanilla. Sift together flour, baking soda, and salt.
Stir into butter mixture, forming a stiff batter. Add chips and nuts.

Use an ice cream scoop to drop batter on ungreased cookie sheet,
averaging 9 cookies per sheet. Bake at 325° for 15–18 minutes, check-
ing periodically to see that they are not overbaked. Yields 27 big cookies!

The Overlake School Cookbook (Washington)

Texas Cow Patties

2 cups margarine, softened
2 cups sugar
2 cups firmly packed brown sugar
4 eggs
2 teaspoons vanilla
2 cups quick-cooking oats
2 cups cornflakes

4 cups all-purpose flour
2 teaspoons baking powder
2 teaspoons baking soda
1 (6-ounce) package semisweet
   chocolate morsels
2 cups chopped pecans

Cream margarine, sugar, and brown sugar together until light and fluffy.
Add eggs, 1 at a time, beating well after each addition. Stir in vanilla.
Add oats and cornflakes to creamed mixture, mixing thoroughly. Sift
flour, baking powder, and baking soda together. Gradually add to
creamed mixture, beating slowly to mix. Stir in chocolate morsels and
pecans. Drop by rounded tablespoons onto greased cookie sheets.

Bake on top rack of oven at 325° for 17 minutes. Cool on wire rack.
Makes 2 dozen.

Changing Thymes (Texas II)

Chocolate Chocolate-Chip Cookies

1 cup butter, softened
$^1/_4$ cup sugar
$^3/_4$ cup brown sugar
1 teaspoon vanilla
2 eggs

1 ($4^1/_2$-ounce) package milk
  chocolate instant pudding
$2^1/_4$ cups flour
1 teaspoon baking soda
1 (12-ounce) package chocolate chips

Combine butter, sugars, and vanilla, and beat until fluffy. Add eggs and pudding; beat well. Combine flour and baking soda and add to batter. Drop by spoonfuls on cookie sheets. Bake at 375° for 8–10 minutes.

Centennial Cookbook (Wisconsin)

Chocolate Drop Cookies

$^1/_2$ cup shortening
2 (1-ounce) squares unsweetened
  chocolate
1 cup brown sugar
1 egg
1 teaspoon vanilla
$^1/_2$ cup buttermilk

$1^1/_2$ cups sifted all-purpose flour
$^1/_2$ teaspoon baking powder
$^1/_2$ teaspoon baking soda
$^1/_4$ teaspoon salt
$^1/_2$ cup chopped walnuts
1 (6-ounce) package semisweet
  chocolate morsels

Melt shortening and unsweetened chocolate together in saucepan. Cool 10 minutes. Stir brown sugar and chocolate together. Beat in egg, vanilla, and buttermilk. Sift together dry ingredients and add to chocolate mix. Stir in nuts and chocolate pieces. Drop from teaspoon on greased cookie sheet. Top with walnut halves, if desired. Bake at 375° for 10–12 minutes. Makes $3^1/_2$ dozen.

Home Cookin': First Congregational United Church of Christ
(Michigan)

Go on a wild goose chase to the small town of Sumner, Missouri, which claims to be the Wild Goose Capital of the World. There you'll find the statue of Maxie, the World's Largest Canadian Goose. Maxie is 40 feet tall, weighs 5,500 pounds and has a 65-foot wingspan.

★★★★★★★★★★   ★★★★★★★★★★

Peanut Butter Middles

. . .with chocolate on the outside! A grandchildren favorite.

1½ cups flour
½ cup cocoa
½ teaspoon baking soda
½ cup brown sugar
½ cup granulated sugar

½ cup margarine, softened
¼ cup peanut butter
1 egg
1 teaspoon vanilla

Combine flour, cocoa, and baking soda, and set aside. Beat together brown and granulated sugars, margarine, peanut butter, egg, and vanilla. Add flour mixture. Form mixture into 40 balls.

FILLING:
1 cup peanut butter   1 cup powdered sugar

Blend peanut butter and powdered sugar and form into 40 balls. Wrap the chocolate mixture balls around the filling mixture balls and place on ungreased baking sheet. Flatten with a glass dipped in granulated sugar. Bake at 375° for 7–9 minutes or until slightly cracked.

In the Kitchen with Kate (Great Plains/Kansas)

★ **Editor's Extra:** I use a large square of wax paper to mix the dry ingredients on—easy to pour (gradually) into butter mixture. Use same wax paper for rolled balls.

Blow Out Cookies

2 cups flour
1 teaspoon baking powder
¼ teaspoon salt
½ cup chunky peanut butter
½ cup soft butter
½ cup brown sugar
½ cup granulated sugar

1 egg
1 teaspoon vanilla
¼ cup milk
¾ cup chocolate chips
¾ cup honey-roasted peanuts
¾ cup coarsely chopped frozen
   miniature peanut butter cups

Combine flour, baking powder, and salt. Beat peanut butter and butter until fluffy. Add both sugars; beat until light. Add egg. Beat 3 minutes. Add vanilla. Stir in dry ingredients, then add milk. Beat thoroughly. Fold in chips, nuts, then peanut butter cups. Drop by 2-tablespoon clumps on ungreased baking sheet. Bake at 375° for 10–12 minutes.

Recipes & Remembrances II (Michigan)

Chocolate Angel Kisses

1 (4-ounce) package sweet baking
  chocolate (semisweet)
1 tablespoon butter
2 eggs
3/4 cup sugar
1/3 cup unsifted all-purpose flour

1/4 teaspoon baking powder
1/8 teaspoon salt
2 cups flaked coconut
1/2 teaspoon cinnamon
1 teaspoon vanilla

Melt chocolate and butter over low heat. Set aside. Beat eggs until foamy and light in color. Add sugar, 2 tablespoons at a time, beating constantly until mixture is thick and light in color (about 5 minutes). Fold in flour, baking powder, and salt. Stir in chocolate, coconut, cinnamon, and vanilla. Drop dough on well-greased and lightly floured baking sheet. Bake 15 minutes at 325°. Remove from oven and let stand a few minutes. Yields 3 dozen.

Cookies and Bars (Michigan)

Butter Dreams
(Snow Balls)

This is an attractive Christmas Cookie.

1 pound butter
1 cup sugar
4 1/2 cups flour
4 teaspoons vanilla

2 regular-size jars maraschino
  cherries, cut in halves and
  drained

Cream butter and sugar; add flour and vanilla. Roll into small balls. Place 1/2 cherry on top and press down. Bake at 350° for 12–15 minutes. Tops will be white and bottoms slightly browned; cool.

ICING:
1/2 pound margarine
Dash of lemon juice
1/2 teaspoon vanilla

1/2 cup evaporated milk
1 box powdered sugar
1 can Angel Flake coconut

Mix all but coconut. Spread Icing around cookie, leaving cherry uncovered. Cover Icing with coconut.

From our Kitchens with Love (Michigan)

★ **Editor's Extra:** You can use 1/2 the Icing recipe and have plenty. This is a delicious cookie, even without the Icing.

★★★★★★★★★★★ ★★★★★★★★★★★

Lemon Pie Cookies

1½ cups flour
½ cup powdered sugar
¾ cup margarine, softened
3 eggs

1½ cups sugar
3 tablespoons flour
3 tablespoons lemon juice
Powdered sugar

Mix first 3 ingredients and pat into 9x13x2-inch pan. Bake at 350° for 20 minutes. Mix remaining ingredients and pour into baked crust. Bake ½ hour longer. Cool and cut into squares. Sprinkle with powdered sugar.

Home Cookin': First Congregational United Church of Christ
(Michigan)

Meringue Raspberry Bars

¾ cup softened butter or margarine
1 cup sugar, divided
2 eggs, separated
1½ cups all-purpose flour

1 tablespoon milk
½ cup flaked coconut
1 (10-ounce) jar raspberry preserves
¾ cup chopped pecans

Cream margarine and ¼ cup sugar until light and fluffy. Beat in egg yolks. Stir in flour and milk. Spread evenly in ungreased 9x13x2-inch pan. Bake at 350° for 15–18 minutes. Remove from oven. Place on rack while preparing meringue.

Beat egg whites in small bowl until foamy. Add ¾ cup sugar gradually until meringue forms stiff peaks. Stir in coconut. Spread preserves on baked layer. Sprinkle with nuts. Dot meringue on raspberry-nut layer. Spread evenly. Bake at 350° for 25 minutes. Cool in pan on rack. Cut into bars. Makes 24 bars.

Home Cookin' is a Family Affair (Illinois)

Chocolate Praline Cookies

$\frac{2}{3}$ cup butter
2 cups brown sugar
2 eggs
1 teaspoon vanilla
$1\frac{1}{2}$ cups flour

$\frac{1}{4}$ teaspoon salt
2 teaspoons baking powder
$\frac{1}{2}$ cup chopped nuts
2 cups chocolate chips

Melt butter and add to brown sugar, eggs, and vanilla. Mix in flour, salt, and baking powder. Add nuts and chocolate chips. Bake in greased 7x11-inch pan for 35 minutes in 350° oven. When cool, cut into bars.

Note: One and one-half this recipe makes a 9x13-inch pan of cookie bars.

Parties & Pleasures (Tennessee)

★ **Editor's Extra:** I baked one-half the recipe in a loaf pan—just right for an after-school snack.

World's Best Cookie Bars

LAYER 1:
1 cup flour
$\frac{1}{2}$ cup butter

$\frac{1}{4}$ cup sugar

Mix with pastry blender and press into 9x13-inch baking pan. Bake at 375° for 10 minutes.

LAYER 2:
1 cup graham cracker crumbs
1 teaspoon baking powder
1 can condensed milk

$\frac{1}{2}$ cup chocolate chips
$\frac{1}{2}$ cup chopped nuts (optional)

Melt together and pour over crust. Bake at 325° for 25 minutes. Cool.

LAYER 3:
$\frac{1}{2}$ cup butter, softened
$1\frac{1}{2}$ cups powdered sugar

1 teaspoon vanilla

Whip, and frost Cookie Bars.

New Beginnings Cookbook (Iowa)

★ ★ ★ ★ ★ ★ ★ ★ ★ ★ ★   ★ ★ ★ ★ ★ ★ ★ ★ ★ ★ ★

Nanaimo Bars

1/2 cup butter, softened
1/4 cup sugar
5 tablespoons cocoa powder
1 teaspoon vanilla

1 egg
1 cup graham cracker crumbs
1 cup flaked coconut
1/2 cup finely chopped nuts

Place butter, sugar, cocoa, vanilla, and egg into top of double boiler. Place over hot water; cook, stirring, until mixture is of custard consistency. Remove from heat and stir in crumbs, coconut, and nuts; blend well. Pack mixture into a buttered 9-inch-square pan.

ICING:
1/2 cup butter
2 tablespoons vanilla pudding mix
  (instant)

3 tablespoons milk
2 cups powdered sugar

Cream butter; blend pudding powder and milk and stir in. Add powdered sugar; mix until smooth and creamy. Spread over cookie base. Refrigerate until firm, about 15 minutes.

TOPPING:
4 squares semisweet chocolate   1 tablespoon butter

Melt chocolate and butter. Spread over Icing layer. Refrigerate until firm; cut in squares.

A Fork in the Road (New Mexico)

★ **Editor's Extra:** I like these without the coconut, too. Just add 1/2 cup more graham cracker crumbs.

Chocolate Mint Bars

CAKE:

½ cup butter, softened
½ cup sugar
4 eggs

1 cup flour, sifted
1 pinch salt
1 can Hershey's Chocolate Syrup

Cream butter and sugar. Add eggs, one at a time. Fold in flour and salt. Stir in chocolate syrup. Bake at 350° for 20–25 minutes in a greased 9x13-inch pan. Cool.

FILLING:

½ cup butter, softened
2 cups powdered sugar

3 tablespoons creme de menthe
   syrup (found in ice cream section)

Cream butter, powdered sugar, and creme de menthe and spread on top of cooled bars.

FROSTING:

1 (6-ounce) package semisweet
   chocolate chips

6 tablespoons butter

Melt chocolate chips and butter. Spread or pour while warm on top of filling.

Cooking with Grace (Wisconsin)

★ **Editor's Extra:** Add green food coloring to Filling, if desired.

★★★★★★★★★★★   ★★★★★★★★★★★

Soda Cracker Bars

Soda crackers may sound like an unlikely ingredient, but once these cookies are baked, no one knows what the crust is. These bars are quick and easy—and unbelievably delicious. You may use unsalted crackers, if you wish.

Saltine crackers
1 cup (2 sticks) butter or margarine, melted

1 cup dark brown sugar
1 (12-ounce) package semisweet chocolate morsels

Line a jellyroll pan (or cookie sheet with sides) with foil. Cover foil with 1 layer of crackers (breaking them as necessary to have sides touching). Mix melted butter and brown sugar in saucepan. Bring to a boil and continue boiling for 3 minutes. Remove from heat and spread mixture over crackers.

Bake 5 minutes in a 400° oven. While cookies are hot, sprinkle chocolate morsels over them. As chips melt, spread chocolate evenly with a spatula. Store in refrigerator or a cool place. Makes 30 bars. Best to cut while still warm.

USO's Salute to the Troops Cookbook (Missouri)

Salted Nut Roll Bars

1 package yellow cake mix
⅓ cup butter

1 egg
3–4 cups miniature marshmallows

Mix together cake mix, butter, and egg. Press into a 9x13-inch pan and bake at 350° for 12–18 minutes. Remove from oven and sprinkle with marshmallows. Return to oven for 1–2 minutes. Cool while preparing Topping.

TOPPING:
⅔ cup corn syrup
¼ cup margarine
1 (12-ounce) package peanut butter chips

2 teaspoons vanilla
2 cups Rice Krispies
2 cups salted peanuts

In pan heat syrup, margarine, chips, and vanilla until melted and smooth. Stir in cereal and nuts. Immediately spoon warm Topping over marshmallows and spread.

Madison County Cookbook (Iowa)

Festive Fudge Filled Bars

2 cups quick oats, uncooked
1½ cups flour
1 cup chopped nuts
1 cup packed brown sugar
1 teaspoon baking soda
1 teaspoon salt

1 cup margarine, melted
2 tablespoons vegetable shortening
1 (1-pound) package plain M&M's,
  divided
1 can condensed milk
½ cup coconut

Mix together first 7 ingredients to resemble coarse crumbs. Reserve 1½ cups; press remaining crumb mixture into bottom of 9x13-inch pan. Bake at 375° for 10 minutes.

Melt vegetable shortening with 1½ cups plain M&M's in heavy pan or microwave, stirring and pressing with spoon to break up chocolate mixture. This mixture will be almost melted and pieces of color coating remain. Remove from heat and stir in condensed milk; mix well. Spread over partially baked crust within ½ inch of edge. Combine reserved crumb mixture and approximately 1 cup M&M's and coconut. Sprinkle on top and press. Continue baking 20–25 minutes.

Appanoose County Cookbook (Iowa)

Polka Daters

1 (8-ounce) package chopped dates
1 cup hot water
1¼ cups sugar
1 cup butter
2 eggs
1¾ cups flour

1½ teaspoons baking soda
1 teaspoon vanilla
1 (6-ounce) package chocolate
  chips, divided
½ cup nuts

Mix dates and hot water. Set aside to cool. Beat sugar, butter, and eggs until smooth. Stir in flour and baking soda. Mix in dates, vanilla, and ½ of chips. Spread in a greased jellyroll pan. Top with remaining chocolate chips and nuts. Bake 30 minutes at 350°.

A Dish to Pass (Minnesota)

Fabulous Pecan Bars

Wherever and whenever you want to serve (or give) about the best cookie ever, do consider this recipe.

CRUST:

½ cup cold butter

¼ cup ice water

1½ cups flour

Use a pastry blender to cut butter into the flour. Mixture should resemble cornmeal. Add water and toss with a fork. Gather dough into a ball. Wrap in plastic wrap and refrigerate for 1 or 2 hours. Butter and flour a 9x13-inch pan. Roll out the dough on floured surface to about 11x15-inch rectangle. Place dough into the prepared pan and let it come up about 1 inch on all sides. Pierce dough with a fork. Chill while making Filling.

FILLING:

1½ cups packed light brown sugar

1 cup butter

½ cup honey

⅓ cup sugar

1 pound pecans, chopped (but not too fine)

¼ cup whipping cream

Preheat oven to 400°. Combine brown sugar, butter, honey, and sugar in a heavy saucepan and bring to a boil over medium heat, stirring constantly. Boil until thick and dark, 3–4 minutes. You must stir constantly. Remove from heat. Stir in pecans and whipping cream. Pour over dough in pan. Bake for 25 minutes. Check after about 15 minutes. If the Filling is browning too much, reduce oven heat to 375° and continue baking. Cool cookies in the pan. Cut into strips. Makes 5 or 6 dozen strips, depending on how large you cut them. Almost better than pecan pie!

Christmas Thyme at Oak Hill Farm (Indiana)

The Cornish-Windsor Bridge, in Cornish, New Hampshire, is the longest wooden covered bridge in the United States and the longest two-span covered bridge in the world. The bridge is 449 feet 5 inches long and has a maximum vertical clearance of 12 feet 9 inches.

Chocolate Marshmallow Bar

3/4 cup margarine
1 1/2 cups sugar
3 eggs
1 teaspoon vanilla
1 1/3 cups flour
1 teaspoon baking powder
1/2 teaspoon salt

3 tablespoons cocoa
1/2 cup chopped nuts
4 cups miniature marshmallows
1 1/3 cups chocolate chips
3 tablespoons margarine
1 cup peanut butter
2 cups Rice Krispies cereal

Cream margarine and sugar. Add eggs and vanilla; beat until fluffy. Combine flour, baking powder, salt, and cocoa; add to creamed mixture. Stir in nuts. Spread in greased jellyroll pan. Bake at 350° for 15–18 minutes. Sprinkle marshmallows evenly over cake. Return to oven 2–3 minutes. Using a knife dipped in water, spread melted marshmallows evenly over cake.

Combine chocolate chips, 3 tablespoons margarine, and peanut butter in small pan (in double boiler for better results); cook over heat, stirring constantly, until melted. Stir in cereal. Mix. Spread over cake and cut into bars.

Old-Fashioned Cooking (Illinois)

Turtle Caramel Brownies

Tastes like chocolate turtle candy. Delicious!

1 (14-ounce) package caramels
2/3 cup evaporated milk, divided
1 (18 1/4-ounce) box German
  chocolate cake mix

3/4 cup butter, melted
1 cup chopped pecans
1 (6-ounce) package chocolate chips

Preheat oven to 350°. Melt caramels and 1/3 cup evaporated milk in a heavy saucepan. Use low heat, stirring often. Keep warm.

In a large bowl, mix remaining ingredients except chocolate chips. Press 1/2 the dough into a lightly greased and floured 9x13-inch pan. Bake for 6 minutes. Sprinkle with chocolate chips. Spread caramel mixture over chips. Spread remaining dough evenly over caramel. Bake 15–20 minutes more. Cool completely before cutting. Yields 3 dozen.

Wild About Texas (Texas II)

Cream Cheese Brownies

1 package German chocolate cake
  mix
1 (8-ounce) package cream cheese,
  softened

1 egg
$^1/_2$ cup sugar
$^1/_2$ cup milk chocolate chips

Heat oven to 350°. Grease and flour jellyroll pan. Prepare cake mix as directed on package. Pour batter into pan. Mix remaining ingredients. Drop by tablespoons onto batter. Cut through batter with knife for marbled effect. Bake until cake tests done in center, 25–35 minutes.

Special Recipes from our Hearts (Iowa)

Almond Fudge Brownies

Easy one-pan mixing—a White Grass favorite!

$^2/_3$ cup margarine
$^3/_4$ cup cocoa powder
2 cups sugar
4 eggs
$^1/_2$ teaspoon almond extract
$^1/_2$ teaspoon vanilla

$1^1/_4$ cups unbleached white or
  all-purpose flour
1 teaspoon baking powder
1 teaspoon salt
1 cup chopped nuts (optional)

Preheat oven to 350°. Grease and flour a 9x13x2-inch baking pan. In medium saucepan, melt margarine, then remove from heat. Add cocoa, sugar, eggs, and extracts, in that order, stirring after each addition. Then add remaining ingredients until just moistened. Spread into pan and bake 20–25 minutes.

    Brownies are done if the center springs back when touched, and edges pull away from pan. It may be difficult to wait, but cool at least 20 minutes before cutting.

White Grass Cafe Cross Country Cooking (West Virginia)

★★★★★★★★★★★★ ★★★★★★★★★★★★

Snow White Chocolate Fudge

The dried apricots are an added surprise and neutralize the sweetness.

2 cups sugar
³/₄ cup sour cream
¹/₂ cup margarine
1 (12-ounce) package white
  chocolate bits

1 (7-ounce) jar marshmallow crème
³/₄ cup chopped walnuts
³/₄ cup chopped dried apricots

Mix together sugar, sour cream, and margarine in heavy saucepan. Bring to a boil and boil 7 minutes, stirring constantly, or until candy thermometer reaches 234°. Remove from heat; stir in white chocolate bits until they are melted. Add other ingredients and beat until well blended. Pour into greased 9-inch pan and cut into squares when cool. Makes 2¹/₂ pounds candy, about 48 (1-inch) squares.

Home at the Range IV (Great Plains/Kansas)

Ooee Gooey Marshmallow Cream Fudge

Just as good as it sounds. Ooee!

1¹/₂ cups sugar
¹/₂ pound (32) marshmallows
1 cup evaporated milk
¹/₄ cup margarine
¹/₈ teaspoon salt

1 (12-ounce) package semisweet
  chocolate morsels
1 teaspoon vanilla
¹/₂ cup chopped nuts

Combine sugar, marshmallows, evaporated milk, margarine, and salt in saucepan. Bring to a full boil, stirring constantly. Remove from heat. Stir in chocolate morsels until melted. Add vanilla and nuts. Pour into greased 8-inch-square pan. Chill until firm. Makes about 2¹/₄ pounds candy.

A Taste of Fayette County (West Virginia)

★★★★★★★★★★★ ★★★★★★★★★★★

Smoothest Divinity

½ cup Karo syrup (red label)
2½ cups sugar
¼ teaspoon salt
½ cup water

2 large egg whites
1 teaspoon vanilla
1 cup chopped nuts

Combine first 4 ingredients in saucepan. Cook over medium heat, stirring constantly, until sugar is dissolved. Cook, without stirring, to firm-ball stage (248°). Be sure to use candy thermometer. Just before syrup reaches 248°, beat egg whites until stiff, not dry. Pour about ½ of the syrup over the egg whites, beating constantly. Cook the remainder of the syrup to soft-crack stage (272°). Add syrup slowly to first mixture, beating constantly. Continue beating until mixture holds shape. Add vanilla and nuts; drop from spoon onto wax paper or tin foil. Makes about 1¾ pounds. Never try to make this on a rainy day or without a candy thermometer.

The Hors D'Oeuvre Tray (Georgia)

Chocolate Meringues

2 egg whites
⅛ teaspoon salt
⅛ teaspoon cream of tartar
1 teaspoon vanilla

¾ cup sugar
1 (6-ounce) package (1 cup)
  semisweet chocolate pieces
¼ cup chopped pecans

Beat egg whites, salt, cream of tartar, and vanilla until soft peaks form. Add sugar gradually, beating until peaks are stiff. Fold in chocolate pieces and nuts. Cover cookie sheet with plain (parchment) paper. Drop mixture on by rounded teaspoons. Bake in slow oven (300°) about 25 minutes. Cool slightly before removing from paper. Makes about 2 dozen cookies.

A Cook's Tour of Shreveport (Louisiana II)

In 1850, two-thirds of America's millionaires were planters on the Great River Road between Natchez, Mississippi, and New Orleans, Louisiana. Many antebellum homes still stand as tribute to this great wealth.

★★★★★★★★★★★★ ★★★★★★★★★★★★

Buttery Almond Roca

Scrumptious.

1 cup butter	1 cup almond halves, toasted
1 cup sugar	8 ounces milk chocolate

Melt butter in a heavy skillet. Add sugar and bring to a boil. Stir constantly after it comes to a boil. Boil for 5 minutes or until caramelized. (If butter separates from sugar, keep stirring until butter blends back in.) Save a few almonds to grind on top; stir in the rest of almonds. Pour into 8x8-inch pan lined with waxed paper. When cool, melt chocolate and spread on top. Sprinkle with ground almonds. Break into bite-size pieces. Keep refrigerated.

Winning Recipes from Minnesota with Love (Minnesota)

Orange Pecan Pralines

Make plenty of these beauties; they go fast!

3 cups sugar	1 teaspoon vanilla
²/₃ cup milk	1 tablespoon butter
¹/₃ cup evaporated milk	1 cup chopped pecans
Grated rind of 1 orange	2 drops yellow food coloring
Dash salt	2 drops red food coloring

Combine sugar, milk, evaporated milk, orange rind, and salt in a large saucepan. Bring to a boil and cook over medium heat, stirring occasionally until soft-ball stage (235°). Remove from heat. Add vanilla, butter, pecans, and food coloring. Beat until mixture has thickened. Drop by spoonfuls onto waxed paper. Yields 3 dozen pralines.

Louisiana LEGACY (Louisiana)

Pies & Other Desserts

★★★★ ★★★★

A hiker's paradise, Fall Creek Falls State Resort Park in Tennessee is a spectacular recreation area where paths lead to caves and creeks and bridges. Gwen's grandson, Corey, gets a little help from his dad, but made it across the swinging bridge, "all by myself."

Rich Chocolate Pie

One of the most requested recipes.

³⁄₄ cup powdered sugar	3 eggs
¹⁄₄ pound butter, softened	1 (9-inch) pie shell, baked
¹⁄₄ pound semisweet chocolate	Whipped cream for garnish
¹⁄₂ teaspoon vanilla	Chocolate shavings for garnish

Cream sugar and butter, blending very well. Melt chocolate in double boiler and beat into mixture. Add vanilla. Add eggs, one at a time, beating well after each addition at high speed. Pour into cooled baked pie shell. Garnish with whipped cream and chocolate shavings. Refrigerate.

Winning Recipes from Minnesota with Love (Minnesota)

Three's Company Chocolate Mousse Pie

CRUST:

1¹⁄₄ cups Oreo cookie crumbs	¹⁄₄ cup butter, melted

Combine Crust ingredients and press into bottom of 10-inch pie plate, quiche dish, or shallow casserole; set aside.

FILLING:

2 (1-ounce) squares unsweetened chocolate	2 cups heavy cream for whipping, divided
1 (7-ounce) jar marshmallow crème	1–2 tablespoons sugar
1 teaspoon vanilla	¹⁄₂ ounce semisweet chocolate for garnish
2 tablespoons cream or milk	

In small bowl, melt chocolate in microwave; or melt in small saucepan on low heat. Remove from heat. In mixing bowl, combine marshmallow crème, vanilla, and melted chocolate. Mix until well blended. Gradually add milk, blending until smooth. Beat 1 cup of cream just till stiff peaks form; fold into chocolate mixture. Spread in Crust.

Whip remaining cream, sweetening slightly with sugar. Gently spread over mousse layer. Grate chocolate evenly over whipped cream topping. Cover and refrigerate at least 2 hours. Refrigerate leftovers. Makes 1 (10-inch) pie.

Enjoy at Your Own Risk! Cookbook (West Virginia)

Black Forest Pie

1 package Pillsbury refrigerated
  pie crusts
3/4 cup sugar
1/3 cup cocoa
2 tablespoons flour
1/4 cup margarine
1/3 cup milk

2 eggs, beaten
1 (21-ounce) can cherry pie filling,
  divided
1 (8-ounce) carton Cool Whip,
  divided
1 (1-ounce) square unsweetened
  chocolate, coarsely grated

Prepare 1 pie crust according to directions for filled pie. Heat oven to 350°. In medium saucepan, combine sugar, cocoa, and flour. Add margarine and milk. Cook until mixture begins to boil, stirring constantly. Remove from heat. Add small amount of hot mix to eggs, then slowly stir egg mix into pan. Fold in 1/2 can pie filling. Reserve the rest of the filling for topping. Pour chocolate mix into pie crust-lined pan. Bake at 350° for 35–45 minutes, or until center is set but still shiny. Cool. Chill 1 hour.

Combine 2 cups of Cool Whip and grated chocolate; spread over chilled pie. Top with remaining pie filling and Cool Whip. Chill at least 1/2 hour before serving.

Thunderbird Cookers of AT&T (Oklahoma)

Turtle Pie

12 caramels, unwrapped
1 (14-ounce) can sweetened
  condensed milk, divided
1 (9-inch) pie shell, baked
2 (1-ounce) squares unsweetened
  chocolate

1/4 cup butter or margarine
2 eggs
2 tablespoons water
1 teaspoon vanilla extract
Dash of salt
1/2 cup chopped pecans

Preheat oven to 325°. In a small heavy saucepan, over low heat, melt caramels with 1/3 cup condensed milk. Spread this mixture evenly on bottom of the prepared pie shell.

In a medium saucepan over low heat, melt chocolate with butter or margarine. In large mixer bowl, beat eggs with remaining condensed milk, water, vanilla, and salt. Add chocolate mixture and mix well. Pour into prepared pie shell; top with pecans. Bake 35 minutes or until center is set. Cool. Chill. May be topped with whipped cream. Refrigerate leftovers.

Asbury Cooks 1799–1999 (New York)

Chocolate Caramel Pecan Pie

CARAMEL SAUCE:

1 teaspoon butter
1 teaspoon flour
⅛ teaspoon salt

⅓ cup whipping cream
¼ cup sugar
¼ cup firmly packed brown sugar

In a glass bowl, melt butter. Stir in flour and salt. Stir in whipping cream. Add sugar and brown sugar. Mix well. Microwave on HIGH until mixture boils; microwave at a boil for 2 minutes longer. Set aside.

FILLING:

⅔ cup sugar
½ teaspoon salt
⅓ cup butter, melted
1 cup light corn syrup
3 eggs

1 cup pecan halves
2 ounces unsweetened chocolate,
  melted
1 (9-inch) pie crust, unbaked

In a large bowl, combine sugar, salt, melted butter, corn syrup, and eggs. Beat well. Stir ½ cup of Filling mixture into Caramel Sauce; blend well. Set aside.

Stir pecans and chocolate into remaining Filling mixture; blend well. Pour into crust-lined pan. Pour Caramel Sauce evenly over Filling. Bake at 375° for 45 minutes or until outer edge of Filling is set and center is partially set. Cool on wire rack. Serve with whipped cream.

Great Recipes from Redeemer's Fellowship (Oregon)

★★★★★★★★★★★★ ★★★★★★★★★★★★★

Peanut Butter Fudge Pie

1 (8-ounce) package cream cheese
1/2 cup peanut butter
1 cup powdered sugar, sifted
2 tablespoons milk
1 teaspoon vanilla
4 ounces frozen whipped topping,
 thawed

1 graham cracker pie shell
3/4 cup fudge ice cream topping,
 divided
Chopped peanuts for garnish

Soften cream cheese; add peanut butter and beat with mixer until combined. Add sugar, milk, and vanilla, and beat until combined. Fold in whipped topping. Spoon half the cream cheese mixture into pie shell, and spread with 1/2 cup fudge topping. Place remaining mixture in crust; cover and freeze at least 6 hours. Let pie stand at room temperature 15 minutes before serving. Drizzle with remaining topping and sprinkle with chopped peanuts.

Washington Cook Book (Washington)

Peanut Buttercup Pie

1/2 cup sugar
1 tablespoon flour
2 tablespoons cocoa
1/4 cup milk
1 egg, beaten
1 1/2 tablespoons butter, softened
1 teaspoon vanilla, divided
1 (8-inch) pie shell, unbaked

4 ounces cream cheese, softened
4 ounces whipped topping
1/6 cup peanut butter (about
 3 teaspoons)
1/2 cup powdered sugar
Miniature chocolate chips or
 grated chocolate for garnish

Combine sugar, flour, cocoa, milk, egg, butter, and 1/2 teaspoon vanilla. Pour into unbaked pie shell. Bake at 350° for about 20 minutes or until set. Cool and chill.

 Combine cream cheese, whipped topping, peanut butter, powdered sugar, and 1/2 teaspoon vanilla and pour over baked chocolate pie. Sprinkle with miniature chocolate chips or grated chocolate. Chill.

The Miller Cookbook (Oregon)

Charlotte's Peanut Butter Pie

1/2 cup crunchy peanut butter
1 cup confectioners' sugar

1 pie shell, baked and cooled

Blend peanut butter and confectioners' sugar. Spread all but 3 tablespoons on bottom of cooled pie shell. Save remainder for topping.

FILLING:

2/3 cup sugar
1/4 cup cornstarch
1/4 teaspoon salt
2 cups milk, scalded

3 egg yolks, beaten (reserve egg whites for Meringue)
2 tablespoons butter
1 teaspoon vanilla

Blend sugar, cornstarch, and salt. Slowly add scalded milk. Place over medium heat. Cook, stirring constantly. Slowly add yolks and butter. Continue stirring until thickened. Set aside and stir in vanilla. Pour over peanut butter mixture.

MERINGUE:

3 egg whites
3 tablespoons sugar

1/8 teaspoon cream of tartar

Beat egg whites, sugar, and cream of tartar until fluffy. Spread over Filling. Dot Meringue with the remaining peanut butter mixture. Place in 300° oven until Meringue is lightly browned. Serve at room temperature or chilled. Makes 6–8 servings.

Betty Talmadge's Lovejoy Plantation Cookbook (Georgia)

 A 20-foot peanut? Yes. In Ashburn, Georgia, in the heart of peanut country, the world's largest replica of a peanut stands 20 feet tall and was erected in February, 1975.

★★★★★★★★★★★ ★★★★★★★★★★★

Honey Crunch Pecan Pie

4 eggs, slightly beaten	1 cup chopped pecans
1 cup light corn syrup	1 (9-inch) pie shell, unbaked
1/4 cup brown sugar	1/3 cup brown sugar
1/4 cup granulated sugar	3 tablespoons butter
2 tablespoons melted butter	3 tablespoons honey
1 teaspoon vanilla	1 1/2 cups pecan halves
1/2 teaspoon salt	

In large bowl, combine eggs and next 6 ingredients. Mix well. Fold in chopped pecans. Pour into unbaked pie shell. Bake at 350° for 50–55 minutes.

On stove over medium heat, cook remaining ingredients, except pecan halves, until sugar dissolves. Stir in pecan halves. Add to top of pie. Bake for 10 minutes more.

Five Loaves and Two Fishes II (Illinois)

Five Layer Pie

This is a favorite.

2 eggs, separated	1 (9-inch) pie shell, baked, cooled
1/2 teaspoon vinegar	1 (6-ounce) package semi-sweet
1/4 teaspoon salt	chocolate chips
1 teaspoon vanilla, divided	1/4 cup water
3/4 cup sugar, divided	1 cup whipping cream

Separate eggs and set yolks aside. Combine egg whites, vinegar, salt, and 1/2 teaspoon vanilla in mixing bowl. Beat until soft peaks form. Gradually add 1/2 cup sugar and beat until stiff peaks form. Spread meringue over bottom and up sides of baked and cooled pie shell. Bake at 325° for 15–20 minutes, or until light brown. Cool. Melt chocolate chips in top of double boiler. Blend in reserved egg yolks and water, stirring until smooth. Spread 4 tablespoons of this mixture over cooled meringue. Chill remaining chocolate mixture until it begins to thicken. In mixing bowl, beat whipping cream until soft peaks form. Add 1/4 cup sugar and the other 1/2 teaspoon vanilla, beating until stiff peaks form. Spread 1/2 of whipped cream over chocolate layer. Fold chilled chocolate mixture into remaining whipped cream. Spread this over whipped cream layer in pie. Refrigerate until ready to serve.

From a Louisiana Kitchen (Louisiana)

My Secret Apple Pie

The secret is out!

1¼ cups sugar
1¼ teaspoons cinnamon
½ teaspoon nutmeg
½ teaspoon salt
⅓ cup cornstarch

2 (9-inch) pie crusts, unbaked
6–7 cups sliced apples
¼ cup orange juice
¼ cup honey or maple syrup

Mix all dry ingredients in 1-gallon plastic bag. Line pan with 1 crust. Add sliced apples to the plastic bag. Shake quickly to coat apples and dump immediately into crust. Mix orange juice and honey. Spread juice mixture over apples and seal on top crust. Sprinkle drops of water on crust and then a little sugar on the wet spots. Cut a few vent holes in top and bake with edge of crust protected. Uncover edge for the final 10–15 minutes of baking. Bake at 425° for 55–60 minutes.

Taste of the Methow (Washington)

★ **Editor's Extra:** Thin strips of tin foil formed around the crust keeps edges from over browning when a pie has to bake for a long time.

Sue's Apple Pie in a Jar

3 cups sugar
1 teaspoon salt
½ teaspoon nutmeg
2 teaspoons cinnamon
1 cup cornstarch

10½ cups water
3 tablespoons lemon juice (optional)
7 quart jars filled with peeled and
    sliced apples

Mix all ingredients except lemon juice and apples. Put in large saucepan on medium heat and cook until bubbling. Remove; add lemon juice, if desired. Stir well. Pour over jars of apples. Process in hot water bath for 25 minutes or 10 minutes in pressure canner at 10 pounds pressure. Store on shelves with other fruit. When unexpected guests arrive for a visit, place in unbaked pie shell and bake at 400° for 40–50 minutes. (Pictured on cover.)

Cookin' with Capital Press (Oregon)

A tisket, a tasket . . . the World's Largest Apple Basket can be found a few miles outside of Dresden, Ohio, at the Longaberger Homestead facility. It stands about 15 feet tall and is a replica of the apple baskets made by J.W. Longaberger for local orchard owners back in the 1930s.

Apple Blackberry Pie

½ cup sugar
3 tablespoons quick-cooking
  tapioca
1 teaspoon grated lemon zest
½ teaspoon cinnamon
4 cups cored, peeled and thinly
  sliced Granny Smith apples

3 cups blackberries
1 (9-inch) pie shell, unbaked
⅓ cup marshmallow crème
2 tablespoons butter or margarine,
  melted
¼ cup packed brown sugar
½ cup rolled oats

Mix sugar, tapioca, lemon zest, cinnamon, apples, and blackberries in a large bowl. Let stand for 15 minutes. Spoon into the pie shell. Mix marshmallow crème, melted butter, brown sugar, and rolled oats in a bowl until crumbly. Sprinkle over the fruit to within 1 inch of the edge. Bake at 375° for 60–70 minutes or until bubbly. Cover with foil after 45 minutes, if the topping is getting too brown. Yields 8 servings.

Cooking from the Coast to the Cascades (Oregon)

Sour Cream Cherry Pie

PIE CRUST:
1½ cups enriched flour (spooned
  into cup)
1 teaspoon grated orange peel
¾ teaspoon salt

½ cup shortening
3–6 tablespoons cold water
2 tablespoons ground toasted
  almonds

Sift together flour, orange peel, and salt. Cut in shortening until pieces are size of small peas. Sprinkle with water, a tablespoon at a time, mixing lightly until dough begins to stick together. Shape into ball. Roll out ⅛ inch thick on lightly floured surface; fit loosely into 9-inch pie pan. Trim and flute edge. Press almonds into bottom.

FILLING:
1 (21-ounce) can cherry pie filling
1 tablespoon lemon juice
1 teaspoon grated orange peel
3 eggs

⅓ cup sugar
1 teaspoon vanilla extract
½ teaspoon almond extract
¾ cup dairy sour cream

In small bowl, stir together cherry pie filling, juice, and peel; spoon over nuts in crust. Beat eggs, sugar, and vanilla and almond extracts until thick and lemon colored, about 10 minutes. Stir in sour cream. Pour cream mixture over cherries. Bake at 350° on lowest rack for 45 minutes, or until crust is brown. Serve chilled.

Cherries Galore (Georgia)

★ **Editor's Extra:** I toast almonds in my toaster oven on "light toast."

★★★★★★★★★★★   ★★★★★★★★★★★

French Coconut Pie

Delicious, easy, pretty.

1/2 cup butter, softened
1 1/2 cups sugar
3 eggs, slightly beaten
1 tablespoon vinegar
1 teaspoon coconut extract

1 teaspoon vanilla extract
Pinch of salt
1 (6-ounce) package frozen
   coconut
1 (9-inch) pie shell, unbaked

Cream butter and sugar. Add eggs and beat slightly. Add vinegar, extracts, and salt. Mix well. Add frozen coconut and mix. Pour into pie shell. Bake at 325° for 40–50 minutes. Serves 6–8.

Temptations (Mississippi)

Bal'More Rhubarb Pie

It's best to make this fresh when rhubarb is in season, but this authentic recipe will work as well with frozen rhubarb.

1 pastry shell, with extra pastry for
   top
4 tablespoons flour
1 cup sugar (less, if using
   strawberries)

1 egg, beaten
3–4 cups rhubarb, cut up, or
   combination of rhubarb and
   strawberries (fresh or frozen)

Preheat oven to 425°. Thaw pastry shell, if frozen.

Combine flour and sugar. Add egg and mix well. Add rhubarb and strawberries (if using). Pour batter into pastry shell and cover with second shell constructed in a lattice design. Bake at 425° for first 10 minutes. Lower temperature to 350° and continue baking for 35 minutes.

Simple Pleasures (Mid-Atlantic/Maryland)

Incredible Peach Pie

2 eggs
$^1/_2$ cup self-rising flour
$^1/_2$ cup milk
$^1/_2$ cup light corn syrup
$^1/_4$ cup butter, melted
$^1/_4$ cup sugar

1 teaspoon vanilla
2$^1/_2$ cups chopped peaches
1 cup shredded coconut
Nutmeg or cinnamon
$^1/_2$ cup chopped pecans

In large bowl, beat eggs. Add next 6 ingredients; mix until smooth. Stir in peaches and coconut. Pour into a greased and floured 10-inch, deep-dish pie plate. Sprinkle generously with nutmeg or cinnamon. Top with pecans. Bake at 350° for 40–50 minutes, or until custard is set. Let stand for awhile before cutting. This pie makes its own crust and needs to set awhile to make the crust firm.

Head Table Cooks (Georgia)

★ **Editor's Extra:** It works well with a 29-ounce can of peaches, drained, because this is good when peaches are out of season, too! Also good without the coconut.

Peach Praline Pie

Prepare one unbaked pie shell. Heat oven to 350°.

FILLING:
4 cups canned (drained) sliced
  peaches
$^1/_2$ cup sugar

2 tablespoons tapioca
1 teaspoon lemon juice

Mix and let set while you make the Topping.

TOPPING:
$^1/_4$ cup butter
$^1/_2$ cup flour

$^1/_4$ cup brown sugar
$^1/_2$ cup chopped pecans

Mix with hands until crumbly. Put $^1/_4$ of this on the bottom of an unbaked pie shell. Put peach mixture on top. Put the rest of the Topping on top of the peach mixture. Bake at 350° for about 50 minutes.

Braham's Pie Cookbook (Minnesota)

★★★★★★★★★★★★   ★★★★★★★★★★★★

Peaches and Cream Cheesecake Pie

¾ cup flour
1 (3-ounce) package regular
  vanilla pudding mix
1 teaspoon baking powder
⅛ teaspoon salt
1 egg, beaten
½ cup milk
3 tablespoons butter, softened

1 (29-ounce) can sliced peaches;
  reserve juice
1 (8-ounce) package cream cheese,
  softened
½ cup plus 1 tablespoon
  granulated sugar, divided
½ teaspoon cinnamon

Combine flour, pudding mix, baking powder, salt, egg, milk, and butter in large mixing bowl. Beat at high speed for 2 minutes. Pour into greased 10-inch, deep-dish pie plate.

Drain peaches well, reserving the liquid. Arrange peach slices decoratively atop the batter. Combine cream cheese, ½ cup sugar, and 3 tablespoons reserved peach juice in medium bowl. Beat with electric mixer at medium speed 2–3 minutes or until smooth. Carefully spread atop peaches to within 1 inch of edge of pie plate. Stir in 1 tablespoon sugar with ½ teaspoon ground cinnamon; sprinkle over cream cheese mixture. Bake in preheated 350° oven for 35–40 minutes, or until bottom and sides are golden brown. Cool. Serve warm or chilled. Makes 8–10 servings.

Generations of Good Cooking (Iowa)

Cheesecake Pie

Easy and delicious!

1 (8-ounce) package cream cheese,
  softened
¾ cup sugar
1 cup sour cream
2 teaspoons vanilla
1 (8-ounce) carton of Cool Whip

1 (9-inch) graham cracker pie crust
1 small box frozen sweet
  strawberries, thawed, or 1 can
  blueberry pie filling, or 1 can
  cherry pie filling

Beat cream cheese until smooth; gradually beat in sugar. Blend in sour cream and vanilla. Fold in Cool Whip, blending well. Spoon into crust (the crust may be bought—makes it even easier). Chill at least 4 hours. Garnish with strawberries or other topping. Yields 6–8 servings.

Betty is Still "Winking" at Cooking (Arkansas)

Lemon Chess Pie

1½ cups sugar
1 tablespoon flour
2 tablespoons cornmeal
4 eggs
½ cup butter, melted

4 teaspoons grated lemon rind
¼ cup milk
¼ cup lemon juice
1 (9-inch) pie shell, unbaked

Combine sugar, flour, cornmeal and eggs. Blend thoroughly. Add butter, lemon rind, milk, and lemon juice. Mix well. Pour into unbaked 9-inch pie shell. Bake in 425° oven for 10 minutes. Reduce heat to 325° and bake 40–45 minutes longer.

What's Cooking in Kentucky (Kentucky)

Lemon Cream Pie with Apricot Sauce

PIE:

1 envelope unflavored gelatin
⅔ cup sugar, divided
¼ teaspoon salt
2 eggs, separated
6 tablespoons cold water

6 tablespoons lemon juice
2 teaspoons grated lemon peel
1 cup heavy cream, whipped
1 (9-inch) graham cracker crust or
    baked pastry crust

Combine gelatin, ⅓ cup sugar, and salt in saucepan. Beat egg yolks; beat in water and lemon juice; add to gelatin mixture. Mix well. Cook over low heat, stirring constantly until gelatin dissolves and mixture thickens slightly. Remove from heat; add lemon peel. Chill, stirring occasionally, until mixture mounds slightly when dropped from a spoon. Beat egg whites until stiff. Gradually add remaining ⅓ cup sugar and beat until very stiff. Fold into gelatin mixture. Fold in cream. Pour into 9-inch crust. Chill until firm.

SAUCE:

1 (16-ounce) can apricot halves

Drain apricots, reserving ¼ cup syrup. Purée apricots and reserved syrup. Chill. Serve over pie. Garnish with mint leaves. May also be served without the crust as a pudding. Yields 6–8 servings.

The Albany Collection: Treasures & Treasured (New York)

Divine Lime Pie

MERINGUE SHELL:

4 egg whites (reserve yolks)   **1 cup sugar**
¼ teaspoon cream of tartar

Preheat oven to 275°. Generously butter a 9-inch pie plate. In a small mixing bowl, beat egg whites and cream of tartar until foamy. Beat in sugar very slowly, 1 tablespoon at a time, until stiff and glossy, about 10 minutes. Pile into pie pan, pushing up around the sides. Bake for 1 hour. Turn off oven, leaving pie in the oven with the door closed for 1 hour. Remove from oven and let cool.

FILLING:

4 egg yolks   **1 cup chilled whipping cream**
¼ teaspoon salt   **1 tablespoon grated fresh lime peel**
½ cup sugar   **Whipped cream and lime peel for**
⅓ cup fresh lime juice (2–3 limes)   **garnish**

Beat egg yolks until light and lemon colored. Stir in salt, sugar, and lime juice. Cook over medium heat, stirring constantly, until mixture thickens, about 5 minutes. Cool completely. In a chilled bowl, beat cream until stiff. Fold in Filling mixture and grated peel. Pile into Meringue Shell and chill at least 4 hours. Garnish with whipped cream and lime peel twists. Serves 8.

The Star of Texas Cookbook (Texas II)

★★★★★★★★★★★★ ★★★★★★★★★★★★

Oregon Strawberry Pie

1 cup whipping cream
1 (8-ounce) package cream cheese, softened
1½ cups sugar, divided
1 teaspoon vanilla extract
1 (10-inch) pie shell, baked, room temperature

3 tablespoons cornstarch
½ cup water
1 cup mashed fresh strawberries
4 cups whole strawberries

In a small mixing bowl, whip cream; set aside. In a medium bowl, beat cream cheese, ½ cup sugar, and vanilla. Fold in whipped cream and beat lightly by hand. Spoon into baked pie shell.

In medium saucepan, combine remaining 1 cup sugar and cornstarch. Add water and mashed berries. Over high heat, bring to a boil, stirring constantly until mixture begins to thicken (about 1 minute). Let cool.

Arrange whole berries on top of cheese mixture, then spoon on berry topping. Refrigerate 3–4 hours. Garnish with additional strawberries. Serves 8.

Rainy Day Treats and Sunny Temptations (Oregon)

Frozen Strawberry Margarita Pie

GRAHAM CRACKER CRUST:
1½ cups graham cracker crumbs
¼ cup sugar

¼ cup (½ stick) butter, melted

Combine crumbs, sugar, and butter in a small bowl; press into bottom and sides of a 9-inch pie plate.

1 (14-ounce) can sweetened condensed milk
¼ cup freshly squeezed lime juice
3 tablespoons tequila

3 tablespoons Triple Sec
½ cup frozen strawberries with syrup, thawed
2 cups heavy cream, whipped

Beat condensed milk, lime juice, tequila, and Triple Sec in a large bowl with electric mixer at medium speed for 3 minutes until smooth. Lower speed; beat in strawberries with syrup for 1 minute. Fold whipped cream into strawberry mixture until no streaks of white remain. Pour into prepared Graham Cracker Crust, mounding in center. Freeze overnight.

Transfer to refrigerator 30 minutes before serving. Garnish with additional whipped cream (around edge), strawberries, and lime slices, if desired. Makes 8 servings.

Carol's Kitchen (Illinois)

Banana Cream Pie

3 tablespoons cornstarch
1¾ cups water
1 (14-ounce) can sweetened
  condensed milk
3 egg yolks, beaten
2 tablespoons margarine or butter

1 teaspoon vanilla
3 medium bananas, sliced and
  dipped in lemon juice and drained,
  divided
1 (9-inch) pastry shell, baked
1 small container whipped cream

In heavy saucepan, dissolve cornstarch in water; stir in sweetened condensed milk and egg yolks. Cook and stir until thickened and bubbly. Remove from heat; add margarine and vanilla. Cool slightly.

Arrange ⅔ banana slices on bottom of prepared pastry shell. Pour filling over bananas; cover. Chill 4 hours or until set. Spread top with whipped cream; garnish with remaining banana slices. Refrigerate leftovers.

Raider Recipes (Texas II)

Dreamy High Pumpkin Pie

Heavenly.

1 tablespoon gelatin
¼ cup cold water
3 eggs, separated
1 cup sugar, divided
1½ cups canned pumpkin
⅓ cup milk

½ teaspoon salt
½ teaspoon pumpkin pie spice
1½ cups heavy cream, divided
1 (10-inch) pie shell, baked
¾ cup moist shredded coconut,
  toasted

Soften gelatin in cold water. Beat egg yolks until thick and lemon colored; add ½ cup sugar and mix. Add pumpkin, milk, salt, and spice. Cook in double boiler until thick, stirring constantly (about 10 minutes). Add gelatin and stir until thoroughly dissolved; cool.

Beat egg whites stiff; add remaining ½ cup sugar. Gradually beat until stiff peaks will stand up; fold into cooled pumpkin mixture. Beat ½ cup cream stiff; fold into mixture. Spoon lightly into baked pie shell. Chill several hours or overnight.

When ready to serve, spread remaining 1 cup of cream, whipped, on top of pie. Sprinkle toasted coconut on top to decorate. Serves 6–8.

Feast in Fellowship (Oklahoma)

★★★★★★★★★★★ ★★★★★★★★★★★

Favorite Apple Betty

Call it Apple Betty, Brown Betty or Blue Betty, it is absolutely the best Betty!

**4 cups peeled and sliced
  cooking apples**
1/3 cup sugar

1 teaspoon cinnamon
3/4 cup hot water

Combine apples, sugar, cinnamon, and water in saucepan. Simmer 10 minutes or until tender. Pour into ungreased 9-inch pie pan. Sprinkle the Topping over the apples.

TOPPING:
1/2 cup brown sugar
1/4 cup shortening
2 tablespoons butter or margarine

1 cup flour
1 teaspoon baking powder
1/4 teaspoon salt

Blend brown sugar, shortening, and butter. Add remaining ingredients and mix well. Mixture will be crumbly. Sprinkle over apples. Bake at 350° for 25–30 minutes. Serve warm or cold. Yields 6 servings.

From the Apple Orchard (Missouri)

Blackberry Roll

We in Oregon are blessed with abundant blackberries and I am always looking for ways to utilize them. This is a great recipe.

2 cups flour
4 teaspoons baking powder
1/2 teaspoon salt
1/4 cup cold butter or margarine
1 cup grated sharp Cheddar cheese
3/4 cup milk

2 1/2 cups fresh blackberries
**1/2 cup plus 2 tablespoons sugar,
  divided**
1/4 cup brown sugar
1/2 teaspoon grated nutmeg

Preheat oven to 350°. In a mixing bowl, combine flour, baking powder, salt, and butter. Work until butter is fine crumbs. Blend in cheese and milk; do not overmix. Roll dough out lightly into a 10x12-inch rectangle, about 1/3 inch thick. Sprinkle blackberries on top, then add 1/2 cup white sugar, the brown sugar, and nutmeg.

Starting from the long edge, roll up dough like a jellyroll and transfer to a greased baking sheet, placing it seam-side-down. Pinch edges together and fold under. Pat roll into a tidy bundle and sprinkle remaining 2 tablespoons white sugar on top. Bake for 45 minutes, or until the roll is golden brown. Slice and serve warm in bowls with cream. Serves 10.

Then 'til Now (Oregon)

Old-Fashioned Berry Cobbler

This recipe is unbeatable and so attractive.

FRUIT:

4 cups frozen raspberries,
  blackberries, or loganberries
¹/₂ cup seedless raspberry jam

2 tablespoons quick-cooking tapioca
2 tablespoons sugar
2 tablespoons butter

Heat oven to 425°. Grease 10x6-inch baking dish or 1¹/₂-quart casserole. In large bowl, combine berries, jam, tapioca, and sugar; mix gently. Spread in greased dish. Dot with butter. Bake at 425° for 15–20 minutes, or until berries begin to bubble; stir.

TOPPING:

1 cup flour
2 tablespoons sugar
2 teaspoons baking powder
¹/₄ teaspoon salt

¹/₄ cup butter
2–4 tablespoons milk
1 egg
¹/₂ teaspoon sugar

Lightly spoon flour into measuring cup; level off. In large bowl, combine flour, 2 tablespoons sugar, baking powder, and salt; mix well. With pastry blender or fork, cut in butter until crumbly. In small bowl, beat 2 tablespoons milk and egg until blended, adding to flour mixture with additional milk, if necessary, to form stiff dough. On lightly floured surface, roll out dough to ¹/₂-inch thickness. With 2-inch cookie cutter, cut out hearts, stars, circles, or diamonds. Place on top of hot fruit mixture; sprinkle with ¹/₂ teaspoon sugar. Bake at 425° for 15–25 minutes, or until fruit bubbles around edges and biscuits are light golden brown. Serve warm with cream or ice cream.

Bounteous Blessings (Washington)

 Texas leads the nation in functioning farms with approximately 194,000 in operation. Missouri is second with approximately 98,000 farms.

Old Fashioned Peach Cobbler

This is the very popular peach cobbler in our Tea Room. It's an incredible crowd pleaser—enjoy!

FRUIT MIXTURE:
6 tablespoons tapioca
6 or 7 cups sliced fresh peaches
1 cup sugar

¼ teaspoon cinnamon
¼ teaspoon nutmeg

COBBLER DOUGH:
½ cup butter, softened
1 cup sugar
2 cups flour

1½ cups milk
2 teaspoons baking powder
1 teaspoon salt

COBBLER TOPPING:
1½ cups sugar
2 tablespoons cornstarch
Cinnamon

Nutmeg
½ cup boiling water

Preheat oven to 375°. In a mixing bowl, combine all ingredients to make Fruit Mixture. Mix thoroughly. Pour the Fruit Mixture into a buttered 9x13-inch baking dish.

In a bowl, mix thoroughly all ingredients for Cobbler Dough. Spread over Fruit Mixture.

In a medium mixing bowl, stir together dry Cobbler Topping ingredients. Sprinkle evenly over the Cobbler Dough layer. Pour boiling water evenly over the cobbler. Bake for 1 hour and 20 minutes, or until inserted knife comes out clean and the top has a golden crust. Serves 15.

The Peach Tree Family Cookbook (Texas II)

Best-Ever Layer Dessert

¹/₂ cup butter, melted
1 box Famous Chocolate Wafers, crushed
1 (8-ounce) package cream cheese, softened
¹/₃ cup peanut butter
1 cup powdered sugar
1 (12-ounce) carton frozen whipped topping, thawed and divided

1 (3-ounce) package vanilla instant pudding
1 (4¹/₂-ounce) package chocolate instant pudding
2³/₄ cups milk
1 (1.2-ounce) milk chocolate candy bar, shaved

Melt butter and crush wafers. Mix together thoroughly and press into 9x13-inch casserole. Bake for 10 minutes at 350°. Cool crust completely.

Combine cream cheese, peanut butter, and powdered sugar. Beat until fluffy. Stir 1 cup whipped topping into cream cheese mixture. Spread over crust. Chill.

Combine pudding mixes and milk. Beat 2 minutes at medium speed of electric mixer. Spread pudding over cream cheese layer. Spread remaining whipped topping over pudding layer. Sprinkle top with shaved chocolate. Store in refrigerator. Yields about 15 servings.

Bountiful Harvest Cookbook (Pennsylvania)

Chocolate Divine Dessert

Paradise found!

¹/₂ cup slivered almonds
12 ounces semisweet chocolate chips
3 tablespoons sugar
3 large egg yolks, beaten

3 large egg whites, stiffly beaten
2 cups heavy cream, whipped
1 teaspoon pure vanilla extract
1 (8-ounce) angel food cake

Place almonds on ungreased cookie sheet and bake at 350° until light golden brown (a few minutes). Watch carefully so almonds do not burn! Cool and set aside.

In top of double boiler over hot water, melt chocolate chips with sugar. Cool. Mix in beaten egg yolks. Gradually fold in stiffly beaten egg whites. Fold in whipped cream and vanilla.

Tear up angel food cake into ¹/₂-inch pieces. Put half of the cake pieces on bottom of buttered 10-inch springform pan. Cover with half of chocolate mixture. Layer remaining cake and chocolate. Refrigerate at least 24 hours. Remove springform rim. Top with toasted almonds. May be made up to 3 days in advance. Makes 10–12 servings.

Crème de Colorado (Colorado)

★★★★★★★★★★★ ★★★★★★★★★★★

Chocolate Decadence

We do not think there is a dessert on this earth that can top this one for pure unadulterated enjoyment.

CRUST:

½ stick butter

⅓ cup sugar

1 tablespoon flour

1 cup finely chopped pecans

Preheat oven to 325°. Combine ingredients and press into sides and bottom of a 9-inch pie plate.

FILLING:

1 stick butter, softened

1 cup sugar

2 ounces unsweetened chocolate, melted and cooled

⅛ teaspoon salt

¼ cup flour

2 eggs, beaten

1 teaspoon vanilla

Cream butter and sugar; add remaining ingredients. Mix well and pour into Crust. Bake 35–40 minutes, or until Filling is set. Do not overbake!

ICE CREAM TOPPING:

1 cup Kahlúa or to taste

1 quart vanilla ice cream, softened

Stir Kahlúa into ice cream; put in plastic container and freeze.

To serve, pie should be warm or room temperature. Stir ice cream well and spoon over each slice of pie. Serves 6–8 marvelously!

Southern Flavors' Little Chocolate Book (Arkansas)

★ **Editor's Extra**: I use half as much Kahlúa and it is yum-mee!

Chocolate Yummy

A dessert men love.

CRUST:

1 cup flour

1 stick margarine, melted

1 cup finely chopped pecans

Mix all ingredients well. Spread Crust in a 9½ x 13½-inch baking dish. Bake at 350° for 20 minutes. Cool.

FILLING:

4 cups Cool Whip, divided

1 cup confectioners' sugar

1 (8-ounce) package cream cheese, softened

1 (3-ounce) package each: chocolate and vanilla instant pudding

3 cups milk

1 Hershey's bar, frozen, grated

Mix 1 cup Cool Whip, confectioners' sugar, and cream cheese. Spread over cooled Crust. Mix puddings with milk. Let set for a few minutes to thicken. Pour over cream cheese layer and top with remaining Cool Whip. Sprinkle with grated Hershey's bar. Serves 10.

Pirate's Pantry (Louisiana)

★ **Editor's Extra:** Approximately 3 cups of whipped topping can be measured per 8-ounce tub. The 8-ounce designation is a measurement of the weight of the full tub, not the volume in the tub. If a recipe calls for 2 cups whipped topping, we suggest using a measuring cup for that amount.

Chocolate Cloud

3 egg whites
2 teaspoons vanilla, divided
1 teaspoon baking powder
³/₄ cup sugar
1 (4-ounce) package German sweet
  chocolate, grated

1 cup Ritz cracker crumbs
¹/₂ cup chopped pecans
1 cup whipping cream
2 tablespoons sugar

Beat egg whites and 1 teaspoon vanilla to soft peaks. Combine baking powder and ³/₄ cup sugar and gradually add to whites, beating until stiff peaks form. Reserve 2 tablespoons chocolate and add remaining chocolate with crackers and pecans to egg white mixture. Spread in a greased 9-inch pie plate. Bake at 350° for 25 minutes. Cool thoroughly.

Whip cream with 2 tablespoons sugar and 1 teaspoon vanilla and spread on top of pie. Garnish with reserved chocolate. Refrigerate at least 8 hours. Serves 8.

Lone Star Legacy (Texas II)

★ **Editor's Extra:** To save a step, chop chocolate with steel blade in food processor, then crumb Ritz crackers in same bowl.

Strawberries Over Snow

1 large angel food cake
1 (8-ounce) package cream cheese,
  softened

³/₄ cup milk
1 (8-ounce) carton frozen whipped
  topping, thawed

Trim crust from cake. Tear into chunks and place in 9x13x2-inch baking dish. Combine cream cheese and milk, blending until smooth; fold in whipped topping. Spread mixture over cake chunks. Chill. Prepare Glaze.

GLAZE:
1 cup water
1 teaspoon lemon juice
1 cup sugar

2 tablespoons cornstarch
12 drops red food coloring
2 pints strawberries, cut in halves

Combine water, lemon juice, sugar, and cornstarch in saucepan. Bring to a boil; cook until thickened. Remove from heat. Add food coloring and mix well. Fold strawberries into Glaze. Let stand until cool. Pour Glaze over cake. Chill thoroughly. Serves 8–10.

Cane River's Louisiana Living (Louisiana II)

Strawberry Trifle

CUSTARD SAUCE:

1½ tablespoons cornstarch
2¼ cups milk, divided
¼ cup sugar

1 teaspoon vanilla
3 egg yolks, beaten

Mix cornstarch with ½ cup milk. In heavy saucepan or double boiler, heat 1¾ cups milk with sugar just to boiling. Remove from heat. Stir in cornstarch mixture until smooth. Cook, stirring constantly, until thickened. Simmer 3 minutes. Remove from heat and stir in vanilla extract. Add small amount of custard to egg yolks, then stir into mixture. Cover and chill.

TRIFLE:

1 (10-ounce) angel loaf cake
⅓ cup strawberry jam or jelly
⅓ cup orange juice
3 cups strawberries
Custard Sauce

¾ cup whipping cream
2 tablespoons powdered sugar
1 teaspoon vanilla extract
2 tablespoons sliced almonds
  (toasting optional)

Split cake into 3 layers. Spread jam in between layers and reassemble the layers. Cut into 2-inch cubes. Arrange cubes in 2-quart bowl. Sprinkle with orange juice. Wash strawberries. Pick 8–12 berries for garnish. Remove hulls from the remaining strawberries; slice and spoon over cake. Pour chilled custard over berries. Cover and refrigerate for 1 hour or more. Meanwhile, whip cream to soft peaks. Add sugar and vanilla and whip until stiff. Spread cream over the custard. Garnish with whole strawberries and sprinkle with almonds. Chill; serve within a few hours.

Kids in the Kitchen (Arizona)

★ **Editor's Extra:** Substitute sherry for orange juice for a truly authentic trifle flavor.

Fantastic Trifle

This is spectacular, can be made ahead, and serves a crowd.

1 (16-ounce) angel food cake
²⁄₃ cup sugar
3 tablespoons cocoa
1 tablespoon cornstarch
²⁄₃ cup evaporated skimmed milk
¹⁄₄ cup coffee liqueur
3 (1³⁄₁₆-ounce) English toffee
  candy bars, crushed

3 (4-serving) packages instant
  vanilla pudding
3 cups skim milk
2 bananas, peeled and sliced
1 (12-ounce) container frozen light
  whipped topping, thawed

Cube cake and put in bowl. To make chocolate sauce, combine sugar, cocoa, cornstarch, and evaporated milk. Cook over low heat until it thickens. Remove from heat; add coffee liqueur. Cool. Pour chocolate mixture over cake in bowl. Add crushed candy to angel food cake mixture. In mixer, beat pudding and skim milk until thick. Pour over angel food cake mixture. Refrigerate 15 minutes. In trifle dish, layer cake mixture, bananas, and whipped topping. Repeat layers, ending with whipped topping. Yields 16 servings.

Cal 261; Chol 5 mg; Fat 3.8g; Cal from Fat 13.2%.

A Trim & Terrific Louisiana Kitchen (Louisiana II)

Pull Me Up
(Terra-Me-SU)

24 ladyfingers in halves
1½ teaspoons orange extract,
  divided
3 tablespoons finely ground coffee
  beans
2 tablespoons water
1 cup very strong coffee
1 (16-ounce) container mascarpone
  cheese

½ cup plus 2 tablespoons
  confectioners' sugar, divided
½ teaspoon salt
3 ounces dark chocolate, grated,
  divided
1½ cups whipping cream,
  whipped, divided

Place 6 ladyfinger halves in a flat casserole dish. In a small bowl, stir ½ teaspoon orange extract with coffee beans, water, and strong coffee. Brush onto ladyfinger halves. In a separate bowl, place mascarpone, ½ cup confectioners' sugar, salt, 1 teaspoon orange extract, and 2 ounces chocolate and mix well. Fold ⅔ of the whipped cream into mixture. Spoon ⅓ cheese mixture over ladyfingers. Add a layer of ladyfingers, brush with coffee mixture, and spoon ⅓ cheese mixture. Repeat. Top with last 6 halves. Brush with coffee mixture.

Mix remaining whipped cream and 2 tablespoons confectioners' sugar together. Spread on top layer. Sprinkle remaining chocolate on whipped cream. Refrigerate 2 hours before serving.

My Italian Heritage (New York)

Ladyfingers

8 egg yolks
½ pound sugar
8 egg whites

2 cups sifted flour
Powdered sugar

Beat egg yolks and sugar till light and foamy. Beat egg whites until stiff, then add to yolk mixture. Add sifted flour, and stir until smooth. Pour batter into floured finger molds or on waxed paper pressed into finger forms. Bake on cookie sheet in slow (300°) oven for 45 minutes to 1 hour. Dust with powdered sugar. Makes 24.

Cherished Czech Recipes (Iowa)

★ **Editor's Extra:** Easy to make these in muffin tins. Superb! And they freeze well, too.

Luscious Lady

A family tradition to prepare on Christmas Eve, but out of this world any day of the year.

3½ dozen ladyfingers, split
4 squares unsweetened chocolate
¾ cup sugar
⅓ cup milk
6 eggs, separated
1½ cups unsalted butter, softened
1½ cups confectioners' sugar,
  divided
⅛ teaspoon salt
1½ teaspoons vanilla
1 cup maraschino cherries, halved
Garnish: whipped cream, nuts,
  cherries, shaved chocolate

Line a deep 9-inch springform pan with about ⅔ of the ladyfingers (bottom and sides). Chill overnight.

Melt chocolate. Combine sugar, milk, and egg yolks. Add to chocolate and cook until smooth and thickened, stirring constantly. Cool to room temperature.

Cream butter well. Add ¾ cup confectioners' sugar and cream thoroughly. Add chocolate mixture and mix well. Beat egg whites with salt until stiff and gradually beat in remaining ¾ cup confectioners' sugar. Fold in chocolate mixture. Add vanilla and cherries.

Spoon mixture into pan, alternating layers with remaining ladyfingers. Garnish with whipped cream, nuts, cherries, and shaved chocolate. Serves 16.

Still Gathering (Illinois)

★★★★★★★★★★★ ★★★★★★★★★★★

Chocolate Mousse

When you want a dessert that is just a little bit of something . . . this one is extra easy and has the taste of mousses that take hours.

1 (16-ounce) package of chocolate
  chips
2 tablespoons granulated sugar
1 teaspoon vanilla
1 egg

Pinch of salt
¾ cup milk
Whipped cream or whipped
  topping

Put chocolate chips, sugar, vanilla, egg, and a pinch of salt in container of blender. Heat milk just to boiling; pour into container. Blend for 1 minute or until thoroughly blended. Pour into 6 demitasse cups. Chill and serve topped with whipped cream or topping. Makes 6 servings.

What Is It? What Do I Do With It? (North Carolina)

A moose with a sweet tooth—the world's only life-size chocolate moose, "Lenny," draws the tourists to Len Libby Candies in Scarbrough, Maine. He is eight feet tall and over nine feet from nose to tail. But what makes him truly unique is that he is made of 1,700 pounds of milk chocolate!

German Chocolate Pudding

1 (4-ounce) bar German
  sweet chocolate
$\frac{1}{4}$ pound butter
3 eggs, separated

1 cup powdered sugar, divided
1 teaspoon vanilla
1 pint whipping cream, whipped
1 (10-ounce) box vanilla wafers

Melt chocolate and butter together. Add chocolate mixture to beaten egg yolks, then add $\frac{2}{3}$ cup powdered sugar and vanilla. Chill, then fold in whipped cream. Beat egg whites until they begin to stand in peaks. Add remaining $\frac{1}{3}$ cup sugar into egg whites and fold into chocolate mixture.

Grind vanilla wafers and pour $\frac{1}{3}$ into a buttered 9x9-inch deep dish with $\frac{1}{2}$ of chocolate mixture over crumbs, then add another layer of crumbs; repeat chocolate and place remainder of crumbs on top. Refrigerate 24 hours.

Court Clerk's Bar and Grill (Oklahoma)

Banana Pudding

This is a rich and delicious dessert! It is loved by anyone who has tried it.

1½ cups water
1 box (small) instant French vanilla
  pudding
1 box (small) instant regular vanilla
  pudding
1 can condensed milk
½ teaspoon banana flavoring
  (optional)

1 (16-ounce) container Cool Whip,
  thawed
1 box vanilla wafers, crumbled or
  broken
4 bananas, sliced
4 tablespoons graham cracker
  crumbs

Combine first 3 ingredients with mixer. Add milk and flavoring, if desired. Stir in Cool Whip. Layer in serving dish in following order: crushed or broken wafers, bananas, pudding—repeat. Top with additional crumbs (vanilla wafer or graham cracker).

Campbellsville College Women's Club Cookbook (Kentucky)

Bananas Foster Bread Pudding

1 (12-ounce) loaf stale French
  bread, broken in small pieces, or
  9–11 cups any type stale bread
1 cup milk
4 cups half-and-half

2½ cups sugar
8 tablespoons butter, melted
4 eggs
2 tablespoons vanilla
3 bananas, sliced

Combine all ingredients; mixture should be very moist, but not soupy. Pour into buttered 9x13-inch baking dish. Place on middle rack of cold oven. Bake in a 350° oven for approximately 1 hour and 15 minutes, until top is golden brown. Serve warm with Bananas Foster Sauce.

BANANAS FOSTER SAUCE:
½ cup butter
2 cups dark brown sugar
4 ounces dark rum

2 ounces banana liqueur
2 bananas, cut in small pieces

Melt butter and add brown sugar to form a creamy paste. Stir in liqueurs until smooth sauce is formed. Add bananas and simmer for 2 minutes. Serve warm over warm Bread Pudding.

Cooking New Orleans Style! (Louisiana II)

Vanilla Bread Pudding with Butter Rum Sauce

6 eggs
2 cups milk
½ pound or 1⅛ cups sugar
2 teaspoons ground cinnamon
½ cup raisins

2 teaspoons vanilla extract
1 loaf French bread, (approximately)
½ cup chopped walnuts
½ cup brown sugar

In a large bowl, mix together the eggs, milk, sugar, cinnamon, raisins, and vanilla. Cut up enough French bread in small cubes to absorb the mixture. Pour mixture into a greased deep baking pan and top with walnuts and brown sugar. Bake in oven for 45 minutes at 350°.

BUTTER RUM SAUCE:
½ cup butter, melted
¾ cup powdered sugar

¼ cup Myer's rum

Combine all ingredients and cook over medium heat for 15 minutes. To serve, cut bread pudding into squares and serve warm topped with heated rum sauce.

A recipe from Muriel's Restaurant, Newport, Rhode Island
A Taste of Newport (New England/Rhode Island)

★★★★★★★★★★★   ★★★★★★★★★★★

Miniature Cream Cheese Tarts
with Cherry Sauce

PASTRY:

2 (3-ounce) packages cream cheese,
  softened

1 cup butter, softened
2 cups all-purpose flour

Mix cream cheese, butter, and flour by hand. Form into a ball. Cover and chill for 1 hour. Form dough into 1-inch balls and press to fit in ungreased miniature muffin tins.

FILLING:

1 pint sour cream
5 tablespoons sugar

2 teaspoons vanilla extract

Preheat oven to 350°. Blend all ingredients. Fill each muffin cup with a heaping teaspoon of Filling. Bake for 15–20 minutes, or until Pastry is light brown and Filling bubbles. Cool slightly in tins, then remove to cooling racks.

CHERRY SAUCE:

1½ tablespoons cornstarch
⅛ teaspoon ground cinnamon
1 (16-ounce) can pitted dark sweet
  cherries (save juice)

2 tablespoons brandy (optional)
½ teaspoon lemon juice

Combine cornstarch and cinnamon in a small saucepan. Drain cherries, reserving liquid. Gradually add cherry liquid to cornstarch mixture. Cook over medium heat, stirring constantly, until mixture thickens. Remove from heat and stir in brandy, if desired, lemon juice, and cherries. Cool. Spoon a little sauce into each tart. Makes 4 dozen tarts.

Jacksonville & Company (Florida)

With more than 1,600 booths, Flea World, in Sanford, Florida, near Orlando on U.S. 17-92, claims to be America's largest flea market under one roof. Flea World sells only new merchandise including everything from car tires and pet tarantulas to gourmet coffee and beaded evening gowns.

Cream Puffs with Lemon Curd

The food processor makes this easier!

LEMON CURD:

¹⁄₃ cup lemon juice
1 cup sugar
¹⁄₄ cup butter

¹⁄₄ cup cornstarch
3 eggs

Process all ingredients together with steel blade. Cook in saucepan over medium heat on top of range until thickened. Process again until smooth. Refrigerate until ready to use.

CREAM PUFF:

1 cup water
¹⁄₂ cup butter, cut into chunks
1 cup flour

¹⁄₂ teaspoon salt
4 eggs

Heat water and butter on high heat until water boils and butter melts. Add flour and salt all at once; stir over heat until ball of dough is formed and excess moisture has evaporated. Turn into food processor bowl with steel blade. Add eggs all at once and process until smooth. Drop dough by tablespoonfuls onto baking sheet. Bake for 10 minutes at 400°, then at 350° for 25 minutes. Let stay in turned-off oven for 10 more minutes. Let cool; slice off tops and fill. Makes about 10 large puffs or 40 small.

The puffs can also be filled with tuna salad, egg salad, or chicken salad for a "new" sandwich.

Delicioso! (Texas II)

Napoleans

This takes a little time but is well worth it. It will impress anyone!

**3 sheets Pepperidge Farm Puff
  Pastry, thawed**

CUSTARD:

1 cup flour
1 cup sugar
6 egg yolks
$\frac{1}{2}$ cup cold milk

1 quart milk
2 teaspoons vanilla
$\frac{1}{2}$ pint whipping cream

Mix together flour, sugar, egg yolks, and $\frac{1}{2}$ cup cold milk. Bring 1 quart milk and vanilla to a boil. Add other mixture to this; cook over medium heat for 3–4 minutes. Cool. Whip cream and fold into cooled mixture.

ICING:

3 egg whites
$\frac{1}{2}$ cup sugar
2 tablespoons white corn syrup

$\frac{1}{16}$ teaspoon cream of tartar
$\frac{1}{2}$ teaspoon vanilla
$\frac{1}{4}$ cup melted semisweet chocolate

Mix all ingredients (except vanilla and chocolate) together and place over boiling water for about 6 minutes, stirring with finger until too hot to do so. Remove from heat. Beat vigorously with mixer until Icing holds shape, about 10 minutes. Blend in vanilla.

Roll out each sheet of puff pastry to about $\frac{1}{8}$ inch thick and 12 inches long. Prick with fork. Bake on a baking sheet at 350° for about 15–20 minutes. To assemble, layer 1 sheet of baked pastry on a platter, add half the custard, and repeat. Top with third layer and ice. Drizzle top with chocolate. Serves 12–16. Cut with a serrated knife.

Best of Friends Two (Texas II)

★★★★★★★★★★★★ ★★★★★★★★★★★★

Strawberries Bourbonnaise

This deliciously simple recipe is too good to be true. Make it for no reason and it will be something nobody will forget. Make it for a special occasion and it will become a tradition.

2 cups sugar
¼ cup unsalted butter
½ cup heavy cream
½ cup bourbon

1½ quarts strawberries, stemmed
  (the fresher the better)
Whipped cream

Use a heavy cast-aluminum or black iron skillet and make sure bottom of pan fits burner. Place on medium heat until you feel heat penetrate through bottom of pan to hand held over pan. When pan is hot, immediately add sugar. Stir with long-handled wooden spoon. As sugar starts to melt, stir gently until you have golden-colored syrup. Remove from heat and add butter. When butter is melted, add heavy cream a little at a time...very carefully. Stir in bourbon. Let sauce cool down and pour into a glass container. Cover and refrigerate. When cool, this wonderful sauce will be caramelized.

To serve: Place strawberries in individual stemmed glasses. Pour caramel sauce over strawberries. Top with a dollop of whipped cream. Sauce can be kept in refrigerator for several weeks. Yields 8 servings.

Food Fabulous Food (Mid-Atlantic/New Jersey)

★ **Editor's Extra:** This sauce is so good, it is delicious over any berries, and great on bread pudding. Good to add bananas, too! Try a small piece of pound cake underneath thawed frozen berries when fresh aren't available.

Crème Brulée

An easy gourmet dessert! Easy—yet sensational!!

2 cups light cream
5 egg yolks
3¹/₂ tablespoons sugar

2 tablespoons vanilla
¹/₄ cup dark brown sugar

Preheat oven to 325°. Heat cream in top of a double boiler until warm. Do not allow water in bottom of double boiler or the cream to boil!

Use electric mixer to beat egg yolks; gradually add sugar. Very slowly add the warm cream to the egg yolk mixture. Allow mixer to run slowly while adding cream; add vanilla and pour into an uncovered 1¹/₂-quart oven-proof dish. (Do not use a flat dish since the custard will be too thin.) Place dish in a pan of hot water and bake 40–45 minutes or until set. Remove baking dish and pan of water from the oven and sift the brown sugar over the custard immediately; place custard under broiler for 1 or 2 minutes, or until the sugar melts. Chill until very cold! Serves 6.

Note: Do not allow sugar to be thicker in some places than others, or it won't completely melt.

Words Worth Eating (Virginia)

Lime Chiffon Dessert

Plan ahead—this lovely dessert needs to chill.

1¹/₂ cups crushed graham crackers
  (about 24 crackers)

¹/₃ cup sugar
¹/₂ cup butter or margarine, melted

Combine ingredients; set aside 3 tablespoons for topping. Press remaining crumbs onto the bottom of an ungreased 9x13x2-inch baking dish; set aside.

FILLING:
1 (3-ounce) package lime gelatin
1 cup boiling water
11 ounces cream cheese, softened
1 cup sugar

1 teaspoon vanilla
1 (16-ounce) carton frozen whipped
  topping, thawed

In a bowl, dissolve gelatin in boiling water; cool. In a mixing bowl, beat cream cheese and sugar. Add vanilla; mix well. Slowly add gelatin until combined. Fold in whipped topping. Spoon over crust; sprinkle with reserved crumbs. Cover and refrigerate for 3 hours or until set. Yields 12–15 servings.

Treasured Recipes (Oregon)

Cold Lime Soufflé

1 envelope unflavored gelatin	2 drops green food coloring
1/4 cup cold water	(optional)
4 egg yolks	6 egg whites
1 cup sugar, divided	1 cup heavy cream, whipped
1/2 cup lime juice	Grated coconut (optional)
1/2 teaspoon salt	Lime slices (optional)
1 tablespoon grated lime rind	

Wrap and tape wax paper around top of 1 1/2-quart soufflé dish, extending 4 inches above rim. Brush inside paper with oil. Sprinkle gelatin over water. In top of double boiler, mix egg yolks, 1/2 cup sugar, lime juice, and salt. Cook over simmering water, stirring constantly until slightly thickened. Remove from heat. Add gelatin and stir until completely dissolved. Add lime rind and food coloring. Cool.

Beat egg whites until stiff, gradually adding remaining sugar. Fold into lime mixture. Fold whipped cream into mixture. Spoon into prepared dish. Chill until firm. Remove paper to serve. Garnish with coconut and lime slices, if desired. Serves 6–8. (Pictured on cover.)

Fare by the Sea (Florida)

★ **Editor's Extra:** These are fun in custard cups (see cover).

Pumpkin Squares

A Tea House Winner—Served from Halloween 'til Christmas.

1 (1-pound) can pumpkin (2 cups)	1/2 teaspoon nutmeg
1 1/2 cups sugar	1 cup chopped pecans
1 teaspoon salt	1/2 gallon vanilla ice cream (soft)
1 teaspoon ginger	1 box gingersnaps
1 teaspoon ground cinnamon	

Combine pumpkin, sugar, salt, ginger, cinnamon, and nutmeg. Then add pecans. Fold pumpkin mixture into ice cream.

Line a 9x13-inch pan or Pyrex dish with 1/2 of the gingersnaps. Top with 1/2 of the pumpkin/ice cream mixture. Cover with the remaining gingersnaps and spread the balance of the pumpkin mixture over the second layer of gingersnaps.

Freeze; when firm, cut into squares. Top with whipped cream or Cool Whip. Serves 18.

Collectibles II (Texas)

Chocolate Chip Pizza

Fun to make and eat.

1/2 cup sugar	1 egg
1/2 cup packed dark brown sugar	1 1/2 cups flour
1/2 cup butter, softened	2 cups miniature marshmallows
1 cup chunky peanut butter	12 ounces semisweet chocolate chips
1/2 teaspoon vanilla extract	1 cup chopped pecans

In mixing bowl, combine sugar, brown sugar, butter, peanut butter, vanilla, and egg with an electric mixer. Add flour. Press dough into disposable 12- or 14-inch round aluminum pan, forming a rim around edge. Bake in a preheated 375° oven for 10 minutes. Remove and sprinkle with marshmallows, chocolate chips, and pecans. Bake for an additional 5 minutes, or until marshmallows are golden. Remove from oven; slice and cool. Yields 10 servings.

Note: During the holiday season, this pizza topped with chopped candied red and green cherries, or red and green M&M's makes a nice hostess gift.

Capital Celebrations (Mid Atlantic/Washington, DC)

Frozen Chocolate Crunch

This is a delicious and impressive dessert. Can be made days in advance.

8 ounces sweet German chocolate or milk chocolate	1 1/2 cups crushed chocolate Oreo cookies
1/3 cup light corn syrup	1 cup coarsely chopped English walnuts
2 cups whipping cream, divided	

In a double boiler pan, combine chocolate and corn syrup. Stir occasionally until chocolate melts. Remove from heat. Stir in 1/2 cup of the cream until blended. Refrigerate 25–30 minutes, or until cool. Stir in cookies and walnuts.

In a small bowl, with mixer at medium speed, beat remaining 1 1/2 cups cream until soft peaks form. Gently fold in chocolate mixture just until combined. Spread mixture into a 9-inch glass baking dish and freeze 4–6 hours or until firm. Cut into squares to serve.

Note: You can pour this mixture into 12 individual dessert dishes and freeze. You can garnish with chocolate shaves, nuts, or whipped cream, if desired. This will store, covered, in freezer for up to 1 month. Before serving, let sit at room temperature several minutes.

Shattuck Community Cookbook (Oklahoma)

Frozen Peanut Butter Cups

These are rich, delicious and addictive! Must be prepared and frozen several hours ahead, or overnight.

1 cup whipping cream
1 (7- to 7¹/₂-ounce) jar marshmallow
  crème

1 (3-ounce) package cream cheese,
  softened
¹/₂ cup chunky peanut butter

In a small bowl with mixer at high speed, beat whipping cream until stiff peaks form. In a large bowl, with same beaters and mixer now at low speed, beat marshmallow crème, cream cheese, and peanut butter until smooth. Use a rubber spatula and fold whipped cream into the peanut butter mixture.

Line mini-muffin pan cups with fluted paper or foil baking cups. Spoon the mousse into the cups. Set uncovered pans in the freezer for 15–20 minutes (set your timer). Remove pans, wrap well, and immediately place back in freezer. Remove from freezer a few minutes before serving time.

These are wonderful to serve as a light dessert for a luncheon. One or two per serving with coffee is a perfect ending to a holiday (or any day!) luncheon. Makes 24.

Christmas Thyme at Oak Hill Farm (Indiana)

The Natchez Trace Parkway runs 450 miles from Natchez, Mississippi, to Nashville, Tennessee. There are numerous historical and nature sites that can be enjoyed along the way. Gwen's son, Shawn, and her three grandchildren are exploring a portion of the original trace, showing how it was literally sunken from use.

Listed below are the cookbooks that have contributed recipes to the *Recipe Hall of Fame Cookbook II*, along with copyright, author, publisher, city and state. The information in parentheses indicates the BEST OF THE BEST cookbook in which the recipe originally appeared.

Accent One ©1985 Accent Enterprises, Inc., Frank Simpson, Jr., Bentonia, MS (Mississippi)

Albany Collection: Treasures & Treasured ©1997 Women's Council of the Albany Institute of History and Art, Women's Council, Albany Institute of History and Art, Albany, NY (New York)

Allrecipes Tried & True ©2001 Allrecipes, Allrecipes, Seattle, WA (Washington)

Amarillo Junior League Cookbook ©1979 Amarillo Junior League Publications, Amarillo Junior League, Amarillo, TX (Texas)

Amazing Graces ©1993 The Texas Conference Ministers Spouses Association, The Texas Conference Ministers Spouses Association, Houston, TX (Texas II)

Amish Country Cookbook ©2001 Evangel Publishing House, Evangel Publishing House, Nappanee, IN (Indiana)

Angels and Friends Favorite Recipes II ©1991 Angels of Easter Seals, Angels of Easter Seals, Youngstown, OH (Ohio)

Appanoose County Cookbook, Appanoose County Historical Museum, Centerville, Iowa (Iowa)

Applause Applause, Standing Ovation Cooks, Coggon, IA (Iowa)

Apples, Apples, Apples ©1991 by Ann Clark, Marionville, MO (Missouri)

Asbury Cooks 1799-1999, Asbury United Methodist Church, Croton on Hudson, NY (New York)

Becky's Brunch & Breakfast Book ©1983 by Rebecca Walker, Austin, TX (Texas)

Bed & Breakfast Leatherstocking Welcome Home Recipe Collections, New York State Bed & Breakfast Leatherstocking Assn., Utica, NY (New York)

The Best Cranberry Recipes, From the Eagle River Cranberry Fest, Eagle River, WI (Wisconsin)

The Best from New Mexico Kitchens ©1978 New Mexico Magazine, Sheila MacNiven Cameron, New Mexico Magazine, Sante Fe, NM (New Mexico)

Best of Amish Cooking ©1988 Good Books, Phyllis Pellman Good, Good Books, Intercourse, PA (Pennsylvania)

Best of Friends ©2000 Friends School of Baltimore Parents Association, Friends School of Baltimore, Baltimore, MD (Mid-Atlantic)

Best of Friends Two ©1985 by Dee Reiser and Teresa Dormer, Kingwood, TX (Texas II)

Bethel Food Bazaar II ©1988 Bethel United Methodist Women, Bethel United Methodist Women, Spartanburg, SC (South Carolina)

Betty Groff's Up-Home Down-Home Cookbook ©1987 by Betty Groff, Pond Press, Mount Joy, PA (Pennsylvania)

Betty is Still "Winking" at Cooking, Betty J. Winkler, Little Rock, AR (Arkansas)

Betty Talmadge's Lovejoy Plantation Cookbook ©1983 by Betty Talmadge, Atlanta, GA (Georgia)

Beyond Chicken Soup ©1996 Jewish Home Auxiliary, Jewish Home of Rochester Auxiliary, Rochester, NY (New York)

Beyond the Bay ©1985 The Panama City Junior Service League, Inc., Panama City Junior Service League, Panama City, FL (Florida)

Blue Ridge Christian Church Cookbook, Christian Women's Fellowship, Independence, MO (Missouri)

Contributors

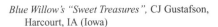

Blue Willow's "Sweet Treasures", CJ Gustafson, Harcourt, IA (Iowa)

The Bonneville House Presents ©1990 The Bonneville House Association, The Bonneville House Association, Fort Smith, AR (Arkansas)

Bounteous Blessings ©2001 by Frances A. Gillette, Yacolt, WA (Washington)

Bountiful Harvest Cookbook, Lancaster Bible College Women's Auxiliary, Lancaster, PA (Pennsylvania)

Bountiful Ohio ©1993 by Susan Failor, James Hope and Susan Failor, Bowling Green, OH (Ohio)

Braham's Pie Cookbook, Pie Day Committee, Braham, MN (Minnesota)

Breakfasts Ozark Style ©1986 by Kay Cameron, Point Lookout, MO (Michigan)

Brunch Basket and Generations ©1984 Junior League of Rockford, Inc., Junior League of Rockford, Inc., Rockford, IL (Illinois)

Bucks Cooks ©1950/1983 Trinity Episcopal Church, Trinity Church, Solebury, PA (Pennsylvania)

By Special Request © by Leu Wilder, Shreveport, LA (Louisiana II)

California Sizzles ©1992 The Junior League of Pasadena, Inc., Junior League of Pasadena, Pasadena, CA (California)

Campbellsville College Women's Club Cookbook ©1987 Circulation Services, Campbellsville College Women's Club, Campbellsville, KY (Kentucky)

Cane River's Louisiana Living ©1994 The Service League of Natchitoches, Inc., The Service League of Natchitoches, Inc., Natchitoches, LA (Louisiana II)

Capital Celebrations ©1997 The Junior League of Washington, DC, Junior League of Washington, DC, Washington, DC, (Mid-Atlantic)

Carol's Kitchen ©1993 by Carol J. Moore, Galesburg, IL (Illinois)

Carolina Cuisine Encore! ©1981 The Junior Assembly of Anderson, SC, Inc., The Junior Assembly of Anderson, SC, Anderson, SC (South Carolina)

A Casually Catered Affair ©1980 by Carole Curlee, Lubbock, TX (Texas II)

Celebration ©1985 Sevier County Cookbook Committee, Sevier County Cookbook Committee, Lockesburg, AR (Arkansas)

Centennial Cookbook, Second Presbyterian Church, Racine, WI (Wisconsin)

Centennial Cookbook, Welcome Corners United Methodist Church, Hastings, MI (Michigan)

Changing Thymes ©1995 Austin Junior Forum, Inc., Austin Junior Forum Publications, Austin, TX (Texas II)

Cheesecakes et cetera ©1989 by Shirley Michaels, Loveland, CO (Colorado)

Chefs and Artists, Black Mountain Memorial Library, Dallas, PA (Pennsylvania)

Cherished Czech Recipes, Penfield Press, Iowa City, IA (Iowa)

Cherries Galore ©1984 The Macon Telegraph Publishing Co., The Macon Telegraph Publishing Co., Macon, GA (Georgia)

Christmas in Washington ©1995 Golden West Publishers, Janet Walker, Golden West Publishers, Phoenix, AZ (Washington)

Christmas Memories Cookbook ©1985 Mystic Seaport Museum Stores, Inc., Lois Klee and Connie Colom, Mystic Seaport Stores, Mystic, CT (New England)

Christmas Thyme at Oak Hill Farm ©1994 Thyme Cookbooks, Marge Clark, West Lebanon, IN (Indiana)

Coastal Cuisine, Texas Style ©1993 Junior Service League of Brazosport, Junior Service League of Brazosport, Lake Jackson, TX (Texas II)

Collectibles II ©1983 by Mary Pittman, Van Alstyne, TX (Texas)

College Avenue Presbyterian Church Cookbook, Presbyterian Women of College Avenue Church, Aledo, IL (Illinois)

The Colophon Cafe Best Soups ©1996 Mama Colophon Cafe, Inc., Ray Dunn & Taimi Dunn Gorman, Mama Colophon, Inc., Bellingham, WA (Washington)

Colorado Collage ©1995 The Junior League of Denver, Inc., The Junior League of Denver, Inc., Denver, CO (Colorado)

Colorado Columbine Delicacies ©1995 Tracy M. Winters and Phyllis Y. Winters, Winters Publishing, Greensburg, IN (Colorado)

Colorado Foods and More... ©1990 by Judy Barbour, Bay City, TX (Colorado)

Comida Sabrosa ©1982 by Irene Barraza Sanchez and Gloria Sanchez Yund, University of New Mexico Press, Albuquerque, NM (New Mexico)

Cook and Deal ©1982 by D.J. Cook, Vero Beach, FL (Florida)

Cook, Line & Sinker, Rocky River Junior Women's Club, Rocky River, OH (Ohio)

A Cook's Tour of Iowa ©1988 University of Iowa Press, Susan Puckett, University of Iowa Press, Iowa City, IA (Iowa)

Cook's Tour of Shreveport ©1964 The Junior League of Shreveport, Inc., The Junior League of Shreveport, Shreveport, LA (Louisiana II)

Cookies and Bars ©1986 by Dorothy Zehnder, Bavarian Inn Restaurant, Frankenmuth, MI (Michigan)

Cookin' for the Crew, Spangler Chapel and Friends Church, Moscow, IA (Iowa)

Cookin' with Capital Press, Capital Press, Salem, OR (Oregon)

Cookin' with the Stars, Bufflao Chapter 150 - Order of the Eastern Star, Fraziers Bottom, WV (West Virginia)

A Cooking Affaire II ©1991 by Jan Bertoglio and JoLe Hudson, Butcher Block Press, Inc., Medicine Lodge, KS (Great Plains)

The Cooking Book ©1978 The Junior League of Louisville, Inc., The Junior League of Louisville, Inc., Louisville, KY (Kentucky)

Cooking...Done the Baptist Way, The First Baptist Church, Abbeville, SC (South Carolina)

Cooking from the Coast to the Cascades ©2002 Junior League of Eugene, Junior League of Eugene, Eugene, OR (Oregon)

Cooking New Orleans Style! ©1991 Episcopal Churchwomen of All Saints, Inc., Episcopal Churchwomen of All Saints, Inc., River Ridge, LA (Louisiana II)

Cooking with Grace, St. Bernard Parish, Wauwatosa, WI (Wisconsin)

Cooking with Mr. "G" and Friends, Kevin Grevemberg, Anacoco, LA (Louisiana II)

Cooking with the Menno-Haven Auxiliary ©1991 Menno-Haven Auxiliary, Menno-Haven Auxiliary, Chambersburg, PA (Pennsylvania)

Cotton Country Cooking ©1972 The Decatur Junior Service League, Inc., Junior League of Morgan County, Decatur, AL (Alabama)

Country Chic's Home Cookin, Christine C. Milligan, Preston, MD (Mid-Atlantic)

Country Classics II ©1995 by Ginger Mitchell and Patsy Tompkins, Karval, CO (Colorado)

The Country Mouse ©1983 Quail Ridge Press, Inc., Sally Walton and Faye Wilkinson, Quail Ridge Press, Brandon, MS (Mississippi)

Court Clerk's Bar and Grill, Tulsa County Court Clerk's Office, Tulsa, OK (Oklahoma)

Créme de Colorado ©1987 The Junior League of Denver, Inc., Junior League of Denver, Denver, CO (Colorado)

The Crowning Recipes of Kentucky ©1986 by Madonna Smith Echols, Marathon International Book Co, Madison, IN (Kentucky)

Cuckoo Too ©1982 Cuckoos, Inc., Nancy Allen, Kay Bruce, Fran Fauntleroy, Pat Glauser, Isla Reckling, and Mary Whilden, Cuckoos, Inc., Houston, TX (Texas)

Culinary Arts & Crafts ©1984 The Park Maitland School, Inc., The Park Maitland School, Inc., Maitland, FL (Florida)

Culinary Classics ©1981 Young Matron's Circle for Tallulah Falls School, Young Matron's Circle for Tallulah Falls School, Roswell, GA (Georgia)

Culinary Creations ©1998 Bnos Zion of Bobov, Bnos Zion of Bobov, Brooklyn, NY (New York)

¡Delicioso! ©1982 The Junior League of Corpus Christi, Junior League of Corpus Christi, Inc., Corpus Christi, TX (Texas II)

The Denton Woman's Club Cookbook, Denton Woman's Club, Denton, TX (Texas II)

Dining in Historic Ohio ©1987 by Marty Godbey, McClanahan Publishing House, Inc., Kuttawa, KY (Ohio)

Dinner on the Diner ©1983 Junior League of Chattanooga, Inc., Junior League of Chattanooga, Chattanooga, TN (Tennessee)

A Dish to Pass, First United Methodist Church, Austin, MN (Minnesota)

Dishes from the Deep, Arizona Perch Base Submarine Veterans, Sun City West, AZ (Arizona)

Dixie Delights ©1983 St. Francis Hospital Auxiliary, St Francis Hospital Auxiliary, Memphis, TN (Tennessee)

A Doctor's Prescription for Gourmet Cooking ©1984 Peanut Butter Publishing, Reba Michels Hill, M.D., Peanut Butter Publishing, Houston, TX (Texas)

Down Memory Lane, Straight Fork Extension Homemakers, Crawford, WV (West Virginia)

The Eagle's Kitchen, Belen Middle School M.E.S.A., Belen, NM (New Mexico)

The Eater's Digest, Scranton Preparatory School Parents' Club, Scranton, PA (Pennsylvania)

The Elsah Landing Restaurant Cookbook ©1981 The Elsah Landing Restaurant, Inc., Helen Crafton and Dorothy Lindgren, The Elsah Landing Restaurant, Inc., Elsah, IL (Illinois)

Encore, Walker School Association, Dot Gibson Publications, Waycross, GA (Georgia)

The Encyclopedia's of Cajun and Creole Cuisine ©1983 The Encyclopedia Cookbook of Cajun and Creole Cuisine, John D. Folse, Baton Rouge, LA (Louisiana)

Enjoy at Your Own Risk! ©1996 by Judy Grigoraci, Charleston, WV (West Virginia)

Entertaining at Aldredge House ©1980 The Dallas County Medical Society Auxiliary, Dallas County Medical Society Auxiliary, Dallas, TX (Texas)

Eufaula's Favorite Recipes ©1985 The Eufaula Tribune, The Eufaula Tribune, Eufaula, AL (Alabama)

Everyday Cakes ©2000 Hill Street Press, Bevelyn Blair, Hill Street Press, Athens, GA (Georgia)

Fare by the Sea ©1983 The Junior League of Sarasota, Inc., Junior League of Sarasota, Sarasota, FL (Florida)

Favorite Herbal Recipes Volume III, Herbs for Health & Fun Club, Centralia, IL (Illinois)

Favorite Recipes, St. Nicholas Orthodox Church, Barton, OH (Ohio)

Favorite Recipes from Poland Women's Club, Poland Women's Club, Poland, OH (Ohio)

Favorite Recipes from Quilters ©1992 Good Books, Louise Stolzfus, Good Books, Intercourse, PA (Pennsylvania)

Favorites for all Seasons, The Desert Foothills Library, Cave Creek, AZ (Arizona)

Feast in Fellowship, First United Methodist Women, Altus, OK (Oklahoma)

Feeding the Faithful ©1983 The Women of Mauldin United Methodist Church, United Methodist Women of Mauldin United Methodist Church, Mauldin, SC (South Carolina)

Feeding the Flock, Havaco Community Church Ladies, Welch, WV (West Virginia)

Festival ©1983 Humphreys Academy Patrons, Humphreys Academy Patrons, Belzoni, MS (Mississippi)

The Fifth Generation Cookbook, Carol L. Wise, Findlay, OH (Ohio)

Fillies Flavours ©1984 The Fillies Inc., The Fillies, Inc., Louisville, KY (Kentucky)

The Fine Art of Cooking ©1989 The Women's Committee of the Philadelphia Museum of Art, The Women's Committee, Philadelphia, PA (Pennsylvania)

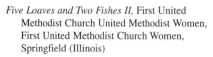
Five Loaves and Two Fishes II, First United Methodist Church United Methodist Women, First United Methodist Church Women, Springfield (Illinois)

Five Star Sensations ©1991 Auxiliary of University Hospitals of Cleveland, Auxiliary of University Hospitals of Cleveland, Cleveland, OH (Ohio)

Flaunting Our Finest ©1982 Junior Auxiliary of Franklin, Franklin Junior Auxiliary, Franklin, TN (Tennessee)

Flavor Favorites ©1979 Baylor Alumni Association, Baylor University Alumni Association, Waco (Texas)

Flavors ©1978 The Junior League of San Antonio, Junior League of San Antonio, San Antonio, TX (Texas)

Flavors of Cape Henlopen, Village Improvement Association, Rehoboth Beach, DE (Mid-Atlantic)

Food Fabulous Food ©1997 The Women's Board to Cooper Health System, Women's Board to Cooper Health System, Camden, NJ (Mid-Atlantic)

A Fork in the Road ©1998 Mimbres Region Arts Council, Mimbres Region Arts Council, Silver City, NM (New Mexico)

The Fortsville United Methodist Church Cookbook, Fortsville United Methodist Church, Gansevoort, NY (New York)

Four Generations of Johnson Family Favorites, Ruth Johnson, Oklahoma City, OK (Oklahoma)

Four Square Meals a Day, Women's Ministries, Lamar, CO (Colorado)

Friend's Favorites, Dover Plains Library, Dover Plains, NY (New York)

From a Louisiana Kitchen ©1983 by Holly Berkowitz Clegg, Baton Rouge, LA (Louisiana)

From Cajun Roots to Texas Boots, Cookie Brisbin, Marfa, TX (Texas II)

From our Kitchens with Love, St. Mark Orthodox Church, Rochester Hills, MI (Michigan)

From Portland's Palate ©1992 Junior League of Portland, Junior League of Portland, Portland, OR (Oregon)

From the Apple Orchard ©1984 by Leona N. Jackson, Maryville, MO (Missouri)

Gallery Buffet Soup Cookbook ©1983 Dallas Museum of Art, Dallas Museum of Art League, Dallas, TX (Texas)

The Garden Patch, Kay Hauser, St. Johns, AZ (Arizona)

Gardeners' Gourmet II ©1985 Garden Clubs of Mississippi, Inc., Garden Clubs of Mississippi, Inc., Yazoo City (Mississippi)

The Gasparilla Cookbook ©1961 The Junior League of Tampa, Inc., Junior League of Tampa, Tampa, FL (Florida)

Gateways ©1990 St. Louis Children's Hospital Auxiliary, St. Louis Children's Hospital Auxiliary, St. Louis, MO (Missouri)

The Gathering ©1987 The Blue Bird Circle, The Blue Bird Circle Shop, Houston, TX (Texas II)

Gator Country Cooks ©1975 The Junior League of Gainesville, Florida, Inc., Junior League of Gainesville, Gainesville, FL (Florida)

Generations ©1984 Junior League of Rockford, Inc., Jr. League of Rockford, Rockford, IL (Illinois)

Generations of Good Cooking, St Mary's Parish, Oxford, IA (Iowa)

Get Cookin' With Sound Construction, Sound Construction, Bend, OR (Oregon)

Golliwogg Cake ©1996 The Red River Radio Network, Katrina Blodgett, Red River Radio Station, Shreveport, LA (Louisiana II)

Gourmet Cooking ©1982 by Earl Peyroux, Pensacola, FL (Florida)

Grandmother's Cookbook ©1990 by Elizabeth Rose von Hohen and Carrie J. Gamble, Doylestown, PA (Pennsylvania)

Granny's Kitchen, Theone L. Neel, Bastian, VA (Virginia)*Great Grandmother's Goodies,* Pennsylvania's State Federation of Negro Women's Clubs, Inc., Erie, PA (Pennsylvania)

Great Recipes from Redeemer's Fellowship, Redeemer's Fellowship Church, Roseburg, OR (Oregon)

Great Tastes of Texas ©1994 by Barbara C. Jones, Bonham, TX (Texas II)

Green Thumbs in the Kitchen ©1996 Green Thumb, Inc., Green Thumb, Inc. Wisconsin Program, Neillsville, WI (Wisconsin)

The Gulf Gourmet ©1978 The Gulf Gourmet, Westminster Academy, Gulfport, MS (Mississippi)

Gulfshore Delights ©1984 The Junior Welfare League of Fort Myers, Florida, Inc., Junior League of Ft. Myers, Fort Myers, FL (Florida)

Hallmark's Collection of Home Tested Recipes, Freeda Rogers Hallmark, Tuscaloosa, AL (Alabama)

Head Table Cooks ©1982 American Camellia Society, Inc., American Camellia Society, Fort Valley, GA (Georgia)

Heavenly Delights, Mothers and Daughters of Zion, Independence, MO (Missouri)

Heavenly Dishes, United Methodist Women of Union Pisgah Church, Attica, OH (Ohio)

Heavenly Recipes, Milnor Lutheran Church WELCA, Milnor, ND (Great Plains)

Herrin's Favorite Italian Recipes Cookbook, Herrin Hospital Auxiliary, Herrin, IL (Illinois)

Historic Lexington Cooks ©1989 Historic Lexington Foundation, Historic Lexington Foundation, Lexington, VA (Virginia)

Holiday Treats, Theone L. Neel, Bastian, VA (Virginia)

Home at the Range Volume IV, Chapter EX.P.E.O., Oakley, KS (Great Plains)

Home Cookin': First Congregational United Church of Christ, First Congregational United Church of Christ, Morenci, MI (Michigan)

Home Cookin' is a Family Affair, Aldersgate United Methodist Women, Marion, IL (Illinois)

Home Cooking II, 49'ers Club of Dana, Hillsdale, IN (Indiana)

Homecoming ©1994 Baylor Alumni Association, Baylor Alumni Association, Waco, TX (Texas II)

Honest to Goodness ©1990 The Junior League of Springfield, Inc., Junior League Publications, Springfield, IL (Illinois)

Hors d'Oeuvre Tray, Valdosta Junior Service League, Valdosta, GA (Georgia)

Hospice Hospitality, The Hospice, Yuma, AZ (Arizona)

Hospitality ©1991 Salem Hospital Aid Association, North Shore Medical Center, Salem, MA (New England)

Hospitality Heirlooms ©1983 South Jackson Civic League, Inc., South Jackson Civic League, Jackson, MS (Mississippi)

Huntsville Entertains ©1983 Historic Huntsville Foundation, Historic Huntsville Foundation, Huntsville, AL (Alabama)

If It Tastes Good, Who Cares? I ©1992 Spiritseekers Publishing, Pam Girard, Spiritseekers Publishing, Bismarck, ND (Great Plains)

In the Kitchen with Kate ©1995 Capper Press, Inc., Capper Press, Topeka, KS (Great Plains)

In the Kitchen with Kendi, Volume I ©1999 by Kendi O'Neill, Diversions Publications, Inc., Frederick, MD (Mid-Atlantic)

In Good Taste ©1983 Department of Nutrition, School of Public Health of the University of North Carolina, Department of Nutrition, Chapel Hill, NC (North Carolina)

Inverness Cook Book ©1963 All Saints Episcopal Guild, All Saints Episcopal Guild, Inverness, MS (Mississippi)

It's Our Serve ©1989 Junior League of Long Island, Inc., Junior League of Long Island, Inc., Roslyn, NY (New York)

It's About Thyme! ©1988 Marge Clark-Thyme Cookbooks, Marge Clark, Thyme Cookbooks, West Lebanon, IN (Indiana)

Jacksonville & Company ©1982 The Junior League of Jacksonville, Florida, Inc., Junior League of Jacksonville, Jacksonville, FL (Florida)

Jasper County Extension Homemakers Cookbook, Jasper County Extension Homemakers, Rensselaer, IN (Indiana)

Jaycee Cookin', Annapolis Jaycees, Inc., Annapolis, MD (Mid-Atlantic)

Jubilee Cookbook ©1991 The United Methodist Women of Highland Park United Methodist Church, Highland Park United Methodist Church, Dallas, TX (Texas II)

The Junior Welfare League 50th Anniversary Cookbook, Maryfield-Graves County Junior Welfare League, Mayfield, KY (Kentucky)

Just Plain Country, Alice Lantz, Glady, WV (West Virginia)

Kay Ewing's Cooking School Cookbook ©1994 by Kay Ewing, Baton Rouge, LA (Louisiana II)

Kids in the Kitchen, Parents Who Care, Ft. Huachuca, AZ (Arizona)

Kiss My Grits ©1984 by Roy Overcast, Jr., Brentwood, TN (Tennessee)

Koinonia Cooking ©1982 by Elaine S. Mynatt, Knoxville, TN (Tennessee)

Kountry Kooking ©1974 by Phila Hach, Clarksville, TN (Tennessee)

La Bonne Louisiane ©1983 by Michele M. Odom, Baton Rouge, LA (Louisiana)

Lasting Impressions ©1988 Saint Joseph's Hospital of Atlanta Auxiliary, Saint Joseph's Hospital of Atlanta Auxiliary, Atlanta, GA (Georgia)

Laurels to the Cook ©1988 Laurels to the Cook, Talus Rock Girl Scout Council, Inc., Johnstown, PA (Pennsylvania)

License to Cook Arizona Style ©1999 Penfield Press, Penfield Press, Iowa City, IA (Arizona)

License to Cook Iowa Style ©1996 Penfield Press, Penfield Press, Iowa City, IA (Iowa)

License to Cook New Mexico Style ©1990 Penfield Press, Penfield Press, Iowa City, IA (New Mexico)

Light Kitchen Choreography ©1994 Cleveland Ballet Council, Cleveland Ballet Council, Cleveland, OH (Ohio)

A Little Taste of Texas ©1990 by Barbara C. Jones, Bonham, TX (Texas II)

Little Dave's Seafood Cookbook, Volume One ©1998 by David J. Harvey, Playa Vista Publishing, Los Angeles, CA (California)

Lone Star Legacy ©1981 Austin Junior Forum, Inc., Austin Junior Forum Publications, Austin, TX (Texas II)

The Long Island Holiday Cookbook, Newsday Books, Melville, NY (New York)

The Louisiana Crawfish Book ©1984 Louisiana Crawfish Cookbook, Inc., Louisiana Crawfish Cookbook, Inc., Lettsworth, LA (Louisiana)

Louisiana Largesse ©1983 Capital City Press, Baton Rouge Morning Advocate, Baton Rouge, LA (Louisiana)

Louisiana LEGACY ©1982 The Thibodeaux Service League, Inc., Thibodeaux Service League, Inc., Thibodeaux, LA (Louisiana)

Love Yourself Cookbook ©1987 by Edie Low, Charlotte, NC (North Carolina)

Lowfat, Homestyle Cookbook ©1995 by Christina Korenkiewicz, Brook Forest Publishing, Conifer, CO (Colorado)

The Lucy Miele Too Good to be Low-Fat Cookbook ©1988 by Lucy Miele, Hill House Publications, Stockton, IL (Illinois)

Madison County Cookbook ©1994 St. Joseph Catholic Church, St. Joseph Catholic Church, Winterset, IA (Iowa)

Manna by the Sea, St. Peter the Fisherman' Lutheran Church, Lincoln City, OR (Oregon)

Maple Hill Cookbook, Maple Hill Senior Citizens and Community Club, Hibbing, MN (Minnesota)

★★★★★★★★★★★ ★★★★★★★★★★★

Market to Market ©1983 The Service League of Hickory, North Carolina, Inc., Service League of Hickory, NC, Inc., Hickory, NC (North Carolina)

Maury County Cookbook ©1964 The Guilded Circle of King's Daughters, The Maury County Union of King's Daughters & Sons, Columbia, TN (Tennessee)

McNamee Family & Friends Cookbook, McNamee Family, Terri Snyder, Colville, WA (Washington)

Mendocino Mornings: A Collection of Breakfast Delights from the Joshua Grindle Inn ©1996 by Arlene and Jim Moorehead, Joshua Grindle Inn, Mendocino, CA (California)

Micro Quick! ©1984 by CiCi Williamson and Ann Steiner, MicroScope, McLean, VA (Texas)

The Miller Cookbook, Carrie Gingerich, Shedd, OR (Oregon)

The Mississippi Cookbook ©1972 University Press of Mississippi, University Press of Mississippi, Jackson, MS (Mississippi)

More Calf Fries to Caviar ©1988 Jan-Su Publications, Janel Franklen and Sue Vaughn, Jan-Su Publications, Lamesa, TX (Texas II)

More Favorites From the Melting Pot, Church of Saint Athansius, Baltimore, MD (Mid-Atlantic)

More Goodies and Guess-Whats ©1981 by Helen Christiansen, Walsh, CO, (Colorado)

More Than Delicious ©1993 Erie Art Museum, Erie Art Museum, Erie, PA (Pennsylvania)

More to Love...from the Mansion of Golconda ©1993 by Marilyn Kunz, Golconda, IL (Illinois)

Mountain Laurel Encore ©1984 Bell County Extension Homemakers, Bell County Extension Homemakers, Pineville, KY (Kentucky)

Mountain Recipe Collection ©1981 Ison Collectibles, Inc., Valeria S. Ison, Ison Collectibles, Inc., Hazard, KY (Kentucky)

Moveable Feasts Cookbook ©1992 Mystic Seaport Museum Stores, Inc., Ginger Smyle, Mystic Seaport Stores, Mystic, CT (New England)

Mad About Muffins ©1998 Andrew McMeel Publishing, Dot Vartan, Andrew McMeel Publishing, knsas City, MO (Illinois)

My Italian Heritage, August E. Corea, East Rochester, NY (New York)

Natchez Notebook of Cooking ©1986 Trinity Episcopal Day School, Trinity Episcopal Day School, Natchez, MS (Mississippi)

Necessities and Temptations ©1987 The Junior League of Austin, Inc., Junior League of Austin, Austin, TX (Texas II)

Neighboring on the Air ©1991 University of Iowa Press, University of Iowa Press, Iowa City, IA (Iowa)

New Beginnings Cookbook, First Congregational United Church of Christ, Candlelight Fellowship, DeWitt, IA (Iowa)

The New Gourmets & Groundhogs ©1968 by Elaine Light, Punxsutawney, PA (Pennsylvania)

New Mexico Cook Book ©1990/1998 by Lynn Nusom, Golden West Publishers, Phoenix, AZ (New Mexico)

Nibbles Cooks Cajun ©1983 by Suzie Stephens, Fayetteville, AR (Arkansas)

North Dakota American Mothers Cookbook, North Dakota American Mothers, Des Lacs, ND (Great Plains)

Nothing Could Be Finer ©1982 The Junior League of Wilmington, Inc., The Junior League of Wilmington, Inc., Wilmington, NC (North Carolina)

Of Tide & Thyme ©1995 The Junior League of Annapolis, Junior League of Annapolis, Annapolis, MD (Mid-Atlantic)

Oklahoma Cookin' ©1995 Barnard Elementary School, Barnard Elementary School, Tecumseh, OK (Oklahoma)

Old Westbrook Evangelical Lutheran Church Cookbook, Old Westbrook WELCA, Lamberton, MN (Minnesota)

Old-Fashioned Cooking, Raleigh Historical Society, Raleigh, IL (Illinois)

Our Favorite Recipes, Professional Clerical Section/WVPHA, Ronceverte, WV (West Virginia)

Our Favorite Recipes, Saint Mary's Hospital Auxiliary, Rochester, MN (Minnesota)

Our Favorite Recipes, The South Carolina Club of Bethel AME Church, Knoxville, TN (Tennessee)

Our Favorite Recipes, Union County Hospital Auxiliary, Anna, IL (Illinois)

The Overlake School Cookbook ©1984 The Overlake School, Pickle Point Publishing, Bellevue, WA (Washington)

The Parkview Way to Vegetarian Cooking, Parkview Memorial Hospital Auxiliary, Brunswick, ME (New England)

Parties & Pleasures ©1985 by Wilma Taylor Sowell, Columbia, TN (Tennessee)

Paul Naquin's French Collection I — Louisiana Seafood © by Paul Naquin, Baton Rouge, LA (Louisiana)

The Peach Sampler ©1983 by Eliza Mears Horton, West Columbia, SC (South Carolina)

The Peach Tree Family Cookbook ©1994 Peach Tree Gift Gallery & Tea Room, Cynthia Collins Pedregon, The Peach Tree Gift Gallery, Fredericksburg, TX (Texas II)

Pig Out, White Eagle Grange # 683, Pilot Rock, OR (Oregon)

Pioneer Pantry, Telephone Pioneers of America, Lucent Technologies Chapter #135, Lisle, IL (Illinois)

Pirate's Pantry ©1976 Junior League of Lake Charles, Inc., Pelican Publishing, Lake Charles, LA (Louisiana)

Plain & Fancy Favorites, Montgomery Woman's Club, Cincinnati, OH (Ohio)

Pleasures from the Good Earth, Rock of Ages Lutheran Women's Missionary League, Sedona, AZ (Arizona)

Pool Bar Jim's Famous Frozen Drinks ©1979 by James D. Lisenby, Hilton Head Island, SC (South Carolina) www.poolbarjims.com

Potluck Volume II, MN Catholic Daughters of the Americas, Medford, MN (Minnesota)

Potlucks and Petticoats ©1986 by Jerry and Becky Cope, Appalachian Cultural Center, Dillard, GA (Georgia)

Quail Country ©1983 The Junior League of Albany, Georgia, Inc., Smith House Publications, Albany, GA (Georgia)

Raider Recipes ©1993 Fleming Publishing, David and Dawn Fleming, Fleming Publishing, Lubbock, TX (Texas II)

Rainy Day Treats and Sunny Temptations, Medical Faculty Auxiliary of the Oregon Health Sciences University, Portland, OR (Oregon)

Raleigh House Cookbook ©1991 San Antonio Cuisine, Martha R. Johnson, Kerrville, TX (Texas II)

Ready to Serve ©1984 Texas National Guard Auxiliary, National Guard Auxiliary of Austin, Austin, TX (Texas)

Recipes & Remembrances, Covenant Women of Courtland Kansas, Courtland, KS (Great Plains)

Recipes & Remembrances II, Rockwood Area Historical Society, Rockwood, MI (Michigan)

Recipes from a New England Inn ©1992 by Trudy Cutrone, Castine, ME (New England)

Recipes from Jan's Cake & Candy Crafts, Janet Travis, Anderson, IN (Indiana)

Recipes from Minnesota with Love ©1981 by Betty Malisow Potter, Strawberry Point, Prior Lake, MN (Minnesota)

Recipes from Smith-Appleby House, Historical Society of Smithfield, RI, Esmond, RI (New England)

Recipes to Remember, St. Joseph's Hospital, Chewelah, WA (Washington)

Red River Valley Potato Growers Auxiliary Cookbook, R.R.V.P.G. Auxiliary, East Grand Forks, MN (Great Plains)

Red, White & Blue Favorites, American Legion Aux. Unit 81, Lake Havasu City, AZ (Arizona)

Reflections Under the Sun: The Brightest Collection of Recipes from the Junior League of Phoenix ©1999 The Junior League of Phoenix, The Junior League of Phoenix, Phoenix, AZ (Arizona)

Rehoboth Christian School Cookbook ©1981 Tse Yaaniichii Promoters, Rehoboth, NM (New Mexico)

Return Engagement ©1989 The Junior Board of the Quad City Symphony Orchestra Assn., Quad City Symphony, Davenport, IA (Iowa)

River Road Recipes II ©1976 The Junior League of Baton Rouge, Inc., Junior League of Baton Rouge, Inc., Baton Rouge, LA (Louisiana)

Rivertown Recipes ©1976 Kennedy Book Club, Kennedy Book Club, Memphis, TN (Tennessee)

Rogue River Rendezvous ©1992 The Junior League of Jackson County, Junior League of Jackson County, Medford, OR (Oregon)

Sam Houston Schoolhouse Cookbook, Sam Houston Schoolhouse Association, Maryville, TN (Tennessee)

San Francisco á la Carte ©1979 The Junior League of San Francisco, Inc., The Junior League of San Francisco, San Francisco, CA (California)

Sandy Hook Volunteer Fire Company Ladies Auxiliary Cookbook, Sandy Hook Volunteer Fire & Rescue Ladies Auxiliary, Sandy Hook, CT (New England)

Sassy Southwest Cooking—Vibrant New Mexico Foods ©1997 by Clyde W. Casey, Pecos Valley Pepper Co., Roswell, NM (New Mexico)

Savannah Collection ©1986 by Martha Giddens Nesbit, Savannah, GA (Georgia)

Savor the Flavor, Holy Cross Ladies Society, Buffalo, NY (New York)

Savor the Flavor of Oregon ©1990 The Junior League of Eugene, Junior League of Eugene, Eugene, OR (Oregon)

Savoring the Southwest, Roswell Symphony Guild Publications, Roswell, NM (New Mexico)

Sawgrass and Pines, Perry Garden Club, Perry, FL (Florida)

Seafood Sorcery, The Junior League of Wilmington, Inc., Wilmington, NC (North Carolina)

Seasons in the Sun ©1976 Beaux Arts, Inc., The Lowe Art Museum, University of Miami Beaux Arts, Inc., Coral Gables, FL (Florida)

Seasoned with Light, First Baptist Church - Baptist Women, Hartsville, SC (South Carolina)

Seasoned with Love, Trinity United Church of Christ, Brookfield, WI (Wisconsin)

Second Round, Tea-Time at the Masters® ©1988 The Junior League of Augusta, Georgia, Inc., Junior League of Augusta, Augusta, GA (Georgia)

The Second Typically Texas Cookbook ©1989 The Association of Electric Cooperatives, Inc., Texas Electric Cooperatives, Inc., Austin, TX (Texas II)

Seminole Savorings ©1982 Seminole Productions, Inc., Seminole Productions, Inc., Tallahassee, FL (Florida)

Serving Up Oregon ©2000 Serving Oregon, Atkinson Graduate School of Management/Willamette University, Salem, OR (Oregon)

Sharing Our Best, The Elizabeth House for Assisted Living, Maumee, OH (Ohio)

Sharing Our Best, Glen Retirement Home, Chico, CA (California)

Sharing Our Best, St. Mary Magdalene Episcopal Church, Boulder, CO (Colorado)

Shattuck Community Cookbook, Shattuck Chamber of Commerce, Shattuck, OK (Oklahoma)

Ship to Shore I ©1983 Ship to Shore, Jan Robinson, Charlotte, NC (North Carolina)

Ship to Shore II ©1985 Ship to Shore, Inc., Jan Robinson, Charlotte, NC (North Carolina)

Simple Pleasures, Jewish Caring Network, Baltimore, MD (Mid-Atlantic)

Simply Colorado ©1989 Colorado Dietetic, Colorado Dietetic Association, Denver, CO (Colorado)

Simply Sensational, Our Lady Queen of Apostles Parish, Hamtramck, MI (Michigan)

Simply Whidbey: A Regional Cookbook from Whidbey Island, WA ©1991 by Laura Moore and Deborah Skinner, Saratoga Publishing, Oak Harbor, WA (Washington)

Sisters' Secrets, Beta Sigma Phi, Ville Platte, LA (Louisiana II)

Sisters Two II, Nancy Barth and Sue Hergert, Ashland, KS (Great Plains)

Six Ingredients or Less: Cooking Light & Healthy ©1992 by Carlean Johnson, CJ Books, Gig Harbor, WA (Washington)

Sleigh Bells & Sugar Plums ©1992 by Frances A. Gillette and Daughters, Frances A. Gillette, Yacolt, WA (Washington)

Some Like it South! ©1984 The Junior League of Pensacola, Inc., Junior League of Pensacola, Inc., Pensacola, FL (Florida)

Somethin's Cookin' at LG&E, Louisville Gas & Electric Co. Employees Association, Louisville, KY (Kentucky)

South Coastal Cuisine, Friends of the South Coastal Library, Bethany Beach, DE (Mid-Atlantic)

Southern Flavors' Little Chocolate Book ©1991 Southern Flavors, Inc., Southern Flavors, Inc., Pine Bluff, AR (Arkansas)

Southern Vegetable Cooking ©1981 Sandlapper Publishing Co., Inc., Sandlapper Publishing Co., Inc., Orangeburg, SC (South Carolina)

Southwest Olé! ©1993 by Barbara C. Jones, Bonham, TX (Texas II)

Special Recipes from our Hearts, The United Methodist Church of DeWitt, DeWitt, IA (Iowa)

The Star of Texas Cookbook ©1983 The Junior League of Houston, Inc., Junior League of Houston, Inc., Houston, TX (Texas II)

Steamboat Entertains ©1991 Steamboat Springs Winter Sports Club, Steamboat Springs Winter Sports Club, Steamboat Springs, CO (Colorado)

Steinbeck House Cookbook © The Valley Guild, The Valley Guild, Salinas, CA (California)

Steppingstone Cookery, Steppingstone Museum, Havre de Grace, MD (Mid-Atlantic)

Still Gathering ©1992 Auxiliary to the American Osteopathic Assn., Auxiliary American Osteopathic Association, Chicago, IL (Illinois)

Stirrin' the Pots on Daufuskie ©1985 by Billie Burn, Daufuskie Island, SC (South Carolina)

Stirring Performances ©1988 The Junior League of Winston-Salem, Inc., Junior League of Winston-Salem, Inc., Winston-Salem, NC (North Carolina)

Take it to Heart ©1989 Stanley E. Evans Heart Institute of Arkansas, Stanley E. Evans Heart Institute of Arkansas, Fort Smith, AR (Arkansas)

Talk About Good!, Junior League of Lafayette, Lafayette, LA (Louisiana)

Taste of Balboa, Balboa Elementary Parent Teacher Group, Spokane, WA (Washington)

A Taste of Fayette County, New River Convention & Visitor's Bureau, Oak Hill, WV (West Virginia)

A Taste of Fishers ©1993 Fishers Tri Kappa, Fishers Tri Kappa, Fishers, IN (Indiana)

A Taste of History, North Carolina Museum of History, Raleigh, NC (North Carolina)

Taste of the Methow, Methow Valley United Methodist Women, Twisp, WA (Washington)

A Taste of Newport ©1990 Gillian Drake, Shank Painter Publishing Co., Provincetown, MA (New England)

A Taste of Salt Air & Island Kitchens, Ladies Auxiliary of the Block Island Volunteer Fire Department, Block Island, RI (New England)

A Taste of South Carolina ©1983 The Palmetto Cabinet of South Carolina, Sandlapper Publishing Co., Inc., Orangeburg, SC (South Carolina)

Taste of the South ©1984 The Symphony League of Jackson, Mississippi, Jackson Symphony League, Jackson, MS (Mississippi)

A Taste of Tillamook, Tillamook Chamber of Commerce, Tillamook, OR (Oregon)

A Taste of Tradition, Sandra Nagler, Georgetown, DE (Mid-Atlantic)

Tasting Tea Treasures ©1984 Greenville Junior Woman's Club, Greenville Junior Woman's Club, Greenville, MS (Mississippi)

A Tasting Tour Through Washington County ©1987 Springfield Woman's Club, Springfield Woman's Club, Springfield, KY (Kentucky)

Tasty Temptations, The Ladies Auxiliary of Knights of Columbus, Fremont, CA (California)

Temptations ©1986 Presbyterian Day School, Presbyterian Day School, Cleveland, MS (Mississippi)

The Texas Experience ©1982 Richardson Woman's Club, Inc., Richardson Woman's Club, Richardson, TX (Texas II)

Texas Historic Inns Cookbook ©1985 by Ann Ruff and Gail Drago, Austin, TX (Texas)

Then 'til Now, Dorothy J. O'Neal, Eugene, OR (Oregon)

Third Wednesday Homemakers Cookbook Volume, Fraziers Bottom Pliny Homemakers, Fraziers Bottom, WV (West Virginia)

Three Rivers Cookbook I ©1973 Child Health Association of Sewickley, Child Health Association of Sewickley, Sewickley, PA (Pennsylvania)

Through our Kitchen Windows ©1980 WMSC Museum of Bay County, Inc., Bahia Vista Mennonite Church, Sarasota, FL (Florida)

Thunderbird Cookers of AT&T ©1986 Telephone Pioneers of America, Oklahoma Chapter 94, Telephone Pioneers-Thunderbird Chapter 94, Oklahoma City, OK (Oklahoma)

Thyme & the River, Too, Sharon Van Loan, Patricia Lee, Steamboat Inn, Idleyld Park, OR (Oregon)

Tony Clark's New Blueberry Hill Cookbook ©1990 by Arlyn Patricia Hertz and Anthony Clark, Tony Clark, Down East Books, Camden, ME (New England)

Top Rankin' Recipes ©1986 Rankin General Hospital Auxiliary, Rankin General Hospital Auxiliary, Brandon, MS, (Mississippi)

Traditionally Wesleyan ©1985 The Wesleyan Business Club, Wesleyan College Business Club, Macon, GA (Georgia)

Treasured Recipes: Western Welcome Newcomers, Western Welcome Newcomers, Grants Pass, OR (Oregon)

Treasures and Pleasures ©1995 Shawnee United Methodist Church, Shawnee United Methodist Church, Lima, OH (Ohio)

Treat Yourself to the Best Cookbook ©1984 Junior League of Wheeling, Junior League of Wheeling, Inc., Wheeling, WV (West Virginia)

★★★★★★★★★★★ ★★★★★★★★★★★

A Trim & Terrific Louisiana Kitchen ©1996 by Holly B. Clegg, New York, NY (Louisiana II)

Trinity Catholic School Cookbook, Trinity Catholic School, Oswego, NY (New York)

Tucson Treasures ©1999 Tucson Medical Center Auxiliary, Tucson Medical Center Auxiliary, Tucson, AZ (Arizona)

225 Years in Pennington & Still Cooking, First United Methodist Church, Pennington, NJ (Mid-Atlantic)

Two Hundred Years of Charleston Cooking ©1976 University of South Carolina, University of South Carolina Press, Columbia, SC (South Carolina)

Uptown Down South ©1986 Greenville Junior League Publications, Junior League of Greenville, Greenville, SC (South Carolina)

USO's Salute to the Troops Cookbook, James S. McDonnell USO, St. Louis, MO (Missouri)

Waddad's Kitchen ©1982 by Waddad Habeeb Buttross, Natchez, MS (Mississippi)

Wandering & Feasting ©1996 Board of Regents of Washington State University, Mary Houser Caditz, Washington State University Press, Seattle, WA (Washington)

Washington Cook Book ©1994 Golden West Publishers, Janet Walker, Golden West Publishers, Phoenix, AZ (Washington)

Watsonville Community Hospital Service League Favorite Recipes 40th Anniversary Edition, Watsonville Community Hospital Service League, Watsonville, CA (California)

We Love Country Cookin', Marlene Grager and Donna Young, Sykeston, ND (Great Plains)

What Is It? What Do I Do With It? ©1978 by Beth Tartan and Fran Parker, TarPar Ltd., Kernersville, NC (North Carolina)

What's Cookin' ©1993 by Arlene Luskin, Goodyear, AZ (Mid-Atlantic)

What's Cookin' at Casa, Casa Arena Blanca Retirement Home, Alamogordo, NM (New Mexico)

What's Cookin' in Melon Country, Rocky Ford Chamber of Commerce, Rocky Ford, CO (Colorado)

What's Cooking in Kentucky ©1982 by Irene Hayes, T. I. Hayes Publishing Co., Inc., Ft. Mitchell, KY (Kentucky)

When Dinnerbells Ring ©1978 Talladega Junior Welfare League, Talladega Junior Welfare League, Talladega, AL (Alabama)

Where There's a Will ©1997 by Evelyn Will, Easton, MD (Mid-Atlantic)

White Grass Cafe Cross Country Cooking ©1996 White Grass Ski Touring Center, Laurie Little and Mary Beth Gwyer, White Grass Ski Touring Center, Canaan Valley, WV (West Virginia)

Wild About Kansas City Barbecue ©1997 Pig Out Publications, Rich Davis and Shifra Stein, Pig Out Publications, Kansas City, MO (Great Plains)

Wild About Texas ©1989 Cypress Woodlands Junior Forum, Cypress Woodlands Junior Forum, Spring, TX (Texas II)

Winning Recipes from Minnesota with Love ©1992 New Boundary Concepts, Inc., Strawberry Point, Prior Lake, MN (Minnesota)

Winterthur's Culinary Collection ©1983 The Henry Francis du Pont Winterthur Museum, Inc., Winterthur, Winterthur, DE (Mid-Atlantic)

The Words Worth Eating Cookbook ©1987 by Jacquelyn G. Legg, Newport News, VA (Virginia)

WYVE's Bicentennial Cookbook ©1989 WYVE Radio, WYVE Radio Station, Wytheville, VA (Virginia)

Years and Years of Goodwill Cooking, Goodwill Circle of New Hope Lutheran Church, Upham, ND (Great Plains)

Zion Lutheran Church Cookbook, Zion Lutheran Church, Readlyn, IA (Iowa)

*The Lamar River is fed by hot springs in Montana's beautiful range
country. It is not unusual to see bears, wolves, foxes, and coyotes
patrolling its swollen boundaries when the river is rushing with snow
melt in the early summer. Gwen's daughter-in-law, Betsy, says it makes
for an interesting swim—the river is icy but the spring is hot!*

A

Almonds:
Almond Fudge Brownies 235
Almond Topped Crab Quiche 130
Almond Turkey Casserole 150
Buttery Almond Roca 238
Luscious Almond Amaretto Cheesecake 213
Almost Pizza 132
Amber Glow 33
Angel Hair Pasta Primavera 123
Appetizers: *(see also Dips)*
Amber Glow 33
Appetizer Chicken Wings 16
Armadillo Eggs 20
Baked Caramel Goodstuff 35
Benedictine 31
Cheese Cookies 24
Cherry Tomatoes Filled with Pesto 25
Chipped Beef Spread 31
Christmas Cheese Ball 25
Coconut Shrimp 21
Crab Quiche Squares 34
Crab Stuffed Mushrooms 20
Cranberry Jalapeño Jelly 36
Helen's Nuts and Bolts 35
Hot Pepper Jelly 36
Kahlúa Pecan Brie 33
Parmesan Chicken Fingers 15
Peter Rabbit's Pizza 22
Please with Cheese 23
Rolled Tortillas 19
Savory Ham Balls 18
Shrimp Appetizer Platter 22
Smoked Salmon Paté 23
Spinach Cheese Pastries 24
Sun-Dried Tomato Spread 32
Tamale Bites 19
Teriyaki Chicken Wings 16
Turkey Tidbits with Cranberry Dip 15
Vidalia Onion Spread 32
Waikiki Meatballs 17
Apples:
Apple Biscuit Coffee Cake 50
Apple Blackberry Pie 247
Apple-Carrot Casserole 104
Apple Dapple Cake 202
Apple Dump Cake 202
Apple Pan Dowdy 56
Autumn Cheesecake 214
Bite-Size Applesauce Muffins 49
Favorite Apple Betty 255
My Secret Apple Pie 246
Sue's Apple Pie in a Jar 246
Sweet Potatoes and Apples 103
Taffy Apple Salad 94
Turkey Waldorf Salad 82
Applesauce Bread Baked in a Jar 42
Applesauce Muffins, Bite-Size 49
Apricot Glazed Carrots 104
Apricot Sauce 251
Armadillo Eggs 20
Autumn Cheesecake 214
Award-Winning Mocha Icing 194

B

Baja Salad 91
Baked Brie with Caramelized Apple Topping 33
Baked Caramel Goodstuff 35
Baked Dijon Salmon 153
Baked Eggs in Pepper Rings 59
Baked Flounder with Crabmeat 156
Baked Mashed Potatoes 101
Bal'More Rhubarb Pie 248
Bananas:
Banana Cream Pie 254
Banana Pudding 267
Bananas Foster Bread Pudding 268
Cooperstown B&B Banana Jam Bread 44
Fantastic Trifle 263
Bar-B-Que Brisket 185
Barbecued Fish 157
Beachcomber's Gold 13
Beans:
Baja Salad 91
Chili Blanco 75
Coyote Caviar 29
Five-Layer Mexican Dip 28
Green Bean Casserole 108
Hearty Split Pea, Bean and Barley Soup 63
Husband Pleasin' Baked Beans 109
Indian-Style Pinto Beans 109
Mexican Casserole 179
Mexican Corn & Bean Sopa 64
Taste of the Rockies Casserole 173
White Grass Chili 74
Beef:
Almost Pizza 132
Bar-B-Que Brisket 185
Beef in a Bread Bowl 30
Biscuit Pie 177
Black-Iron Skillet One Dish Meal 173
Bowl of Red 75
Cajun Chow Mein 184
Chile Relleños Casserole 183
Chimichangas 182
Chipped Beef Spread 31
Crock Pot Barbecued Beef Stew 76
Don't-Cook-The-Pasta-Manicotti 120
Frito Pie 181
Glazed Meatloaf 175
Goulash Soup 62
Hamburger-Spinach Casserole 174
Impossible Cheeseburger Pie 178
Inside Out Ravioli 121
Italian Spiedini 171
Mexican Casserole 179
Nana's Swiss Steak 172
No Peep Stew 76
One Step Tamale Pie 181
Ox-Tail Vegetable Soup 62
Picadillo II 183
Pizza Rice Casserole 127
Popover Pizza 177
Shrimp and Beef Filet Brochettes with Sesame Marinade 170
Skillet Supper 172
Sour Cream Enchiladas 178
Sour Cream Meat Loaf 175

Southwest Taco Soup 65
Strombolis 176
Swiss Bliss Round Steak 171
Taco Bake 180
Taco Ring 182
Taco Smacho 179
Tamale Bites 19
Taste of the Rockies Casserole 173
Waikiki Meatballs 17
Beet Pickles 98
Beet Salad, Pickled 98
Benedictine 31
Best Maryland Crab Cakes 160
Best Pumpkin Bread 45
Best-Ever Layer Dessert 258
Beverages: *(see also Punch, Tea)*
  Beachcomber's Gold 13
  Creamy Hot Chocolate 10
  Frozen Peach Margaritas 14
  Mock Sangria 11
  Peachy Twirl Cooler 12
  Texas Sunrise 12
Biscuit Pie 177
Bisque, Seafood 71
Bisque, Tomato 70
Bite-Size Applesauce Muffins 49
Black Forest Pie 241
Black Russian Cake 197
Black-Eyed Pea and Pepper Salsa 29
Black-Iron Skillet One Dish Meal 173
Blackberry Pie, Apple 247
Blackberry Roll 255
Blend of the Bayou Seafood Casserole 167
Block Island Potatoes 102
Blow Out Cookies 225
Blue Ribbon Barbecued Country Back Ribs 186
Blue Ribbon Carrot Cake 201
Blueberries:
  Blueberry Hill Wild Blueberry Pancakes 55
  Blueberry Salad 96
  Blueberry Streusel Coffee Cake 51
  Leslie's Blueberry Cinnamon Muffins 47
Bob's Barbecued Shrimp 164
Bowl of Red 75
Boxcar Barbecue 187
Bran Muffins with Maple Syrup 46
Breads: *(see also Coffee Cakes, Muffins)*
  Applesauce Bread Baked in a Jar 42
  Best Pumpkin Bread 45
  Bunker Hill Brown Bread 41
  Cheese Biscuits 38
  Classic Bruschetta 40
  Cooperstown B&B Banana Jam Bread 44
  Feather Beds 38
  Glazed Cranberry Orange Nut Bread 44
  Mexican Spoon Bread 39
  Morning Glorious Bread or Muffins 46
  Spicy Pineapple Zucchini Bread 42
  Spinach Corn Bread 39
  Strawberry Bread with Spread 43
Breakfast Bundt Cake 53
Breast of Chicken Veronique 136
Brie, Kahlúa Pecan 33

Broccoli:
  Broccoli Soufflé with Mushroom Cheese
    Sauce 107
  Broccoli-Cheese Casserole 106
  Broccoli-Cheese Soup 69
  Broccoli Salad Supreme 89
  Broccoli-Peanut Salad 89
  Cream of Broccoli Soup 69
  Snow-Capped Broccoli Spears 106
Brownies and Bars:
  Almond Fudge Brownies 235
  Chocolate Marshmallow Bar 234
  Chocolate Mint Bars 230
  Chocolate Praline Cookies 228
  Cream Cheese Brownies 235
  Fabulous Pecan Bars 233
  Festive Fudge Filled Bars 232
  Lemon Pie Cookies 227
  Meringue Raspberry Bars 227
  Nanaimo Bars 229
  Polka Daters 232
  Pumpkin Squares 274
  Salted Nut Roll Bars 231
  Soda Cracker Bars 231
  Turtle Caramel Brownies 234
  World's Best Cookie Bars 228
Bunker Hill Brown Bread 41
Butter Dreams 226
Butter Pecan Cheesecake 212
Butter Rum Sauce 268
Butterscotch Breakfast Ring 52
Buttery Almond Roca 238
Buttery Pound Cake 199

C

Cabbage:
  Cabbage and Onion Casserole 105
  Golden Raisin Coleslaw 90
  Skillet Supper 172
  Sweet and Sour Cabbage Soup 66
  Sweet and Sour Slaw 90
Cajun Chow Mein 184
Cajun Peppered Shrimp and Grits 166
Cakes: *(see also Cheesecakes)*
  Apple Dapple Cake 202
  Apple Dump Cake 202
  Black Russian Cake 197
  Blue Ribbon Carrot Cake 201
  Breakfast Bundt Cake 53
  Buttery Pound Cake 199
  Candy Bar Pound Cake 199
  Carolyn's Coconut Cake 200
  Cherry Walnut Delight 204
  Chocolate Kahlúa Cake 197
  Chocolate Upside-Down Cake 195
  Grant Wood's Strawberry Shortcake 203
  Heavenly Dessert Torte 206
  Milky Way Cake 196
  Pineapple Cheese Torte 205
  Prize Winning Johnson Special Chocolate
    Cake 194
  Rave Review 200
  Somersault Cake 204
  Southern Gingerbread with Caramel Sauce 206

Strawberry Chocolate Mousse Cake 203
Tunnelfudge Muffins 198
Whacky Cake 195
Candies:
Buttery Almond Roca 238
Chocolate Meringues 237
Ooee Gooey Marshmallow Cream Fudge 236
Orange Pecan Pralines 238
Smoothest Divinity 237
Snow White Chocolate Fudge 236
Candy Bar Pound Cake 199
Capt'n 'Fuskie's Lowcountry Boil 162
Caramel:
Baked Caramel Goodstuff 35
Caramel Sauce 206, 242
Chocolate Caramel Pecan Pie 242
Overnight Caramel French Toast 54
Southern Gingerbread with Caramel Sauce 206
Turtle Caramel Brownies 234
Turtle Cheesecake 207
Turtle Pie 241
Carolyn's Coconut Cake 200
Carrots:
Apple-Carrot Casserole 104
Apricot Glazed Carrots 104
Blue Ribbon Carrot Cake 201
Zesty Carrots 105
Catfish Fillets Meuniere 152
Cattle King Potatoes 102
Charlotte's Peanut Butter Pie 244
Cheese:
Broccoli-Cheese Casserole 106
Broccoli-Cheese Soup 69
Cheese Biscuits 38
Cheese Cookies 24
Cheese Strata 59
Christmas Cheese Ball 25
Debbie's Chile Con Queso 28
Down Home Cheddar Cheese Soup 68
Fabulous Easy Quiche 130
Garlic Cheese Grits 57
Herbed Parmesan Chicken 141
Impossible Cheeseburger Pie 178
Kahlúa Pecan Brie 33
Macaroni and Cheese 125
Pineapple Cheese Torte 205
Please with Cheese 23
Quiche Cargo Boat 60
Southwestern Quiche 131
Spinach Cheese Pastries 24
Three Cheese Baked Rice 126
Wild Rice Casserole 127
Cheesecakes:
Autumn Cheesecake 214
Butter Pecan Cheesecake 212
Cheesecake Pie 250
Cherry Cheesecake 216
Hugs and Chips Cheesecake 210
Luscious Almond Amaretto Cheesecake 213
Mon Ami Oreo Cookie Cheesecake 208
Peaches and Cream Cheesecake Pie 250
Peanut Butter Chocolate Chip Cheesecake 211
Strawberry Glazed Cheesecake 215
Three Layered Cheesecake 209
Turtle Cheesecake 207

Cherries:
Black Forest Pie 241
Butter Dreams 226
Cherry Cheesecake 216
Cherry Chip Cookies 222
Cherry Sauce 269
Cherry Walnut Delight 204
Cherry Winks 221
Chocolate Covered Cherry Cookies 222
Miniature Cream Cheese Tarts with Cherry
Sauce 269
Snow Balls 226
Sour Cream Cherry Pie 247
Cherry Tomatoes Filled with Pesto 25
Chicken:
Appetizer Chicken Wings 16
Baja Salad 91
Breast of Chicken Veronique 136
Chicken à la Bethany 136
Chicken Alfredo 142
Chicken and Spinach Enchilada Casserole 149
Chicken and Spinach Casserole 148
Chicken and Wild Rice 128
Chicken Bundles 137
Chicken Salad in Melon Rings 84
Chicken Spaghetti "Carole Curlee Special" 124
Chicken Wedding Salad 84
Chili Blanco 75
Chinese Chicken Salad 83
Crab-Stuffed Chicken Breasts 138
Crescent Chicken Casserole 148
Crispy Parmesan Chicken Strips 144
Crispy Sesame Chicken 135
Dandy Chicken 141
Eddy's Chicken Kiev 139
Fantastic Chicken Fajitas 145
Favorite Chicken Casserole 147
Fiesta Chicken 140
First Place Chicken Casserole 147
Heavenly Chicken Casserole 146
Herbed Parmesan Chicken 141
Italian Stuffed Shells 121
Mini Chicken Pies 145
Monterey Chicken 135
Moo Goo Gai Pan 144
Oven Barbecued Chicken 134
Oven-Fried Chicken with Honey Butter Sauce 134
Parmesan Chicken Fingers 15
Provolone Chicken 139
Santa Fe Chicken 140
Stir-Fried Chicken and Mushrooms 144
Sweet and Sour Baked Chicken 143
Swiss Chicken 142
Teriyaki Chicken Wings 16
Chile Relleno Casserole 113
Chile Relleños Casserole 183
Chilies:
Bowl of Red 75
Chili Blanco 75
White Grass Chili 74
Chimichangas 182
Chinese Chicken Salad 83
Chipped Beef Spread 31
Chocolate:
Almond Fudge Brownies 235

Index

Best-Ever Layer Dessert 258
Black Forest Pie 241
Black Russian Cake 197
Blow Out Cookies 225
Candy Bar Pound Cake 199
Cherry Chip Cookies 222
Chocolate Angel Kisses 226
Chocolate Caramel Pecan Pie 242
Chocolate Chip Pizza 275
Chocolate Chocolate-Chip Cookies 224
Chocolate Cloud 261
Chocolate Covered Cherry Cookies 222
Chocolate Decadence 259
Chocolate Divine Dessert 258
Chocolate Drop Cookies 224
Chocolate Kahlúa Cake 197
Chocolate Marshmallow Bar 234
Chocolate Meringues 237
Chocolate Mint Bars 230
Chocolate Mousse 266
Chocolate Praline Cookies 228
Chocolate Upside-Down Cake 195
Chocolate Yummy 260
Cream Cheese Brownies 235
Creamy Hot Chocolate 10
Festive Fudge Filled Bars 232
German Chocolate Pudding 267
Frozen Chocolate Crunch 275
Hugs and Chips Cheesecake 210
Luscious Lady 265
Milky Way Cake 196
Mon Ami Oreo Cookie Cheesecake 208
Mrs. Overlake's Cookies 223
Nanaimo Bars 229
Napoleans 271
Ooee Gooey Marshmallow Cream Fudge 236
Peanut Butter Chocolate Chip Cheesecake 211
Peanut Butter Fudge Pie 243
Peanut Buttercup Pie 243
Polka Daters 232
Prize Winning Johnson Special Chocolate Cake
  194
Pull Me Up 264
Rich Chocolate Pie 240
Snow White Chocolate Fudge 236
Soda Cracker Bars 231
Strawberry Chocolate Mousse Cake 203
Terra-Me-SU 264
Texas Cow Patties 223
Three Layered Cheesecake 209
Three's Company Chocolate Mousse Pie 240
Tunnelfudge Muffins 198
Turtle Caramel Brownies 234
Turtle Cheesecake 207
Turtle Pie 241
Whacky Cake 195
World's Best Cookie Bars 228
Chowder, Grandma Smith's Clam 73
Chowder, Midwest Corn 73
Christmas Cheese Ball 25
Clam Chowder, Grandma Smith's 73
Classic Bruschetta 40
Cobb Salad with Buttermilk Herb Dressing 79
Cobbler, Old Fashioned Peach 257
Cobbler, Old-Fashioned Berry 256

Coconut:
  Carolyn's Coconut Cake 200
  Coconut Shrimp 21
  French Coconut Pie 248
  Rave Review 200
Coffee Cakes:
  Apple Biscuit Coffee Cake 50
  Blueberry Streusel Coffee Cake 51
  Breakfast Bundt Cake 53
  Butterscotch Breakfast Ring 52
  Peach Pudding Coffee Cake 49
  Pineapple Coffee Cake 50
Coffee Mocha Punch 10
Cold Lime Soufflé 274
Coleslaw, Golden Raisin 40
Company Vegetable Casserole 114
Cookies: (see also Brownies and Bars)
  Blow Out Cookies 225
  Butter Dreams 226
  Cheese Cookies 24
  Cherry Chip Cookies 222
  Cherry Winks 221
  Chocolate Angel Kisses 226
  Chocolate Chocolate-Chip Cookies 224
  Chocolate Covered Cherry Cookies 222
  Chocolate Drop Cookies 224
  Chocolate Praline Cookies 228
  Cream Cheese Cut-Out Cookies 219
  Lemon Pie Cookies 227
  Melting Moments 220
  Mrs. Overlake's Cookies 223
  Painted Cookies 220
  Peanut Butter Middles 225
  Snow Balls 226
  Sugar & Spice Cookies 218
  Sugar Cookies (World's Best) 218
  Texas Cow Patties 223
Cooperstown B&B Banana Jam Bread 44
Corn:
  Capt'n 'Fuskie's Lowcountry Boil 162
  Corn Casserole 115
  Corn Relish 115
  Corn Salad 91
  Mexican Corn & Bean Sopa 64
  Midwest Corn Chowder 73
Coyote Caviar 29
Crab:
  Almond Topped Crab Quiche 130
  Baked Flounder with Crabmeat 156
  Best Maryland Crab Cakes 160
  Crabmeat Au Gratin 158
  Crab Quiche Squares 34
  Crab Salad 85
  Crab Stuffed Mushrooms 20
  Crab-Stuffed Chicken Breasts 138
  Deviled Crabs 158
  Scallops and Crabmeat 159
  Spicy Hot Crab Dip 27
Craisin-Spinach Salad 81
Cranberries:
  Craisin-Spinach Salad 81
  Cranberry Dip 15
  Cranberry Jalapeño Jelly 36
  Glazed Cranberry Orange Nut Bread 44
  Holiday Cranberry Salad 97

Index

Crawfish Dip, Hot 27
Cream Cheese Brownies 235
Cream Cheese Cut-Out Cookies 219
Cream of Broccoli Soup 69
Cream Puffs with Lemon Curd 270
Creamy Frozen Salad 94
Creamy Gazpacho Salad 87
Creamy Hot Chocolate 10
Crème Brulée 273
Creole Jambalaya 129
Crescent Chicken Casserole 148
Crispy Fried Okra 117
Crispy Parmesan Chicken Strips 144
Crispy Sesame Chicken 135
Crock Pot Barbecued Beef Stew 76
Crock Pot Ribs 186
Curried Fruit 53
Curried Lamb Chops 192

D

Dandy Chicken 141
Debbie's Chile Con Queso 28
Desserts: *(see also specific dessert)*
  Best-Ever Layer Dessert 258
  Chocolate Cloud 261
  Chocolate Decadence 259
  Chocolate Divine Dessert 258
  Chocolate Yummy 260
  Crème Brulée 273
  Ladyfingers 264
  Lime Chiffon Dessert 273
  Luscious Lady 265
  Napoleans 271
  Pull Me Up 264
  Strawberries Bourbonnaise 272
  Strawberries Over Snow 261
  Terra-Me-SU 264
Deviled Crabs 158
Deviled Potato Salad 93
Dilled Haddock Parmesan 155
Dips:
  Amber Glow 33
  Beef in a Bread Bowl 30
  Benedictine 31
  Black-Eyed Pea and Pepper Salsa 29
  Chipped Beef Spread 31
  Coyote Caviar 29
  Cranberry Dip 15
  Debbie's Chile Con Queso 28
  Five-Layer Mexican Dip 28
  Hot Crawfish Dip 27
  Kahlúa Pecan Brie 33
  Pepperoni Pizza Dip 30
  Spicy Hot Crab Dip 27
  Spinach Dip 26
  Sun-Dried Tomato Spread 32
  Tonia's Spinach Dip Supreme 26
  Vidalia Onion Spread 32
Divine Lime Pie 252
Dixie Tea 11
Don't-Cook-The-Pasta-Manicotti 120
Down Home Cheddar Cheese Soup 68
Dreamy High Pumpkin Pie 254
Dressing, Southern Corn Bread 150
Dressings, Salad: *(see Salad Dressings)*
Dry Rub 185

E

Easy Strawberry Salad 95
Eddy's Chicken Kiev 139
Eden's Flower 111
Eggplant Parmigiana 114
Eggs: *(see also Quiches)*
  Baked Eggs in Pepper Rings 59
  Cheese Strata 59
  Deviled Crabs 158
  Deviled Potato Salad 93
  Potato Egg Bake 58
  Sausage and Egg Brunch Bake 58

F

Fabulous Easy Quiche 130
Fabulous Pecan Bars 233
Fantastic Chicken Fajitas 145
Fantastic Trifle 263
Favorite Apple Betty 255
Favorite Chicken Casserole 147
Feather Beds 38
Festive Baked Ham 191
Festive Fudge Filled Bars 232
Fettuccine, Seafood 123
Fiesta Chicken 140
First Place Chicken Casserole 147
Fish:
  Baked Flounder with Crabmeat 156
  Barbecued Fish 157
  Catfish Fillets Meuniere 152
  Dilled Haddock Parmesan 155
  Friday Night Fish 157
  Pan-Fried Fish Parmesana 154
  Rockfish Chesapeake 155
  Trout Almondine 156
Fisherman's Wharf Garlic Prawns 161
Five Layer Pie 245
Five-Layer Mexican Dip 28
French Coconut Pie 248
French Toast, Overnight Caramel 54
French Toast, Stuffed 54
Friday Night Fish 157
Fried Green Tomatoes 117
Frito Pie 181
Frostings:
  Buttermilk Glaze 201
  Chocolate Glaze 208, 210
  Coconut Icing 200
  Napolean Icing 271
Frozen Chocolate Crunch 275
Frozen Peach Margaritas 14
Frozen Peanut Butter Cups 276
Frozen Strawberry Margarita Pie 253
Fruit: *(see also specific fruit)*
  Chicken Salad in Melon Rings 84
  Creamy Frozen Salad 94
  Curried Fruit 53
  Texas Sunrise 12

G

Garlic Cheese Grits 57
Garlic Soup 67

German Chocolate Pudding 267
Gingerbread with Caramel Sauce, Southern 206
Glazed Cranberry Orange Nut Bread 44
Glazed Meatloaf 175
Golden Parmesan Potatoes 100
Golden Raisin Coleslaw 90
Goulash Soup 62
Grandma Smith's Clam Chowder 73
Grant Wood's Strawberry Shortcake 203
Greek Salad 80
Greek Shrimp Salad 87
Green and Gold Squash 110
Green Bean Casserole 108
Greenback Tomatoes 116
Greens and Ham Hocks 118
Grilled Citrus Salmon 153
Grits:
　　Cajun Peppered Shrimp and Grits 166
　　Garlic Cheese Grits 57
　　Sausage-Grits Casserole 57
Groff's Potato Salad 92
Gumbo II, Seafood 72

H

Ham:
　　Creole Jambalaya 129
　　Fabulous Easy Quiche 130
　　Festive Baked Ham 191
　　Greens and Ham Hocks 118
　　Hearty Ham Pie 191
　　Hearty Split Pea, Bean and Barley Soup 63
　　Monte Cristo Club 41
　　Savory Ham Balls 18
Hamburger-Spinach Casserole 174
Hazelnut Salad, Roasted 78
Hearty Ham Pie 191
Hearty Split Pea, Bean and Barley Soup 63
Heavenly Chicken Casserole 146
Heavenly Dessert Torte 206
Heavenly Pancakes 55
Helen's Nuts and Bolts 35
Herbed Parmesan Chicken 141
Holiday Cranberry Salad 97
Honey Butter Sauce 134
Honey Crunch Pecan Pie 245
Hot Crawfish Dip 27
Hot Pepper Jelly 36
Hot Pepper Jelly Salad 97
Hugs and Chips Cheesecake 210
Husband Pleasin' Baked Beans 109

I

Impossible Cheeseburger Pie 178
Incredible Peach Pie 249
Indian-Style Pinto Beans 109
Inside Out Ravioli 121
Italian Sausage Soup 66
Italian Shrimp and Pasta Toss 122
Italian Spiedini 171
Italian Stuffed Shells 121

J

Jalapeño Spinach 112
Jambalaya, Creole 129
Jellies and Jams:
　　Cranberry Jalapeño Jelly 36

Hot Pepper Jelly 36
Hot Pepper Jelly Salad 97

K

Kahlúa Pecan Brie 33

L

Ladyfingers 264
Lamb Chops, Curried 192
Lemons:
　　Cream Puffs with Lemon Curd 270
　　Lemon Chess Pie 251
　　Lemon Cream Pie with Apricot Sauce 251
　　Lemon Pie Cookies 227
Lentil Soup 64
Leslie's Blueberry Cinnamon Muffins 47
Limes:
　　Cold Lime Soufflé 274
　　Divine Lime Pie 252
　　Lime Chiffon Dessert 273
Lobster, Merrymount 168
Lower-Fat Pesto 125
Luscious Almond Amaretto Cheesecake 213
Luscious Lady 265

M

Macaroni and Cheese 125
Macaroni Salad 93
Make-Ahead Mashed Potatoes 100
Margaritas, Frozen Peach 14
Meatballs, Waikiki 17
Meatloaf, Glazed 175
Meat Loaf, Sour Cream 175
Meats: *(see Beef, Ham. Pork, Lamb)*
Melting Moments 220
Meringue Raspberry Bars 227
Merrymount Lobster 168
Mexican Casserole 179
Mexican Corn & Bean Sopa 64
Mexican Spoon Bread 39
Midwest Corn Chowder 73
Milky Way Cake 196
Mini Chicken Pies 145
Miniature Cream Cheese Tarts with Cherry
　　Sauce 269
Mint Bars, Chocolate 230
Mocha Icing, Award-Winning 194
Mock Sangria 11
Mom's Stuffed Pork Chops 189
Mon Ami Oreo Cookie Cheesecake 208
Monte Cristo Club 41
Monterey Chicken 135
Moo Goo Gai Pan 144
Morning Glorious Bread or Muffins 46
Mousse, Chocolate 266
Mrs. Overlake's Cookies 223
Muffins:
　　Bite-Size Applesauce Muffins 49
　　Bran Muffins with Maple Syrup 46
　　Leslie's Blueberry Cinnamon Muffins 47
　　Morning Glorious Bread or Muffins 46
　　Raspberry Muffins 48
　　Tunnelfudge Muffins 198
Mushrooms:
　　Crab Stuffed Mushrooms 20
　　Moo Goo Gai Pan 144

Mushroom Cheese Sauce 107
Stir-Fried Chicken and Mushrooms 144
My Secret Apple Pie 246

N

Nana's Swiss Steak 172
Nanaimo Bars 229
Napoleans 271
No Peep Stew 76
Northwest Seafood Salad 86

O

Okra, Crispy Fried 117
Old Fashioned Peach Cobbler 257
Old-Fashioned Berry Cobbler 256
One Step Tamale Pie 181
Onion Spread, Vidalia 32
Ooee Gooey Marshmallow Cream Fudge 236
Orange Pecan Pralines 238
Orange Soufflé Gelatin Salad 96
Oregon Strawberry Pie 253
Oven Barbecued Chicken 134
Oven-Fried Chicken with Honey Butter Sauce 134
Overnight Caramel French Toast 54
Ox-Tail Vegetable Soup 62
Oysters Parmesan 168

P

Painted Cookies 220
Pancakes:
  Blueberry Hill Wild Blueberry Pancakes 55
  Heavenly Pancakes 55
  Sour Cream Rollups 56
Pan-Fried Fish Parmesana 154
Parmesan Chicken Fingers 15
Pasta:
  Angel Hair Pasta Primavera 123
  Chicken Spaghetti "Carole Curlee Special" 124
  Don't-Cook-The-Pasta-Manicotti 120
  Inside Out Ravioli 121
  Italian Shrimp and Pasta Toss 122
  Italian Stuffed Shells 121
  Macaroni and Cheese 125
  Macaroni Salad 93
  Scallops and Green Noodles 122
  Seafood Fettuccine 123
Pastries:
  Chicken Bundles 137
  Cream Puffs with Lemon Curd 270
  Napoleans 271
  Spinach Cheese Pastries 24
Peaches:
  Frozen Peach Margaritas 14
  Incredible Peach Pie 249
  Old Fashioned Peach Cobbler 257
  Peach Praline Pie 249
  Peach Pudding Coffee Cake 49
  Peaches and Cream Cheesecake Pie 250
  Peachy Twirl Cooler 12
Peanut Butter:
  Charlotte's Peanut Butter Pie 244
  Frozen Peanut Butter Cups 276
  Peanut Butter Chocolate Chip Cheesecake 211
  Peanut Butter Fudge Pie 243
  Peanut Butter Middles 225
  Peanut Buttercup Pie 243

Peas, Pot-Luck 108
Pecans:
  Baked Caramel Goodstuff 35
  Butter Pecan Cheesecake 212
  Cheese Cookies 24
  Chocolate Caramel Pecan Pie 242
  Chocolate Praline Cookies 228
  Fabulous Pecan Bars 233
  Helen's Nuts and Bolts 35
  Honey Crunch Pecan Pie 245
  Orange Pecan Pralines 238
  Peach Praline Pie 249
  Turtle Cheesecake 207
  Turtle Pie 241
Pepperoni Pizza Dip 30
Pesto, Lower-Fat 125
Peter Rabbit's Pizza 22
Picadillo II 183
Pickled Beet Salad 98
Pies:
  Apple Blackberry Pie 247
  Bal'More Rhubarb Pie 248
  Banana Cream Pie 254
  Biscuit Pie 177
  Black Forest Pie 241
  Charlotte's Peanut Butter Pie 244
  Cheesecake Pie 250
  Chocolate Caramel Pecan Pie 242
  Divine Lime Pie 252
  Dreamy High Pumpkin Pie 254
  Five Layer Pie 245
  French Coconut Pie 248
  Frito Pie 181
  Frozen Strawberry Margarita Pie 253
  Hearty Ham Pie 191
  Honey Crunch Pecan Pie 245
  Impossible Cheeseburger Pie 178
  Incredible Peach Pie 249
  Lemon Chess Pie 251
  Lemon Cream Pie with Apricot Sauce 251
  Mini Chicken Pies 145
  My Secret Apple Pie 246
  One Step Tamale Pie 181
  Oregon Strawberry Pie 253
  Peach Praline Pie 249
  Peaches and Cream Cheesecake Pie 250
  Peanut Butter Fudge Pie 243
  Peanut Buttercup Pie 243
  Rich Chocolate Pie 240
  Sour Cream Cherry Pie 247
  Sue's Apple Pie in a Jar 246
  Three's Company Chocolate Mousse Pie 240
  Turtle Pie 241
Pineapple:
  Pineapple Cheese Torte 205
  Pineapple Coffee Cake 50
  Spiced Pineapple Pork Roast 189
  Spicy Pineapple Zucchini Bread 42
  Sweet Potato and Pineapple 103
Pizza:
  Almost Pizza 132
  Chocolate Chip Pizza 275
  Pizza Rice Casserole 127
  Pepperoni Pizza Dip 30
  Popover Pizza 177

Index

Please with Cheese 23
Polka Daters 232
Pop's Pepper Poppers 113
Popover Pizza 177
Pork: (see also Ham)
  Armadillo Eggs 20
  Blue Ribbon Barbecued Country Back Ribs 186
  Boxcar Barbecue 187
  Cajun Chow Mein 184
  Crock Pot Ribs 186
  Mom's Stuffed Pork Chops 189
  Picadillo II 183
  Pork Chop 'n' Potato Bake 190
  Pork Chop Skillet 190
  Pork Loin Roulade 188
  Pork Tenderloin with Orange Sauce 188
  Special Indoor Barbecued Spare Ribs with
    Sauce 187
  Spiced Pineapple Pork Roast 189
Pot-Luck Peas 108
Potatoes: (see also Sweet Potatoes)
  Baked Mashed Potatoes 101
  Block Island Potatoes 102
  Deviled Potato Salad 93
  Cattle King Potatoes 102
  Golden Parmesan Potatoes 100
  Groff's Potato Salad 92
  Make-Ahead Mashed Potatoes 100
  Pork Chop 'n' Potato Bake 190
  Potato Egg Bake 58
  Potato Puffs 101
  Sour Cream Potato Salad 92
Poultry: (see Chicken, Turkey)
Pralines, Orange Pecan 238
Prize Winning Johnson Special Chocolate Cake 194
Provolone Chicken 139
Puddings:
  Banana Pudding 267
  Bananas Foster Bread Pudding 268
  German Chocolate Pudding 267
  Vanilla Bread Pudding with Butter Rum Sauce 268
Pull Me Up 264
Pumpkin:
  Best Pumpkin Bread 45
  Dreamy High Pumpkin Pie 254
  Pumpkin Squares 274
Punch Bowl, Yuletide 13
Punch, Coffee Mocha 10

Q
Quiches:
  Almond Topped Crab Quiche 130
  Crab Quiche Squares 34
  Fabulous Easy Quiche 130
  Quiche Cargo Boat 60
  Southwestern Quiche 131

R
Raspberries:
  Meringue Raspberry Bars 227
  Old-Fashioned Berry Cobbler 256
  Raspberry Muffins 48
Rave Review 200
Ravioli, Inside Out 121
Red Pepper Soup, Sweet 68

Relish, Corn 115
Rhubarb Pie, Bal'More 248
Rice:
  Chicken and Wild Rice 128
  Creole Jambalaya 129
  Pizza Rice Casserole 127
  Rice Pilaf 126
  Shrimp in Wild Rice 128
  Three Cheese Baked Rice 126
  Wild Rice Casserole 127
Rich Chocolate Pie 240
Roasted Hazelnut Salad 78
Rockfish Chesapeake 155
Rolled Tortillas 19

S
Salad Dressings:
  Buttermilk Herb Dressing 79
  Cumin-Lime Dressing 91
  Greek Salad Dressing 80
  Poppy Seed Dressing 81
  Sesame Dressing 83, 86
  Turkey Salad Dressing 82
Salads:
  Baja Salad 91
  Blueberry Salad 96
  Broccoli Salad Supreme 89
  Broccoli-Peanut Salad 89
  Chicken Salad in Melon Rings 84
  Chicken Wedding Salad 84
  Chinese Chicken Salad 83
  Cobb Salad with Buttermilk Herb Dressing 79
  Corn Salad 91
  Crab Salad 85
  Craisin-Spinach Salad 81
  Creamy Frozen Salad 94
  Creamy Gazpacho Salad 87
  Deviled Potato Salad 93
  Easy Strawberry Salad 95
  Golden Raisin Coleslaw 90
  Greek Salad 80
  Greek Shrimp Salad 87
  Groff's Potato Salad 92
  Holiday Cranberry Salad 97
  Hot Pepper Jelly Salad 97
  Macaroni Salad 93
  Northwest Seafood Salad 86
  Orange Soufflé Gelatin Salad 96
  Pickled Beet Salad 98
  Roasted Hazelnut Salad 78
  Sour Cream Potato Salad 92
  Strawberry & Romaine Salad 78
  Strawberry Pretzel Salad 95
  Sweet and Sour Slaw 90
  Taffy Apple Salad 94
  Tomato Well Stuffed 88
  Turkey Salad with Strawberries 82
  Turkey Waldorf Salad 82
  Twenty-Four Hour Spinach Salad 81
  Veggie Lovers' Salad 88
Salmon:
  Baked Dijon Salmon 153
  Grilled Citrus Salmon 153
  Salmon Cakes 154
  Smoked Salmon Paté 23

Salted Nut Roll Bars 231
Sangria, Mock 11
Santa Fe Chicken 140
Sauces:
  Apricot Sauce 251
  Bananas Foster Sauce 268
  Brisket Sauce 185
  Butter Rum Sauce 268
  Caramel Sauce 206, 242
  Cheese Sauce 135
  Cherry Sauce 269
  Chinese Mustard Sauce 21
  Honey Butter Sauce 134
  Mushroom Cheese Sauce 107
  Praline Sauce 212
  Sauce Meuniere 152
  Shrimp Scampi Sauce 161
  Sweet and Sour Sauce 163
Sausage:
  Armadillo Eggs 20
  Cabbage and Onion Casserole 105
  Capt'n 'Fuskie's Lowcountry Boil 162
  Italian Sausage Soup 66
  Sausage and Egg Brunch Bake 58
  Sausage-Grits Casserole 57
Savory Ham Balls 18
Scallops:
  Scallops and Crabmeat 159
  Scallops and Green Noodles 122
  Shrimp and Scallops Gruyère 167
Seafood: (see also specific Seafood)
  Blend of the Bayou Seafood Casserole 167
  Northwest Seafood Salad 86
  Seafood Bisque 71
  Seafood Fettuccine 123
  Seafood Gumbo II 72
Shrimp:
  Blend of the Bayou Seafood Casserole 167
  Bob's Barbecued Shrimp 164
  Cajun Peppered Shrimp and Grits 166
  Capt'n 'Fuskie's Lowcountry Boil 162
  Coconut Shrimp 21
  Creole Jambalaya 129
  Fisherman's Wharf Garlic Prawns 161
  Greek Shrimp Salad 87
  Italian Shrimp and Pasta Toss 122
  Shrimp and Beef Filet Brochettes with Sesame
    Marinade 170
  Shrimp and Scallops Gruyère 167
  Shrimp Appetizer Platter 22
  Shrimp Creole 165
  Shrimp Etouffée 165
  Shrimp Florentine 164
  Shrimp in Wild Rice 128
  Shrimp Scampi Sensation 161
  Succulent Shrimp Cakes 160
  Sweet and Sour Shrimp 163
  Tequila-Lime Shrimp 162
Skillet Supper 172
Slaw, Sweet and Sour 90
Smoked Salmon Paté 23
Smoothest Divinity 237
Snow Balls 226
Snow White Chocolate Fudge 236
Snow-Capped Broccoli Spears 106

Soda Cracker Bars 231
Somersault Cake 204
Sopa de Tortilla 65
Soups: (see also Bisques, Chowders)
  Broccoli-Cheese Soup 69
  Cream of Broccoli Soup 69
  Down Home Cheddar Cheese Soup 68
  Garlic Soup 67
  Goulash Soup 62
  Hearty Split Pea, Bean and Barley Soup 63
  Italian Sausage Soup 66
  Lentil Soup 64
  Mexican Corn & Bean Sopa 64
  Ox-Tail Vegetable Soup 62
  Seafood Gumbo II 72
  Sopa de Tortilla 65
  Southwest Taco Soup 65
  Sweet and Sour Cabbage Soup 66
  Sweet Red Pepper Soup 68
Sour Cream Cherry Pie 247
Sour Cream Enchiladas 178
Sour Cream Meat Loaf 175
Sour Cream Potato Salad 92
Sour Cream Rollups 56
South of the Border Casserole 110
Southern Corn Bread Dressing 150
Southern Gingerbread with Caramel Sauce 206
Southwest Taco Soup 65
Southwestern Quiche 131
Spaghetti, Chicken "Carole Curlee Special" 124
Special Indoor Barbecued Spare Ribs with Sauce 187
Spiced Pineapple Pork Roast 189
Spicy Hot Crab Dip 27
Spicy Pineapple Zucchini Bread 42
Spinach:
  Chicken and Spinach Enchilada Casserole 149
  Chicken and Spinach Casserole 148
  Craisin-Spinach Salad 81
  Hamburger-Spinach Casserole 174
  Jalapeño Spinach 112
  Lower-Fat Pesto 125
  Spinach and Bacon Bake 112
  Spinach Stuffed Squash 111
  Spinach and Bacon Bake 112
  Spinach Cheese Pastries 24
  Spinach Corn Bread 39
  Spinach Dip 26
  Spinach Stuffed Squash 111
  Tonia's Spinach Dip Supreme 26
  Twenty-Four Hour Spinach Salad 81
Squash:
  Green and Gold Squash 110
  South of the Border Casserole 110
  Spinach Stuffed Squash 111
Stir-Fried Chicken and Mushrooms 144
Strawberries:
  Cheesecake Pie 250
  Easy Strawberry Salad 95
  Frozen Strawberry Margarita Pie 253
  Grant Wood's Strawberry Shortcake 203
  Oregon Strawberry Pie 253
  Strawberries Bourbonnaise 272
  Strawberries Over Snow 261
  Strawberry & Romaine Salad 78
  Strawberry Bread with Spread 43

Strawberry Chocolate Mousse Cake 203
Strawberry Glazed Cheesecake 215
Strawberry Pretzel Salad 95
Strawberry Trifle 262
Turkey Salad with Strawberries 82
Stew, Crock Pot Barbecued Beef 76
Stew, No Peep 76
Strombolis 176
Stuffed French Toast 54
Succulent Shrimp Cakes 160
Sue's Apple Pie in a Jar 246
Sugar & Spice Cookies 218
Sugar Cookies (World's Best) 218
Sun-Dried Tomato Spread 32
Sweet and Sour Baked Chicken 143
Sweet and Sour Cabbage Soup 66
Sweet and Sour Shrimp 163
Sweet and Sour Slaw 90
Sweet Potato and Pineapple 103
Sweet Potatoes and Apples 103
Sweet Red Pepper Soup 68
Swiss Bliss Round Steak 171
Swiss Chicken 142

T

Taco Bake 180
Taco Ring 182
Taco Smacho 179
Taco Soup, Southwest 65
Taffy Apple Salad 94
Tamale Bites 19
Tarts with Cherry Sauce, Miniature Cream
  Cheese 269
Taste of the Rockies Casserole 173
Tea, Dixie 11
Tequila-Lime Shrimp 162
Teriyaki Chicken Wings 16
Terra-Me-SU 264
Texas Cow Patties 223
Texas Sunrise 12
Three Cheese Baked Rice 126
Three Layered Cheesecake 209
Three's Company Chocolate Mousse Pie 240
Tomatoes:
  Cherry Tomatoes Filled with Pesto 25
  Fried Green Tomatoes 117
  Greenback Tomatoes 116
  Sun-Dried Tomato Spread 32

Tomato Bisque 70
Tomato Pie 116
Tomato Well Stuffed 88
Tonia's Spinach Dip Supreme 26
Torte, Heavenly Dessert 206
Torte, Pineapple Cheese 205
Trifle, Fantastic 263
Trifle, Strawberry 262
Trout Almondine 156
Tunnelfudge Muffins 198
Turkey:
  Almond Turkey Casserole 150
  Monte Cristo Club 41
  Turkey Salad with Strawberries 82
  Turkey Tidbits with Cranberry Dip 15
  Turkey Waldorf Salad 82
Turtle Caramel Brownies 234
Turtle Cheesecake 207
Turtle Pie 241
Twenty-Four Hour Spinach Salad 81

V

Vanilla Bread Pudding with Butter Rum Sauce 268
Vegetables: *(see also specific vegetable)*
  Angel Hair Pasta Primavera 123
  Company Vegetable Casserole 114
  Ox-Tail Vegetable Soup 62
  Peter Rabbit's Pizza 22
  Veggie Lovers' Salad 88
Vidalia Onion Spread 32

W

Waikiki Meatballs 17
Whacky Cake 195
White Grass Chili 74
Wild Rice Casserole 127
World's Best Cookie Bars 228

Y

Yuletide Punch Bowl 13

Z

Zesty Carrots 105
Zucchini:
  Black-Iron Skillet One Dish Meal 173
  Eden's Flower 111
  Green and Gold Squash 110
  Spicy Pineapple Zucchini Bread 42

BEST OF THE BEST STATE COOKBOOK SERIES

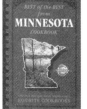

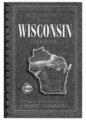